WHAT
AMERICANS
REALLY
THINK

ALSO BY BARRY SUSSMAN:

*The Great Coverup: Nixon and the Scandal
of Watergate*

WHAT AMERICANS REALLY THINK

AND WHY OUR POLITICIANS PAY NO ATTENTION

Barry Sussman

Pantheon Books   New York

Library of Congress Cataloging-in-Publication Data

Sussman, Barry.
What Americans really think.
Includes index.
1. Public opinion—United States. 2. United States—Politics and government—1981– — Public opinion. 3. United States—Economic conditions—1981– —Public opinion. 4. United States—Social conditions—1980– —Public opinion. 5. Public opinion polls.
I. Title.
HN90.P8S88 1988 306'.0973 87-46069
ISBN 0-394-56303-4

Book design by Guenet Abraham

Manufactured in the United States of America

First Edition

In memoriam
Samuel and Esther Sussman

I WOULD LIKE TO THANK SOME PEOPLE:

Kenneth E. John, for his extensive research
assistance and suggestions.

Kim Willenson and John Hanrahan,
who read the manuscript
and made helpful recommendations.

Jeffrey Alderman, for encouragement and
for making material
available to me.

André Schiffrin, who asked me
to do this book.

My wife, Peggy, and my daughters,
Seena and Shari, for all their help
and forbearance.

CONTENTS

PART TWO

The Opinion Polls

PART THREE

What Americans Really Think

PART FOUR

Scandals and Political Realignment

CHARTS

WHAT AMERICANS REALLY THINK

INTRODUCTION

THE FIRST NEWS THAT THE UNITED STATES HAD been sending weapons to the regime of the Ayatollah Khomeini came from a Beirut magazine on November 3, 1986, causing furor and confusion that threatened to wreck the presidency of Ronald Reagan. In a period of nineteen days, Reagan went on television five times in attempts to persuade the people that there was less to the story than met the eye.

On December 2, in his fifth appearance, Reagan said, "The American people—you—will be the final arbiters of this controversy. You will have all the facts and will be able to judge for yourselves."

I watched the president on TV each time, trying to guess at how the public would respond to his appeals. I did that when any president gave a speech or held a press conference; it was in my line of work as a pollster and public opinion analyst for the *Washington Post*.

Reagan's aim was to have the people accept his understated version of events, and not the ugly ones offered by press reports and some Democratic and Republican political leaders. If he could rally the citizenry, the possibility existed that he could blunt or slow down investigations by the news media and critics in Congress. The tactic had worked for Reagan several times in the past, once only weeks earlier when he turned what had first appeared to be a disastrous summit meeting with Soviet leader Mikhail Gorbachev in Iceland into a minor political victory. Criticism of Reagan had come in a burst then, but it melted and disappeared as opinion polls suggested that the public thought the president had done well, not poorly.

Anyone paying attention to Reagan in November and December, 1986, and in the ensuing months of the Iran-contra affair, could see that he regarded public opinion as crucial in his struggle to overcome the scandal that was enveloping him. He behaved as though an election was being held every day.

But even in quieter times what Americans think is of extreme concern to national leaders. To put it directly, politicians as a rule tend to regard the people with terror. Public opinion may erupt at any moment. The citizenry is often condemned as selfish, ignorant, fickle, demanding, easily duped. It is all those things, packaged in sticks of TNT. From time to time in recent years, surging public opinion— spurred by indignation, outrage, or a sense of urgency—has stopped government leaders in their tracks, pushing them into unexpected, sometimes gradual, sometimes abrupt, changes in policy.

It was the mounting flood of public opinion that forced an end to the war in Vietnam, overrunning one president, Lyndon Johnson, in its path. It was public opinion that finally made a reluctant Congress move toward the impeachment of

Richard Nixon, forcing him to resign. In large part it has been public opinion that has brought the nuclear-power industry to its knees, leaving it gasping.

In early 1984, it was public opinion that made Reagan bring the U.S. Marines home from Lebanon only days after saying he would never "cut and run." Public opinion made Reagan stop crusading against the Social Security system; public opinion, cleverly focused by a small group of American black activists, set in motion the reversal of national policy toward South Africa.

It was public opinion in this country, kept alive by a few leaders and some tentative but highly moving TV news coverage, that made Reagan finally change position and push Ferdinand Marcos out of the Philippines, altering forever the course of events in that country. Perhaps it was only the threat of a firestorm in public opinion that kept Reagan from sending American troops into Nicaragua; it was the fear of public opinion that forced him to resort to secrecy in his dealings with the regime of the Ayatollah Khomeini, an action so repugnant to ordinary Americans that he could not have done it openly.

I would go as far as to state that the nuclear-arms treaty between the United States and the Soviet Union, signed by Reagan and Gorbachev in a love feast in Washington in December, 1987, was also in the main the result of pressure applied by the citizenry. Posterity may look on the pact, which called for the destruction of all intermediate-range nuclear missiles, as Reagan's finest achievement. But many at the time saw it as a step he was forced to take if he was ever to restore a presidency that was flagging badly because of the Iran-contra scandal.

Along the same lines, I suggest in this book that what provided the necessary thrust for the sweeping tax reforms in 1986 was a sharp decline in Reagan's approval rating in the spring of 1985. Unlikely as it may seem, the progression of events argues strongly for such reasoning.

▪ ▪ ▪

I first took an interest in public opinion as a political force in the early 1970s in connection with the Watergate scandal. As city editor of the *Washington Post* in 1972 and 1973, I was in charge of the newspaper's coverage of Watergate, and I wrote a book, *The Great Coverup: Nixon and the Scandal of Watergate,* in 1974. One of my conclusions was that the scandal itself arose because Richard Nixon thought of the public as a hostile force—an enemy, if you will.

I was persuaded that most members of Congress had no intention of punishing Nixon severely, not even when the House of Representatives began considering impeachment. What forced the matter, I felt, was enormous public pressure. Americans were slow to become aroused by Watergate, but once they were, their outrage could not be contained. They bent Congress to their will.

As I came to the determination that Congress had to be forced to do what it should have done on its own, I began looking for books that would explain the relationship between public opinion and political power. I found very few. The best I came across was a 1961 book by the noted political writer and teacher V.O. Key, *Public Opinion and American Democracy*, which I commend to anyone interested in the subject. But Key only touched on what concerned me most: the communication and interplay between national leaders and the citizenry, and the effect of public opinion on government policies.

After Watergate, the chief editors at the *Post* recommended that I study and get into public opinion polling, which we all saw as a valuable reporting tool. I began the *Washington Post* poll in 1975, focusing on politics and other national issues. In 1981, the *Post* and the ABC television network formed the *Washington Post/ABC News* poll, with me in charge for the *Post*.

Over the years, I have come to see why it was so difficult to find adequate material on the role of public opinion in decision-making. It simply is not something leaders may be expected to discuss candidly. We will wait a long while before hearing Reagan say he sold arms to the Ayatollah in secret because he couldn't have gotten away with it in public, or for members of Congress to say they intentionally mislead constituents to win votes. Interviewing politicians along such lines is futile.

What I have done instead is to seek out what some social scientists refer to as an "elegant fit," incidents in which the relationship between public opinion and the actions of leaders seems indisputable, at least to me. Here and there, it takes a leap in reasoning to draw a particular conclusion, but not much of one.

Because public opinion is so powerful, national leaders of all leanings look on it as the great gorilla in the political jungle, a beast that must be kept calm. In election campaigns, most office-seekers generally talk to the people in the code of thirty-second commercials; once elected they talk in platitudes, if at all. The tactic is practiced equally by Republicans and Democrats.

Most politicians prefer to deal among themselves, quietly. An issue of such ascendant importance and enormous cost as Star Wars, or what Reagan euphemism experts named the Strategic Defense Initiative, for example, should have been the subject of continuing national debate, discussed vigorously by supporters and opponents from its conception. It has not been. Some in Congress think the plan for an antinuclear space shield is futile and have been working against it. But seldom have they put their views before the broad public. Leaders choose not to roil the people. Even in election campaigns, when office-seekers want to give the appearance of speaking out forcefully, they usually have the latest opinion polls in hand, to tell them which subjects are safe, which must be dealt with warily.

The two political parties pay handsomely for regular opinion surveys whose aim is to keep the politicians a step ahead of the public. Richard Wirthlin, Reagan's private pollster, has gotten millions of dollars from the Republican National Committee to help the president shape his message. The Democratic National Committee spends less—but then again, it has had less money. Its aim is the same: to stay a step ahead, to keep the public tame.

Generally speaking, Republicans and Democrats have

been very successful at that. On the average, adult Americans watch television more than four hours every day. News reports are highly popular, the ratings agencies show, but issues of national importance seldom make it past the eyes and ears. Most people retain hardly any of what they see on TV about public affairs.

Along with such apparent apathy exists enormous public cynicism. We have heard over and over in recent years that it is "morning in America" and that "America is back," slogans signifying a supposed new national spirit and trust in government. What the opinion polls have repeatedly shown, however, even long before the news about Reagan's secret dealings with Iran, was that trust in government has remained very low—about as low in 1985 and 1986 as in 1974, during the worst of the Vietnam-Watergate years.

Distrust is more than a generalized, abstract sentiment; people have particular grievances. For years, eighty percent of all Americans have considered the income-tax system to be unfair, and new surveys show few thinking the sweeping changes enacted in 1986 will provide equity. A majority feel the criminal-justice system mainly benefits the wealthy, a terrible indictment. Distrust and cynicism are leading to the extinction of the American voter: the United States has the lowest turnout record of any industrial nation.

Opinion polls keep reminding us that it is wrong to view most people as politically pliable on sensitive issues even though they know so little about public affairs. With exceptions at some rare moments, polls during Reagan's first six years in office disclosed that only twenty-five to thirty-five percent of the people knew he supported the "contra" rebels in Nicaragua. Yet the same polls also showed a stubborn unwillingness to bend under the president's constant plea for support in his goal of overthrowing the Sandinista government.

When it came to taking a position, there was no difference to speak of in the views of those who knew what Reagan wanted and those who did not. Well-to-do people held essentially the same views as the poor on intervention in Nicaragua, blacks the same as whites, and Republicans were not far from Democrats. In all instances, large majorities were against Reagan's stated policies.

What these polls were tapping was a national consensus, an almost immovable position. The sentiment could well be labeled "No more Vietnams."

There are a number of issues, concerns, and beliefs on which Americans are similarly unified. Put together, they yield an important list of priorities that may be termed the public's agenda. Included high on the list are a desire to maintain a strong national defense, to reduce or eliminate nuclear weaponry, to protect the environment. Also present are concerns over education, crime and drugs, public health, ethics and morality, a fear that the economy will go poof, a desire to bring blacks and the poor into the mainstream, to protect the Social Security and Medicare programs, to have competence and honesty in government and a fair tax system.

Yuppies share these beliefs and concerns; so do Jews, born-again Christians, welfare mothers. Thus the same public that knows so little about government and most issues of the day, that is easily divided into frequently quarreling blocs, has nevertheless for many years, in opinion poll after opinion poll, been laying out a consistent if somewhat idealistic national agenda. Only bits and pieces of it form the agenda of those who govern.

In this book I have tried to examine a few broad issues, such as race relations and views toward blacks, what Americans really think about the news media, how disgust with the income-tax system made us a nation of petty tax cheats, the ups and downs in public sentiment toward Israel, and the political realignment of the 1980s. I have drawn mainly on studies I have been personally involved in, and in many areas I have been able to go only slightly beneath the surface. Nevertheless, it is my sense that even such a limited examination draws a portrait of a people whose hopes and fears and priorities are far different from the picture presented by our leaders, day by day.

It is through scientific public opinion polling, created and developed by George Gallup and a few others just over fifty years ago, that we know as much as we do about what Americans really think. Early on, Gallup envisioned his polls as a means of improving the machinery of democracy, giving the "citizen a way to make his wishes known to government" and thereby countering "the organized minorities in America, with their pressure organizations and their lobbyists in Washington."

Pollsters have not always lived up to that lofty goal. The technique of polling became suspect, wrongly, after 1948, when Gallup and others failed to see that Harry Truman had turned things around against Thomas Dewey. The problem was not with the instrument but with the pollsters, who stopped interviewing in mid-October, thinking that Dewey's five-point lead was insurmountable.

In some instances, the polls—including ones done by Gallup—may have obstructed the democratic process. In 1968, early polls by Gallup and Louis Harris showed Richard Nixon far ahead of Hubert Humphrey, so much so that financial contributions to Humphrey dried up, making him unable to buy close-of-campaign television time. Humphrey ended up losing by one point and was convinced for the rest of his life that those polls had cost him the election.

Despite such shortcomings, the polls in general have made a worthy contribution in exactly the way Gallup had in mind. They keep putting before the people and the government a genuine citizens' agenda. They certainly are not perfect, but we are far better off with them than without them.

Each election year there are more opinion polls, not fewer, done both privately for candidates and publicly for the news media. The ambitious men seeking the presidency in 1988 seldom let a day pass without consulting either their own pollsters or campaign strategists, who are in constant touch with the pollsters. "May the best pollster win" could have been the starting cry for the race to lead the nation.

In these pages, I describe in lay terms how polls work and what some of the pitfalls are. That discussion, I hope, will enhance for some readers the sense of how the game of politics is played, and, perhaps, better attune them to the real meaning behind candidates' campaign utterances and strategy.

In other ways, too, I regard *What Americans Really Think* as a 1988 voters' guide. One important measure of any presidential campaign is whether candidates strive for informed debate on real issues—or deal with such issues at all.

The situation of black Americans springs to mind. In writing about blacks I was struck, as I hope readers will be, by just how important holding down a job is, how black men's having jobs, or their failure to hold one, explains so much about living conditions for blacks in the United States. Yet in the 1984 presidential campaign, when the problem was as urgent as it is today, there was virtually no discussion of a jobs program, for blacks or for anyone else.

Would that occur again this time? Could such an important issue continue to be ignored by the candidates? That and other matters dealt with here, I believe, could form a reader's campaign checklist. Are candidates addressing them at all? And, if they are, is it merely to create an impression of concern? Or are they seriously trying to deal with the issues?

Naturally, I like to think that what usefulness this book may have will extend well past November 8, 1988. The items in the public's agenda will not disappear with the election. Nor will the force of public opinion in our democracy wane, or the fear that so many leaders have of it.

In their daily jobs, most Washington reporters are forced during working hours to take the pronouncements of government leaders literally—to record what they say, no matter how outlandish—as serious expressions of their views and intentions. That is very frustrating work in a capital where, not long ago, Nixon's attorney general John Mitchell told friends, "Watch what we do, not what we say."

Those words serve as good advice, a guide for judging leading Democrats as well as Republicans. A stamp should be prepared for newspaper editors: FOR PUBLIC CONSUMPTION ONLY, NOT TO BE BELIEVED. It would be used every day.

At the same time, however, these reporters in the Washington press corps, dealing as closely as they do with the nation's leaders, often come to know many of them personally as men and women coping with often intransigent problems. A natural sympathy and respect arises from that.

My job has been different. I have followed the news closely, but from inside an office. I have met a good number of national leaders, but I know very few of them personally. What I notice about them in the main are their public statements, which often appear to have jumped right out of that day's printout of opinion-poll data. I have become engrossed with the way leaders speak to the people; few casual remarks are made into Washington microphones.

I am regularly fascinated at the words, words, words in every political assault, the foreplay in the execution of power. Ronald Reagan spoke about keeping the government off the backs of the people. Those are the kinds of words I have in mind. They have a genuine appeal. But as a friend of mine once put it, and as has been amply demonstrated, what Reagan meant to do was keep the people off the backs of the government. The words cannot always be taken at face value.

Nonetheless, I have tried throughout not to read more into certain leaders' statements and actions than was justified. That was not easy for me, having the impression that for most in government, especially those of great prominence, almost every action is aimed at a particular public reaction.

My main hopes are that readers will regard my impressions as fair ones, and that here and there I have found a decent fit, if not an elegant one. Barry Sussman
Washington, D.C.
March, 1988

PART ONE

THE PEOPLE
V.
THE
GOVERNMENT

The force of public opinion cannot be resisted, when permitted freely to be expressed. The agitation it produces must be submitted to. It is necessary to keep the waters pure.

—Thomas Jefferson, 1823,
in a letter to Lafayette

AN IRRESISTIBLE FORCE

IT WAS AUGUST 28, 1974, AND GERALD FORD HAD been president for nineteen days. He was holding his first press conference since the resignation of Richard Nixon. It opened with a question from Helen Thomas, the reporter for the United Press International news service.

"Mr. President," she asked, "do you agree with the bar association that the law applies equally to all men, or do you agree with Governor Rockefeller that former President Nixon should have immunity from prosecution? And specifically, would you use your pardon authority, if necessary?"

To many, the question was like a bolt from the blue. Ford

had given no hint that he was thinking of a pardon; his only public comment on the matter, made nine months earlier, was to scoff at the idea. "I do not think the public would stand for it," he had said then, at a congressional hearing on his appointment as vice-president.

In response to Miss Thomas, Ford again invoked the name of public opinion. He said: "The expression made by Governor Rockefeller, I think, coincides with the general view and the point of view of the American people. I subscribe to that point of view, but let me add, in the last ten days or two weeks I have asked for prayers for guidance on this very important point."

Thus did Ford first suggest that he might pardon Nixon— by asserting that there was broad public support for him to do so. But there was no such support.

A few days later, the Gallup organization released the results of a nationwide public opinion poll taken before the press conference. In it, a substantial majority, fifty-six percent of the people interviewed, favored putting Nixon on trial. Gallup had not asked a direct question about a pardon; to do so would have been premature—a pardon is usually considered only after a person has been indicted, tried, and convicted.

On Sunday, September 8, 1974, Ford pardoned Nixon: "I was certain in my own mind and in my own conscience that it is the right thing to do," he commented.

As for public opinion, Ford had this to say: "My customary policy is to try and get all the facts and to consider the opinions of my countrymen and to take counsel with my most valued friends. But these seldom agree, and in the end, the decision is mine. . . . I do believe the buck stops here, that I cannot rely upon public opinion polls to tell me what is right."

There is a saying about lawyers—that when they don't have the facts they argue the law; when they don't have the facts or the law, they argue principle. So it is with many national leaders and public opinion. When they don't have it on their side, they assert that in fact it is; when they can't even do that, they argue principle, the principle being that they were elected to lead, not follow.

Within days, the Gallup poll reported new findings, from a survey done between the time of the press conference and the issuance of the pardon. Instead of being moved by Ford's hints, sentiment had remained constant: fifty-eight percent approved putting Nixon on trial, thirty-six percent opposed it.

This time Gallup added a question about a pardon. "If Nixon is brought to trial and found guilty," it was phrased, "do you think he should or should not be granted a pardon by President Ford?" Thirty-eight percent favored a pardon, fifty-three percent were opposed.

In the months that followed, there was speculation that the pardon had been part of a deal to obtain Nixon's resignation. A House of Representatives Judiciary subcommittee looked into the matter briefly by summoning Ford to testify at an extraordinary hearing. But there was no formal investigation. The pardon rapidly receded from scrutiny by Congress and the press.

By and large, the nation's major news media began referring to the new president as "decent, honest Jerry Ford." His short term in office was marked by soft coverage, an extended honeymoon.

The American people were less kind. They penalized Ford for trifling with them.

In the most often cited measure of a president's popularity, the approval rating, the Gallup poll showed Ford plummeting from seventy-one percent at the time he took office in August, to sixty-six percent in early September, fifty percent in late September, and forty-two percent by the end of the year.

These declines were steeper than any previously recorded, worse even than Nixon's during the Watergate scandal. The approval rating is a faulty measure of presidential popularity; it is superficial and sometimes misleading. But when it drops that precipitously, there is no misreading it.

As for the pardon, an opinion poll by the Louis Harris organization in late September, 1974, showed sixty percent saying it was wrong for Ford to have issued it, only thirty-three percent saying it was right.

In November, 1974, the Democrats picked up three seats in the U.S. Senate and forty-three in the House. In all, there were ninety-two new House members, including seventy-five freshman Democrats. It was one of the largest influxes of new members ever, and the group came to be known as the "Watergate class."

Few commentators at the time linked the Republican losses to the pardon, seeing them more as a rejection of the party of Richard Nixon. But Ford had a chance to alter perceptions of the Republicans, and he blew it. So a good share of the blame for his party's losses may be laid directly to the pardon, as well.

In 1976 Ford was defeated for the presidency by Jimmy Carter, a political unknown. The election was one of the closest in history, with Carter getting 50.1 percent of the vote and Ford 48.0. In all tight elections, any number of individual factors may be said to account for the difference. In 1976, the pardon was one of them.

Opinion polls showed eight percent of the Carter voters saying the pardon was the main factor in their vote, more then enough to determine the result. (One percent of the Ford voters said the pardon was their main reason for supporting him. *Chacun à son goût.*)

In addition, in some states, such as New York and Pennsylvania, many Republicans simply stayed home. A normal Republican turnout in either place would have turned the election around.

Ford was punished despite the fact that the pardon was seldom mentioned throughout the presidential campaign. Once Carter made a wisecrack, saying to someone, "Pardon me." Mostly, he deliberately avoided the subject.

The pardon did not come up in the three televised debates between the candidates. Toward the end of the campaign, with private polls showing how damaging it had been to him, Ford himself spoke about it briefly, defending his action.

Reporters hardly ever asked either candidate about the

matter; commentators did not dwell on it. They did not have to. It stuck in people's minds. Even today, when people think back on Gerald Ford, one of the few vivid recollections is that he pardoned Nixon.

It seems certain that had Carter or main elements in the news media chosen to home in on the pardon, the margin of the Democrats' victory would have been greater. Conceivably, they could have cruised. Pollster Patrick Caddell said afterward that he and other advisers told Carter in mid-October that he could "blow the election wide open" by focusing on the pardon as an issue. At that point the race had taken a downturn for the challenger, and was judged a tossup by many observers. Carter declined nevertheless, Caddell said, because "he thought he would be elected president and he didn't want blood all over the floor."

Thus, for those who determined the campaign agenda—the candidates and the news media—the pardon was a non-issue, or the next thing to it.

The brief presidency of Gerald Ford holds important lessons on the formation and power of public opinion:

- *It is common for leaders to deal contemptuously with the citizenry, as Ford did when he suggested, misleadingly, that what the people wanted would carry great weight with him.*
- *Most Americans have short political memories. As the Gallup polls showed, large majorities opposed the Nixon pardon and many were outraged by it. But fewer than one in ten voters took their anger out on Ford in the voting booth twenty-seven months later.*
- *Those with the power to keep important issues alive— the nation's political leaders and the news media— often choose not to do so. Their reasons are diverse, at times as apparently well-meaning as Carter's in avoiding discussion of the pardon, but often more self-serving. The effect is almost uniformly the same: to*

*stifle public debate on matters that people care about,
or should care about.*

- *Perhaps most importantly, what the reaction to the
  Nixon pardon demonstrated was the potent, independent side of public opinion. With no concerted drive
  involved, no major advertising campaign—and, probably, no great dislike of Ford, either; simply a judgment that his standards were too low—there were still
  enough people caring about the pardon to force Ford
  out of office.*

The Nixon pardon was of such magnitude that citizens responded with hardly any prodding or interpretation from
leaders or opinion-molders or proof that a deal had been
struck. The pardon was repugnant and memorable. People
felt Ford had cheated them and enough of them remem-
bered, on their own, to see that he was punished for it. It was
that simple, and that awesome.

There have not been many such tidal displays of public
power in recent American history, but there have been some.
Almost all were equally dramatic. One was the response to
the Watergate scandal itself.

In the years since 1974, the myth has grown that Richard
Nixon was forced to resign or be impeached because of an
aggressive press, a responsive Congress, and an independent
justice system. It is now commonplace to think of Watergate
as proof that the "system" worked.

It would be more accurate to say that the system barely
survived. And that without enormous, essentially self-
inspired public pressure it might well have failed.

Most news agencies turned away from Watergate until
they could no longer ignore it. The three television networks
assigned not a single reporter to the story for the first six
months or longer. According to a study by journalism profes-
sor and media critic Ben Bagdikian, there were 433 reporters
in the larger press bureaus in Washington but fewer than 15

were assigned full-time to Watergate in that period, and most of them for only a few days.*

Congress was just as bad. From sworn testimony and Nixon's own public statements, there was sufficient evidence to impeach Nixon in May, 1973. Instead, the Senate then began the celebrated Ervin Committee hearings, which went on for months, were stunning in their impact, but ended with Nixon hardly any closer to being brought to judgment than at their outset.

As for the justice system, the first Watergate trial was crippled by a weak FBI investigation, perjured testimony, and prosecutors who obediently allowed Justice Department higher-ups to narrowly define their inquiry. It concluded with an irate, frustrated judge lamenting his failure to get to the bottom of things and complaining that the system was failing.

Watergate was uncovered for three reasons, none having to do with the integrity of the system. For one thing, the judge, John Sirica, locked up some liars and threatened to throw away the key unless they had a change of heart. For another, so many culprits were involved in the coverup that it began to collapse under its own weight, especially because of Sirica's poking at it.

But of at least equal, and perhaps overriding, importance was the role of public opinion. It was the people that forced Congress finally to move seriously against Richard Nixon, starting with an unprecedented dumping of some three million letters and telegrams on Capitol Hill in one crucial two-week period in October, 1973.†

---

* Ben Bagdikian, *Columbia Journalism Review*, January-February, 1973.
† The occasion was the firing of Watergate special prosecutor Archibald Cox, ordered by Nixon on Saturday, October 20, 1973, in what came to be known as the Saturday Night Massacre. Attorney General Elliot Richardson resigned rather than fire Cox; so did the number-two official in the Justice Department, William Ruckelshaus. The next in line, Solicitor General Robert Bork, did fire Cox, and Nixon's press secretary then announced that the office of special prosecutor had been abolished, precipitating the torrent of public outrage. (Bork's action did not help him any when, years

The public, as is so often the case, was slow to become aroused, much slower than it should have been. But once convinced of Nixon's guilt, no amount of legal nitpicking or protective politicking from friends on Capitol Hill could save him. He was done for. The people, unaided, made it clear there would be a mass ouster of elected leaders who failed to move against the president.

It was almost two years from the time of the break-in before most of the institutions that were supposed to protect the national interest were doing their jobs well. The courts had overcome their problems, the Congress had become diligent. The press was dutifully reporting what was happening. But without an enraged public it is extremely doubtful that Nixon would have been forced out of office.

This view—that public opinion led to Nixon's downfall—has not been given wide circulation. That should come as no surprise. As rare as it is for the citizenry to rise up and force extreme governmental action, it is rarer still for the public to get credit for wielding such power. Politicians do not go around saying, "The people backed me into a corner." Neither does the press.

There are exceptions. It is generally recognized, for example, that gradually swelling public anger finally brought U.S. involvement in the Vietnam war to an end, forcing a proud and powerful president, Lyndon Johnson, to become a virtual prisoner in the White House along the way, afraid to seek reelection. But seldom is it that the raw power of public opinion is cited for what it is: the single strongest motivating force behind many major government decisions—a power so strong that, once put in motion, it will overrun the normal governing process almost every time.

During the Reagan administration, some of the most important government actions were ones that the public forced on the president against his will.

---

later in 1987, the U.S. Senate overwhelmingly rejected him as a nominee for a seat on the Supreme Court.)

In May of 1981, for example, Reagan opened what was no doubt for him a long-considered assault on the Social Security system. On May 12, his first secretary of health and human services, Richard S. Schweiker, announced plans to reduce initial benefits for all future retirees, with sharper reductions in benefits for people who chose to retire before the age of sixty-five, and more stringent requirements for collecting disability insurance.

At the time I was codirector of the *Washington Post/ABC News* public opinion poll. Two days after Schweiker's announcement, we interviewed 1,003 adults nationwide and found sentiment running very strongly against the proposals.

Administration officials had proclaimed that the purpose of the changes was to rescue Social Security from bankruptcy. The people we interviewed agreed that the system was in financial trouble; only eight percent in the poll felt it was in "good financial shape." But by almost two to one among those expressing an opinion, they felt they themselves would be hurt, not helped, by the proposed changes.

At that moment Reagan was in the midst of his early, successful drive to reorder national economic priorities. He had introduced legislation curbing other social programs, creating a massive military buildup and reducing taxes, all at once. Some members of Congress were said to be so impressed by his popularity that they voted in favor of his programs only because he commanded such great public support.

But in attacking Social Security, the most revered of government programs, Reagan had overplayed his hand. By ninety-six to zero, the Senate passed a resolution condemning the administration proposals, forcing Reagan to back down. Older Americans as a group had been his strongest supporters; they began to distrust him and afterward were his weakest backers. Younger people did not leap to criticize Reagan's overall policies, but they too expressed displeasure with the planned Social Security changes.

For a long time, advisers referred to the events of May, 1981, as Reagan's worst blunder. Coasting so smoothly until then, perhaps the president could not envision such a public backlash, although his pollster, Richard Wirthlin, was said to have cautioned him. In retrospect, the sharpness of the outcry may have helped Reagan in one sense, making him more careful in the future.

A year later he engineered a new, successful foray on Social Security, getting Democratic leaders involved by appointing a bipartisan commission, hoping thereby to avoid political recriminations. But the cuts recommended and won were not as extensive as originally sought, and in the end other Republicans, if not Reagan himself, suffered. The public to this day regards the Republican party as unreliable when it comes to the protection of the Social Security system.

From then on Reagan sparred with the citizenry like a crafty boxer, jabbing and sidestepping. He had to. He was in the process of instituting programs that were decidedly unpopular. His experience in May, 1981, taught him to back away when necessary, and he did so repeatedly.

Some of his retreats under the pressure of public opinion were shameless.

On October 23, 1983, a suicide terrorist in Beirut crashed a truck into a four-story building that was being used as quarters for a contingent of U.S. Marines, causing 241 deaths. The Marines at that point had no clear-cut role in Lebanon. Their presence had been sharply criticized by some in Congress and questioned by a great many Americans even before the terrible incident.

After it, the demand that the remaining Marines be removed grew steadily. First to succumb to public pressure was House Speaker Thomas P. (Tip) O'Neill, Jr., but not before considerable waffling. In the days after the calamity, O'Neill urged fellow Democrats to stand by Reagan, demanding that they put "patriotism above partisanship," and saying, in early November, that "it would be a disaster to pull out. It would be a victory for the Syrians and the Soviets in the Mideast."

Polls showed a majority of Americans agreeing that a pullout would benefit hostile powers. But the majority also believed there was no clear goal for the Marines in Lebanon, and growing numbers of people sought a withdrawal regardless of the consequences. In a January, 1984, *Washington Post/ABC News* poll, sixty percent of the people interviewed said they disapproved of Reagan's handling of the situation in Lebanon; only thirty percent approved.

Reagan, in an interview with *Post* reporters in the middle of the month, dealt directly with this problem of public opinion. Speaking of the terrorists in Beirut, he said, "They are trying to take advantage of what they see as criticism here, lack of public support, in the hope that public opinion will force the withdrawal. . . . It would be a disaster if they succeeded."

It became clear that the Marines, if left in Lebanon, would be an issue in the 1984 presidential campaign; Walter Mondale and other Democratic candidates were already attacking Reagan on it. On February 1, House Democrats, in a non-binding resolution, demanded a "prompt and orderly" withdrawal of the troops.

"We, as the opposition, have a duty to tell the American people of the failure of policy," O'Neill said in bowing to pressure from his colleagues. "When the president makes a mistake, we would be derelict if we did not speak out."

In response, Reagan gave the appearance of holding firm. "He may be ready to surrender," the president said of O'Neill in an interview with the *Wall Street Journal*. "If we get out, that means the end of Lebanon."

In a radio broadcast on February 4, Reagan said, "Yes, the situation in Lebanon is difficult, frustrating, and dangerous. But that is no reason to turn our backs on friends and to cut and run."

All along, Reagan tried to give the impression that the Marines were fulfilling a necessary function by being in Lebanon, and that he was guided by principle, not expediency, in his military actions. He said at one point that he would never use American boys for political purposes.

For weeks, however, chief Reagan aides had been preparing a pullout; on January 26 Reagan was presented a plan developed by the Joint Chiefs of Staff that called for removal of the troops. He approved it in principle on February 1, before his criticism of O'Neill, and announced on February 7 that the Marines would be "redeployed" to ships off-shore.

It cannot be proven that Reagan had his eye on the presidential campaign when he ordered the Marines out; the smoking gun here awaits some future White House memoir. But there seems little doubt about it. Most Americans apparently believed he did. In a *Post/ABC News* opinion poll in February, 1984, fifty-two percent said Reagan ordered the withdrawal "more because keeping them there was hurting him politically at home"; only thirty-four percent said it was "more because of what has been happening in Lebanon."

The pattern was the same, with a stunningly different outcome, in the matter of Reagan's policy toward Nicaragua. Events have shown that it was the fear of public opinion that pushed Reagan into a great debacle of secret, illegal maneuvering in Nicaragua. Reagan and the American people were totally at odds over intervention in that poor, miserable country.

From the start, Reagan's aim appeared to be the overthrow of the Sandinista government in Nicaragua, to make its leaders "cry 'Uncle,' " as he put it. The public simply would not accept that; Vietnam was too fresh a memory.

For years the president kept pushing for acceptance of his goals. He built a strong case: Soviet and Cuban military advisers in Managua, no free elections, no free press, mistreatment of the Catholic church, of the Miskito Indians, the likely spread of communism in the hemisphere and a resultant flood of refugees to this country, along with the possibility of the seas turning red with blood on Florida shores. Once again, he appointed a bipartisan commission to report on the situation; he hammered away on the subject, sometimes every day for months at a time, trying to rally support.

It was to no avail. The public had mixed feelings toward Nicaragua, and was especially concerned about the spread of communism in the Americas. But the great majority had no heart at all for U.S. intervention.

Routinely in public opinion surveys, two out of three people would say the United States should not engage in attempts to overthrow the Sandinistas. At one point, when El Salvador was as much in the news as Nicaragua, half the respondents in a *Post/ABC News* poll said they did not believe Reagan when he said he had no intention of sending American troops to fight in either country.

Such sentiments, expressed in dozens of highly publicized public opinion polls, put major constraints on the president. Congress was emboldened by them and, for various periods, refused the president's requests to supply the contras with military aid, or, on occasion, any aid at all. Reagan himself had to keep cutting down the amount he requested.

But the president only half-bowed to public opinion on Nicaragua. Publicly, he kept putting his case to the people, hoping to sway them. Privately he chose to defy Congress and the citizenry, having his emissaries coerce or beg money from foreign leaders to support the contras, and setting up in the White House an illegal control center for the war.

Beginning in November, 1986, the exposure of these and other deceitful, repugnant actions sapped the strength of the Reagan presidency. His approval ratings slid, dropping from around seventy percent in October, 1986, to the low forties by the end of the year.

Stunned by his rapid decline, Reagan flailed for ways to recover his standing. He appeared in TV speeches or news conferences five times in less than three weeks, then avoided such events for months. Alternately he adopted a hard line, attacking Congress and the press, then a soft one, taking popular actions which, in an earlier time, he had absolutely rejected.

In April, 1987, for instance, Reagan, who had made a great show of sending medium-range nuclear missiles to Europe years earlier, agreed without a murmur to withdraw them. The following month, having rejected similar requests in previous years, he went to Tuskegee, Alabama, to give a com-

mencement address at a black college. In June, he spoke
forcefully for the first time on the need for an ambitious,
sympathetic approach to the AIDS epidemic, a problem that
was searing the nation but that he previously had hardly ever
mentioned. A month later he named a twelve-member panel
to make recommendations on national policy toward AIDS
(although the merits of some selected were highly questionable).

Reagan began to speak more about human rights abroad.
Month by month, his negotiators in Geneva went further out
on a limb toward negotiating a major nuclear-arms limitation
treaty with the Soviet Union.

In August, 1987, Reagan stunned supporters on the right by
offering a peace plan for Nicaragua that would put the contra
rebels out of business. Critics on the left charged that the
offer was a phony one that would end in rejection by one
side or the other, resulting in a renewed call for congressional funding of the contras. But it was unlike any offer
Reagan had made previously and it may well have been an
effort by a fading president to regain stature with his countrymen. It, and Reagan's other reversals in direction, may very
well have been caused by his drastic slide in the polls.

To all appearances, Reagan—perceived for so long as a
master at manipulating public opinion—was being manipu-
lated by it, forced to take popular actions in order to survive.
The culmination came on December 8, 1987, at a glorious
moment in the White House when Reagan and Soviet leader
Mikhail Gorbachev signed a treaty calling for the destruction
of 2,611 intermediate-range nuclear missiles and pledged to
work toward further reductions.

Literally, Reagan could claim that he had long sought the
elimination of nuclear weaponry; he had cited it as a goal as
far back as his 1980 election campaign. In actuality, however,
the move was seen as a stunning departure from the president's past performance. In the days just before the pact was
signed, Reagan was severely censured by some of his strongest supporters in the Republican right wing, who simply
could not believe that any treaty agreeable to the Russians

would be acceptable to the United States. These supporters-turned-critics laid Reagan's willingness to sign directly to his desire for a boost in popularity. And indeed, a few days after the pact was signed, a *Washington Post/ABC News* poll showed his approval rating had suddenly risen by eight percentage points.

MANIPULATION

"When you bring your head up and start talking, bring your head up and look at the camera for a moment . . ."
"Yeah," Richard Nixon nodded.

—Joe McGinnis, *The Selling of the President*, 1968

POLITICIANS KNOW THE POWER OF PUBLIC opinion and try their best to stay ahead of it.

One day in 1981 I ran into Richard Wirthlin, President Reagan's pollster, on K Street, three blocks from the White House. He mentioned that he had read my account of a poll having to do with the fundamentalist preacher Jerry Falwell and his organization, the Moral Majority. Falwell was one of several preachers seeking to move their born-again flocks into political activism, making them key figures in a political realignment that was edging the Republican party to parity with the Democrats.

The thrust of my poll findings was that while Falwell was viewed by many in Washington as a force to be reckoned with, only half the public even recognized his name, and among those who did, most disapproved of his goals and those of the Moral Majority. That did not exactly strip Falwell as a figure to be contended with, but it did diminish him some.

Wirthlin told me his polling firm, Decision Making Information, was in the midst of its own survey of Americans' views toward Falwell.

Wirthlin was then being paid about $900,000 a year by the Republican National Committee—a lot of money for polling, especially since there were no elections taking place. His main work was for the president. He met regularly with Reagan, with Nancy Reagan, and with high White House aides.

Some time later, on July 7, Reagan named Sandra Day O'Connor to the Supreme Court. News accounts revealed that before making the appointment public, Reagan had put in a phone call to Falwell. A matter of concern was O'Connor's position on abortion. As a legislator in Arizona, she had voted for legalizing abortion there, and against antiabortion measures. The purpose of Reagan's call, as reported, was to assure Falwell that, despite her votes, O'Connor opposed abortion, and to seek Falwell's support.

My assumption was that Wirthlin's poll findings helped Reagan in his approach to Falwell. Later on a *Post* reporter asked Wirthlin if there had been such a connection; the pollster would not comment one way or the other. But a pollster's job is to report findings, not hold them back. Wirthlin's aim was to help the president stay a step ahead of public opinion, to ensure that whatever the president did, he was able to put his actions in the best possible light, to either get the public on his side, or, at a minimum, to keep from antagonizing large numbers of people.

It was market research applied to politics, practiced not only in election campaigns but in the everyday conduct of government affairs.

Use of opinion polls in the Oval Office did not begin with

Reagan. Jimmy Carter had a pollster, Patrick Caddell, to help frame his message. I hardly knew Caddell, but once, after a televised Reagan speech, he complained to me that almost every sentence had come out of public opinion polls and was aimed at manipulating public opinion. He offered to do a textual analysis of the talk, demonstrating his contention.

I thought the complaint disingenuous, in that Caddell had helped Carter prepare speeches with the same aim in mind. But what he said was not exactly news to me or any public opinion analyst. As it happened, in December, 1983, a good bit before he called, I had written just such an analysis of statements Reagan made in a press conference, and it ran as an article in the *Washington Post*.*

Carter wasn't the first president to make extensive use of opinion polls, either. One amusing sidelight to the Watergate scandal, if any of it could be called amusing, had to do with so-called "secret" opinion polls.

In 1972, it was revealed that the Nixon reelection team kept a slush fund, believed at the time to total perhaps $700,000. That money funded the Watergate break-in and other illegal campaign activities. White House aides denied illegal use of the money and said that $350,000 of it went to "secret" public opinion polling.

The campaign had a large, publicly reported budget for polling. It may well be there was some that went unreported, too. After all, the polling of ordinary citizens could be seen as an extension of campaign spying, or vice versa. Both were

---

* In the article, I took the liberty of matching some of Reagan's statements against *Washington Post/ABC News* poll findings that were only a few days old. I was thus able to put this lead on the article:

> While President Reagan said yesterday that "we're going to do what we can" to alleviate hunger in America, a majority of citizens say they believe that his cutbacks in federal social programs have created serious hardship for many people.

The article, which ran on December 15, also noted that while Reagan had said about the situation in Lebanon, "I think we're making more progress than appears on the surface," a five-to-three majority of the people polled felt the administration had no clear goals for the U.S. Marines there.

methods of gathering intelligence in the war of politics, providing ammunition for swaying public opinion.

Before Nixon, Lyndon B. Johnson was legendary for using opinion polls to cajole people. Any number of them described how LBJ, trying to get his way, would yank an opinion poll from his pocket to prove a point in whatever argument he was making.

The first president to use scientific public opinion polls just happened to be the first who could: Franklin Delano Roosevelt, in 1939 or 1940, only a few years after polling as we know it today came into existence.

By then almost all of Europe was at war or about to be. Roosevelt committed resources to the allies but he faced strong isolationist sentiment at home, with much of it opposed to those efforts. The president knew what he wanted to do but he sought help from the new researchers of mass opinion in determining how to frame his message. What he did not have was a private pollster, like Wirthlin or Caddell. But there was the public pollster, George Gallup.

Through an intermediary, Roosevelt asked that Gallup elicit Americans' views toward U.S. involvement in the war, and convey the findings to the White House. I first heard about this arrangement from an old-time academic and political pollster, Lloyd Free. In the mid-seventies I asked Gallup about it, and he readily confirmed the story. The intermediary, Gallup told me, was Eugene Meyer, publisher of the *Washington Post*.

Ideally, presidents and other national leaders need no public opinion polls to govern; simple explanations of just policies should garner support.

But that is not the way things work. Presidents look at the public as a "market" and use whatever tools they can to sell themselves. Constituents are sales targets, speeches and presidential announcements are advertising. This is especially true in a president's first term, and in all political campaigning. It is hard, sometimes impossible, to discern whether policy announcements are genuine or are merely shams for public relations, aimed at letting a president take a popular stand on one issue so as to gain the latitude for an unpopular move on another.

The marketing approach cannot help but instill in national leaders the same wariness of the citizenry that advertisers often have for potential customers. Schooled in imagery, presidents and other high officials mince their words and patronize the people. The public that turned on government over Vietnam, over Watergate, looms ominously, ever threatening.

Public officials naturally become isolated from ordinary people. The higher their position, the more they become bound to coteries of aides, lobbyists, expert advisers, consultants, large campaign donors, and, perhaps, as Gerald Ford said, a few "valued friends." Often the friends are from back home, but they are members of the local establishment and not ordinary citizens at all.

It took years for the average American to turn against the Vietnam war, but it took high officials in Washington even longer. One reason was their isolation from the people, their failure to understand the feelings of ordinary citizens. Democratic Senator Eugene McCarthy ran for president in 1968 only after being persuaded by his children that the war was so destructive. Other powerful people in Washington stayed with the war longer yet, even though their positions gave them access to the best information available.

Most citizens have nothing to contribute in any discussion of military weaponry or the status of U.S. strength versus that of the Russians. It makes no sense at all for a leader to expect guidance from the public on complicated foreign-policy issues. Public opinion is of no help in those areas. But that is only part of the picture. With little understanding of details, ordinary people have something else to offer: a set of hopes and fears, of priorities and values.

Isolation from the people means losing touch with that, and it is one heavy price leaders pay. The longer a person holds high office, the tighter the cocoon.

Leaders generally treat public opinion as something to keep off their backs. They have important agendas. They may lean toward the left or the right; they may have their hearts in the right place or be captives of special interests. It makes little difference. Once in office, they tend to see public opinion more as a threat than a help.

The Washington power structure has developed elaborate, expensive machinery to deal with that threat, aside from taking the public temperature through opinion polls. An enormous sum of government money is spent on public relations. The president has a White House spokesperson and an entire communications staff. So does his wife. Every office in the executive branch has a public-affairs department; every U.S. senator and member of the House has a budget for publicity and public information, much of which is pure propaganda. The Library of Congress, through its Congressional Research Service, keeps up to date on major media opinion polls, making them available, at a moment's notice, to legislators who want to stay abreast of public thinking on any issue.

Throughout Reagan's years in office, there was hardly a week that Wirthlin was not sampling public opinion for him. Day in and day out, the odds were that interviewers for Decision Making Information were on the telephone asking Americans about the latest foreign crisis, or the death penalty, or whether a president should run for reelection at age seventy-three.

Wirthlin had many other clients; his firm handled Republican candidates in more than a hundred of the 1982 congressional campaigns. But his work for Reagan alone amounted to as much, or almost as much, as the telephone interviewing done for all the news media combined, including the efforts of Gallup, Louis Harris, NBC, the *Washington Post* and ABC, the *New York Times* and CBS, the *Los Angeles Times*, and others.

In the first six or seven weeks of 1987, with the scandal of the secret Iran arms shipments and the contra funding in full throttle, Wirthlin reportedly interviewed more than 25,000 people in a virtually endless round of polling. That would have been more polling than any of the public pollsters were likely to do all year.

Efforts like that were not aimed at helping Reagan determine policy, although on some occasions they may have had that result. Presidents don't take polls to find out what their policies should be. They know what they want to do; they sample public opinion only to find out how best to accomplish it, or to alert themselves to rising storms.

Because Wirthlin polled almost all the time, Reagan became aware of sudden outbursts of concern and was in position to deal with them almost immediately. That happened at the time of the 1983 massacre of the Marines in Lebanon, too. In rapid sequence, Reagan dove in the public opinion polls, then took emergency action and recovered strongly.

The Marines were killed on a Sunday. On Monday we geared up our *Washington Post/ABC News* poll for a quick sampling of public opinion.

On Tuesday, as we were preparing our questionnaire, there was another major event: American troops invaded the Caribbean island of Grenada, population 110,000. A main stated purpose of the attack was to protect several hundred American medical students who were said to be threatened by a violent, erratic Marxist ruler and his militia. The latter had been killing off political opponents and terrorizing ordinary citizens.

For Reagan the timing of the invasion could not have been better. It helped take the focus off Beirut.

We began our opinion poll on Wednesday, including in it questions on Lebanon and Grenada. That evening we interviewed 729 people and found most of them distraught over what had happened in Lebanon, puzzled over Grenada, and decidedly unhappy with Reagan's adventurism.

Only a minority, forty-four percent, approved Reagan's overall handling of foreign policy. Six people in ten took the view that "the United States is trying to do too much with its armed forces overseas." Only four in ten approved Reagan's handling of the situation in Lebanon, and only a slim majority, fifty-three percent, approved of the invasion of Grenada despite its having been advertised as a mission to rescue American youngsters.

Two of every three people interviewed blamed lax security for the deaths of the Marines; hardly more than one in three said the administration had clear goals for the Marines in Lebanon.

In comments after the Marines' deaths, Reagan deplored the incident but said the mission in Lebanon had been "successful overall." By sixty-six to twenty-six percent, the random sample of Americans we interviewed disagreed.

All this, of course, was bad news for a president who relied on public support—or the appearance of public support—to help him have his way with Congress. Wirthlin told reporters that he himself was polling as those events occurred, and I assume he got similar results.

How to turn things around? Part of the answer, as on numerous other occasions, was for Reagan to address the nation on TV.

That Thursday evening, October 27, 1983, Reagan delivered what many considered a consummate appeal to the American people. It was filled with remarks on stopping the spread of communism, and with highly emotional anecdotes.

"Why should our young men be dying in Lebanon?" Reagan asked. "Why is Lebanon important to us?" Among his answers: The Middle East must not fall to "a power or powers hostile to the free world"; "If we turned our backs on Lebanon now, what would be the future of Israel?"

Never mind that Reagan's actions were seen as unsettling by Middle East nations, and thereby served Soviet ends, or that Israel, since its founding, had made it clear that U.S. troops were the one kind of assistance it did not want.

"I received a message from the father of a Marine in Lebanon," Reagan said. "He told me: 'In a world where we speak of human rights, there is a sad lack of acceptance of responsibility. My son has chosen the acceptance of responsibility for the privilege of living in this country. . . .'

"A Lebanese mother told one of our ambassadors that her little girl had only attended school two of the last eight years.

Now, because of our presence there, she said, her daughter could live a normal life."

As for Grenada, Reagan said, "We got there just in time." He described what he termed a "Soviet-Cuban colony being readied as a major military bastion to export terror and undermine democracy."

The *Post* and ABC polled again on Friday, interviewing 517 people and asking many of the same questions as on Wednesday. We found the public mood sharply changed, in some regards radically changed. Suddenly a strong majority, fifty-seven percent, said they approved Reagan's overall handling of foreign policy, an improvement of thirteen points. What that meant, translating poll percentages into actual numbers, was that between twenty million and twenty-five million adult Americans had a change in heart and had fallen in line behind the president.

Approval of Reagan's handling of the situation in Lebanon rose eleven points in the two days, so that a slim majority, fifty-two percent, backed him despite the deaths of the Marines. Support for the invasion of Grenada rose by ten points, with nearly two in every three people now persuaded that it had been the right thing to do. Before Reagan spoke, only a minority, forty-five percent, believed that the American students had been in a fair amount or a great deal of danger. Afterward, fifty-eight percent felt that way.

No longer was there a six-to-four majority thinking that Reagan was trying to do too much with the armed forces overseas. Instead, people were evenly divided, with forty-eight percent saying he was attempting too much militarily but forty-nine percent saying he was not.

I marveled as I watched Reagan's speech, and was not surprised by the change in attitudes a day later. An actor, the president could be counted on to give a splendid performance. He also had the benefit of Wirthlin's polls, which were instructive on which strings to pluck.

But Reagan had a great deal more going for him than his gift for acting and the advice of a pollster. He never could have gone so far in winning over the public without the acquiescence of many other national leaders, including some who were regarded as his major political opponents, both in October, 1983, and through most of his presidency.

When it comes to public affairs, average Americans are properly modest about their interpretive ability. In large degree, they view major national events as they would a tennis match, with political leaders the players. Eyes move to one side of the court, then the other. The people may want a tough contest between Republicans and Democrats, conservatives and liberals, but they seldom get it.

When the Marines were killed there was an understandable hush on Capitol Hill. There was probably a good deal of shame as well, for Congress could have seen to it that the troops were removed before the massacre, or at least pushed the president harder.

As noted earlier, leaders like Tip O'Neill came to Reagan's defense at first, saying that politics stopped at the water's edge. There was no real criticism of Reagan, no attempt at that crucial moment at any serious debate over American policy. Under such circumstances it was no surprise that millions accepted what the president had to say. He had the tennis court to himself.

Much the same occurred in regard to the invasion of Grenada. Skeptics like me had harsh questions about the timing and circumstances of the attack. There was no doubt that the situation on the tiny island had become more tense and that plans for the invasion had been laid several days before the slaughter of the Marines in Lebanon. Nevertheless, it was questionable whether the American students, numbering about seven hundred, were truly endangered. If so, they could have left the island on their own, as some had already done.

So one important and terrible question was whether the attack was aimed at diverting attention from the events in Beirut—that is, whether the timing of the move on such a dot in the ocean was politically motivated.

Some on Capitol Hill clearly had the same nasty thought and were highly critical of Reagan as the raid took place. Fourteen House members went to the island on a fact-finding mission. By the time they came back, Reagan had made his televised speech, public sentiment had turned in his favor, and the invasion of Grenada had become a big hit. Few had the heart to pursue any public criticism further.

House Speaker O'Neill had earlier referred to the incursion as "gunboat diplomacy." When the House delegation returned, he met with them and reversed his position, saying it had been "justified under these particular circumstances."

Reagan had captured the day, and opponents were willing to let it go at that. That does not mean they had decided to stop fighting Reagan on his Caribbean policies, only that they were not willing to go public with the fight, in light of Reagan's success.

As a rule, national leaders prefer to deliberate and bargain among themselves and reach some sort of compromise rather than to create a national debate. Having been elected to high office, they become part of a cozy establishment. They learn quickly to deal among themselves and keep things quiet.

True debate stirs up the citizenry and is mostly an insurgent's tactic. Sometimes, during election campaigns, incumbents are forced to conduct a genuine debate, but even that is rare. More and more, political campaigns consist of poll-driven television advertising, prepared by experts and consisting of political symbolism.

At any given moment, some important matter—unemployment, federal budget deficits, race relations, the SALT treaty with the Soviet Union, acid rain, the federal tax system, Star Wars space weaponry, a national health plan, abortion, needed fixing of the Social Security system, AIDS, drugs, crime—may be the subject of intense debate and lobbying in Washington. For public consumption, one issue or another becomes a cause of the day or week, emerging briefly as the subject of Sunday TV talk shows or commentary in leading newspapers.

Presidents, vice-presidents, cabinet members, senators, members of the House take to television and, regardless of which side of an issue they support, focus on making themselves appear concerned, serious, knowledgeable, and, almost always, restrained. They aim to create an impression.

Helter-skelter, like shards in a kaleidoscope, complicated matters catch the public eye for a day, a week, a month. Issues spout like Yellowstone geysers, then subside, sometimes dealt with, sometimes not, in congressional committees.

Under such circumstances it is impossible for even extremely concerned citizens, let alone ordinary ones, to come to intelligent judgments on many public-policy issues. Their own experience is too circumscribed and the leaders they look to are unhelpful, unwilling to bring to the fore even excruciating national problems.

Thus the matter of unemployment, afflicting at least eight million Americans throughout the Reagan era, is important mostly to the jobless or the marginally employed, but not to average working people. Life-threatening toxic-waste dumps should be a major concern but are not much more than an abstraction to most Americans. Foreign-policy decisions that shape the world's future engage the average person only when it looks like someone in the family may be called to arms; for the most part they stay off to the side. In just such a manner was the Vietnam war fought for many years.

The need for people to be active in public affairs was seen as crucial by Thomas Jefferson, who wrote in a 1789 letter that "every government degenerates when trusted to the rulers of the people alone." The caution is still valid two hundred years later.

Surely, people should pay more attention to politics than they do, even without prodding by leaders. But it is understandable if they do not. Most have enough difficulty getting by from day to day in coping with their own problems; they cannot wade through the web of confusion spun by political leaders. They need some help and encouragement.

Jefferson came back to the theme in 1820, again in a letter, writing, "I know of no safe depository of the ultimate powers of the society but the people themselves; and if we think them not enlightened enough to exercise their control with a wholesome discretion, the remedy is not to take it from them, but to inform their discretion by education."

A little test I conducted in a *Washington Post/ABC News* poll in December, 1983, demonstrates how loose the ties are for most people when it comes to political convictions and ideas, and how strongly debate, even minimal debate, can sway many of them.

Typically in our polls we would ask the presidential-popularity question—"Do you approve or disapprove of the way Ronald Reagan is handling his job as president?"—right off the bat, as the first or second item.

The reasoning was that in such a way the people we interviewed would give their first impressions of Reagan, allowing us to track a genuine trend from month to month, year to year. Had we asked this question in the middle or toward the end of a poll, some people's responses might have been influenced by the line of thinking advanced by previous questions. We could have thrown in a few hardballs, asking, for example, about Reagan's support for James Watt in the early days of his presidency, or the Iran arms deal in the latter stages, creating a sort of brainwashing effect. It is easy for a pollster to bounce the results around intentionally by setting up respondents in this manner through what is called a "question-order bias," or "question-order effect."

In December, 1983, with the agreement of our colleagues at *ABC News*, I altered our procedure. We asked the approval-rating question first, as usual, but then we asked it again, toward the end of the interview. In line with our standard format, we asked people not only whether they approved or disapproved, but whether they felt that way "strongly" or "somewhat."

We interviewed 1,506 people in the survey, and in response to our first question, twenty-nine percent said they approved Reagan's handling of the presidency strongly, thirty percent approved somewhat, fifteen percent disapproved somewhat, twenty-two percent disapproved strongly, and four percent expressed no opinion. The overall fifty-nine-percent approval rating was in the "good" range—not outstanding but safely above the danger point for a president.

The survey then asked opinions on a wide variety of issues: Reagan's handling of the economy, foreign affairs, relations with the Soviet Union, the situation in Lebanon, the federal budget deficit. These were followed by more questions on the economy, on Lebanon, on Democratic candidates for the presidency, on preferences between the leading Democrats and Reagan, and on a number of other matters.

Finally, question number sixty-one went back to the presidential-popularity item, with this preface read by interviewers: "I've asked you some questions on how Reagan has handled a number of issues. With that in mind, let me repeat one of the first questions I asked. Do you approve or disapprove of the way Reagan is handling his job as president?" Again, people also were asked if they approved or disapproved "strongly" or "somewhat."

At a glance, the differences were so small as to appear nonexistent: fifty-nine percent approved, the same as in the first instance, and there was only a two-point increase in disapproval, to thirty-nine percent, with two percent expressing no opinion.

But the consistency existed only on the surface. There had been astonishing movement underneath. Almost a third of the respondents, thirty-one percent, changed positions. Half the time the change was slight, such as movement from approving somewhat to approving strongly. But for the other half, the second answer was different in kind. People who earlier said they approved Reagan's handling of the presidency were now saying they disapproved, and vice versa.

In all, sixteen percent of the people in the survey—a figure equivalent to more than twenty-five million citizens age eighteen or older—had thus changed their views on Reagan from positive to negative or the other way around in the course of a twenty- or twenty-five-minute telephone interview.

There were no loaded questions, no brainwashing, only

references to a number of current issues. Had we wanted to lead people, we could probably have bounced Reagan's ratings up or down by ten points.

The lessons here are several. Many Americans have fragile political convictions; in late 1983, a time when Reagan was seen as being extremely popular, about one-third of the population could be said to have only superficial feelings about him, readily subject to change.

Sharp leadership debate by political opponents surely would have created such change. But most Democrats in Washington rarely showed interest in reaching out for such debate. Some supported Reagan; others remained silent, thereby abetting him. It was only in periods when the public led the way, such as in 1982, during the economic recession, and 1987, spurred by the calamitous revelations of Reagan's deceitful dealings with Iran and Nicaragua, that the opposition spoke up forcefully.

At other times, even in a debate format, Democrats tended to treat Reagan gently.

In the first televised presidential campaign debate of 1984, for example, Walter Mondale was given a golden opportunity to criticize Reagan. A questioner asked, "What do you think the most outrageous thing is your opponent has said in this debate tonight?" The question was a green light, but Mondale's answer, when more Americans had their eye on him than ever before in his lifetime, put on the brakes:

"I'm going to use my time a little differently," he said. "I'm going to give the president some credit. I think the president has done some things to raise the sense of spirit, morale, good feeling in this country, and he's entitled to credit for that. . . . I like President Reagan."

During the following year, Sen. Edward M. Kennedy took the same line, praising Reagan for what he called "his capacity to move the nation," for having "reminded us of the enduring truth that we are Americans first and only then are we Democrats or Republicans."

A third partner in what many would regard as the liberal Democratic triumvirate of the 1980s, House Speaker O'Neill, was often critical of Reagan—more so than either Mondale or Kennedy—but he too was given to lavish praise. In January, 1985, a year after Reagan had called him a coward for advocating withdrawing the Marines from Beirut, O'Neill absolutely fawned over Reagan:

"In my fifty years of public life I've never seen a man more popular than you are with the American people," O'Neill told the president at a meeting after Reagan's second inaugural. Lest the word not get out, O'Neill afterward repeated to others what he had said.

Such remarks both overstated Reagan's popularity, which rose and fell according to events, and served to prop him up. Kind words from Mondale, Kennedy, O'Neill, and other leading Democrats could only help Reagan in his quest for high ratings.

As for these leading Democrats, their approach seems to have been quite cynical, and much too coy. One assumes their aim was not to endorse Reagan's policies but to get in on the flag-waving and cheering that Reagan himself inspired. If even McDonald's hamburger commercials played on the theme of "Morning in America," then why shouldn't the Democrats?

What we had here was a chorus in praise of government, not political debate. Leading the charge at all times was Reagan himself. "Thirty-eight straight months of economic improvement," he would say; "thirty-nine straight months," "forty straight months," "a miraculous fifty-odd months of bringing inflation down."

All the while, statistics showed unemployment to be a worse problem for a longer period than at any time since the Great Depression. Nominally, the jobless rate stayed at about seven percent month after month, year after year, except for the recession of 1982, when it was higher, and finally, in 1987, when it came down a notch to six percent.

The statistics themselves gave too rosy a picture of the employment situation in that countless numbers of the unskilled had quit looking for work, given up altogether, and thus were not included in the statistics; others had lost industrial jobs and gone back to lower-paying work, often finding only part-time positions.

Even as Republicans and Democrats were extolling the recovery of the national spirit, in New York, Washington, Atlanta, Dallas, San Francisco—every large city—a new group, the homeless, or street people, came to be identified as a major national problem. No longer was a bag lady a rare, disturbing spectacle. In July, 1984, each afternoon as the Democrats met in the San Francisco hall for their presidential nominating convention, scores of the homeless would queue up across the street, at a mission, for a bite to eat.

In 1987, a day or so after the Democrats chose Atlanta as the site for their 1988 convention, a United Press International reporter went to that city's convention hall, the Omni, and did a story on the hundreds of homeless who had taken up residence under an elevated highway a block away.

Focusing on the bright side, national leaders have tried to keep the mass of Americans in the dark on serious issues, rarely explaining or even addressing them. The federal budget deficit first came into focus as a major concern only because Mondale made it an election issue. Problems in race relations, never far beneath the consciousness of all Americans, were discussed only during periods of confrontation. Meanwhile, enrollment of blacks in the nation's colleges declined with hardly any notice.

For years, economic circumstances have forced mothers of young children to find jobs. That these women must return to work within weeks or a few months of giving birth is a national problem, not a sign of liberation.

The public perceives a national scandal in the lack of equity in the justice system. This country must find effective ways of dealing with crime and drugs, protecting the environment, restoring the infrastructure, making water sanitary, improving enormously expensive, frequently second-rate education, eliminating gross tax inequities, reducing unaffordable utility rates.

People care deeply about such issues; they would get involved if they were better informed and minimally encouraged. To quote Jefferson once more: "The people cannot be all, and always, well informed. The part which is wrong will be discontented, in proportion to the importance of the facts they misconceive. If they remain quiet under such misconceptions, it is a lethargy, a forerunner of death to the public liberty."*

But leaders seldom take these problems to the people; their efforts go toward keeping the citizenry disengaged. The result, again as Jefferson envisioned it, in a letter written in 1788: "The natural progress of things is for liberty to yield and government to gain ground."

Most leaders look on the people with apprehension, many with contempt. The people recognize that, and they respond accordingly.

---

* From a letter to Colonel William S. Smith, in 1787.

RESENTMENT AND DISTRUST

El Salvador is in Louisiana, near Baton Rouge.

OUR LEADERS' PRACTICE OF TALKING DOWN TO the public and avoiding true national debate has helped create a largely dulled citizenry, turning people away from public affairs and building in them resentment and distrust of government. One result is that where eighty percent of the people voted in presidential elections a hundred years ago, hardly more than half do so today.

This distrust and disengagement are the distinguishing features of Americans' views toward government and national politics, almost unchanged in the past fifteen or twenty years. In the end, citizenship is every individual's responsibility, and only so much blame may be laid to the political establishment. Nevertheless, the leaders' deliberate avoidance of true debate, the contempt they show the public during political campaigning, their use and refinement of propaganda techniques, the attentiveness of so many of them to moneyed interests and not to the people generally, all are major causes of the resentment and distrust.

Very few Americans follow matters closely; most know hardly anything about the details of public affairs. The bulk of the citizenry does little more than form vague impressions about events as they occur.

Throughout most of the Reagan presidency, no single foreign-policy issue was more in the news than the administration's attempts to unseat the Sandinista government in Nicaragua. Yet the opinion polls repeatedly showed that fewer than three in ten people knew which side—the Sandinista government or the contra rebels—Reagan was supporting.

Again, it was a dramatic turnabout when the U.S. Senate went Republican under Reagan; the Democrats had held a majority there for three decades. Yet the change in power passed unnoticed by most people: fewer than half were able to tell interviewers in our *Washington Post/ABC News* poll that the Republicans had a majority in the Senate. Conversely, the Democrats had enjoyed an enormous majority in the House of Representatives for decades, but during the early 1980s, fewer than half of the population knew which party had the most members there. And only one-quarter held both those pieces of information in their heads—that Republicans had the majority in the Senate, and Democrats in the House.

The crowning achievement of Jimmy Carter's presidency was to bring together Menachem Begin and Anwar Sadat at Camp David, and the resulting peace agreement between Israel and Egypt. But repeatedly in polls I helped conduct, fewer than forty percent of the people interviewed were able to tell pollsters which two foreign nations took part in the Camp David peace talks when Carter was president.

Almost since its founding, Israel has been largely supported by American aid. It gets more aid than any other country, and has for many years—a touchy matter for its supporters, especially at a time when Americans are thought to be opposed in principle to foreign aid because there are so many problems at home requiring money. Not to worry. Asked which country gets the most in American foreign aid, fewer than one person in five can single out Israel.

Fewer than half the people in our polls could state which two nations took part in the SALT talks, and fewer than half knew that, geography and reams of newsprint notwithstanding, it is the United States and not the Soviet Union that belongs to the North Atlantic Treaty Organization.

Through 1985 and 1986, reform of the income-tax system was widely considered the main piece of domestic legislation before Congress, affecting every American. But when change was finally enacted, after more than a year of discussion and debate and the innovation of televised Senate hearings, only one-third of the people felt they knew enough to express an opinion one way or the other on the merits of the reforms.

One of the liveliest arguments in Washington in the year 1986 came over the appointment of William Rehnquist as chief justice of the Supreme Court. But at the height of the controversy, only one person in three felt strongly enough to have an opinion either for or against Rehnquist.

Once I discussed with a pollster for *CBS News* the abysmal lack of information stored in people's heads, going over findings like these. "Here's one for you," she said, "We asked people where El Salvador was. One person said it was in Louisiana, near Baton Rouge."

Not everyone is equally ill informed. There are wide differences in the attention paid by men and women, whites and blacks, people who have had education beyond high school and those who have not. Responses to one question, asked in a *Washington Post/ABC News* poll in March, 1983, were typical of the pattern:

Q. *Can you tell me which two countries, aside from the United States, were involved in the Camp David peace talks when Jimmy Carter was president?*

Percentage of those in 1983 correctly naming Israel and Egypt as Camp David participants among . . .

. . . all people interviewed	38%
. . . men	49%
. . . women	28%
. . . whites	42%
. . . blacks	16%
. . . less than high-school graduates	19%
. . . high-school graduates	36%
. . . those with some college education	58%

The gap that appears in this table between men and women and between blacks and whites shows up on all educational levels—for example, in comparisons between college-graduate men and women, and college-graduate whites and blacks—in this and other "knowledge" questions. As a group, white men, who don't do all that well themselves, simply seem to follow current events more than other segments of the population. In my experience the pattern has been broken only on rare occasions, such as during Jesse Jackson's candidacy in 1984, when blacks tended to be watching the Democratic presidential debates at a slightly higher rate than whites.

Americans today are better educated than any past generation, and, in this age of immediate mass communication, much better informed. Studies show that the average adult watches four hours of television a day during the week, and more on weekends. News reports are extensive; the public-affairs program *Sixty Minutes* has been one of the longest-running, most popular shows in TV history. How can it be that a public with such advantages can know so little about what is going on?

The answer, simply put, is that people have tuned out on government and public affairs. The disdain that political leaders show the ordinary citizen is reciprocated. Distrust of government, disregard for it—and for all authority, in fact—sets the tone.

The signs are all around us. A main message in almost every half-hour presentation of the extremely popular TV series *M*A*S*H* was that small groups or individuals could do good things for society in spite of government's stupidity and bungling. The movie *Rambo,* a main box-office attraction in 1985, displayed ceaseless violence—and the message that one man could rectify what the government had messed up. Sex is an integral part of the movies aimed at teenagers, but not any more than defiance of authority.

The public opinion polls portray a nation whose majority sees government as having betrayed basic American values. In June, 1985, the *Washington Post/ABC News* poll asked a random sample of Americans which of the two following statements they tended to agree with more:

A. *The justice system in the United States mainly favors the rich,*

OR

B. *The justice system in the United States treats all Americans as equally as possible.*

The result: The large majority, just under six in ten, said justice favors the rich.

On another matter, Nicaragua once again, the same survey revealed widespread distrust of President Reagan. "The Reagan Administration," one question stated, "says it has no intention of sending American soldiers to fight in Nicaragua. Do you think the Reagan administration is telling the truth about that, or not?"

The result: More people thought the administration was lying than telling the truth, by forty-seven percent to forty-three, with ten percent expressing no opinion. I think it is safe to say that people who felt the "Reagan administration" was lying were thinking of the president as much as any of his executive-branch assistants. And that was long before Reagan's Iran-contra deceits, when large majorities repeatedly told pollsters they felt he was lying.

The same 1985 survey included a battery of seven agree-disagree questions having to do with Congress. Do you agree or disagree with this statement? the first one asked: "To win elections, most candidates for Congress make campaign promises they have no intentions of fulfilling." Three of every four people said they agreed.

Not one of the seven questions elicited a response that showed a high degree of respect for Congress; a majority of its members were seen as not caring about the problems of ordinary citizens, as resorting to lies if the truth would be politically damaging, as caring more about their own power than the good of the country, as making a lot of money improperly through holding public office, as caring more about special interests than the average person.

The same poll showed sharp resentment of the way the government runs the tax system. Four out of every five people agreed with the statement that "many rich people pay hardly any taxes at all"; almost nine in ten agreed that "the government is wasting too much of the tax money it collects."

The public challenged government priorities as well, with only a minority, thirty-seven percent, saying that too much tax money was being spent on social programs but a majority, fifty-six percent, saying that too much was being spent on the military. Then, as always, the Reagan administration was looking to cut social spending and increase military outlays.

The findings in that June, 1985, survey were in no way unusual. Quite the contrary. Responses to questions on justice in America, on Reagan, Congress, and the tax system, were in line with responses given to similar questions for years, since roughly the late 1960s, or the time in which many turned against the government because of its conduct of the Vietnam war.

One question asked in many polls since the 1950s is most expressive of the long-term trend. First asked as part of continuing election studies by the Institute for Social Research at the University of Michigan, the wording goes like this:

Q. *How much of the time do you trust the government in Washington to do what is right: just about always, most of the time, or only some of the time?*

The first time Michigan interviewers asked it, in 1958, seventy-three percent said they trusted the government most of the time or just about always. In 1964, the next time the question was asked, seventy-six percent trusted the government most of the time or always. Two years later, about the time concern over Vietnam began to climb, and coinciding with the profound social change that had just begun, the number expressing that level of trust in government dropped to sixty-five percent. It fell to sixty-one percent in 1968, fifty-four percent in 1970, and fifty-three percent in 1972.

Then, with the arrival of Watergate, the bottom fell out.

In 1974, only thirty-seven percent in the Michigan study said they trusted the government to do the right thing most or all of the time. In 1976, the figure stood at thirty-three percent; in 1978 at thirty percent, in 1980, the low point, at twenty-five percent. There was a slight rebound afterward, back to thirty-three percent expressing trust most of the time or just about always in 1982; forty-four percent in 1984.

The *Post/ABC News* poll began asking the same question in early 1985. In five consecutive surveys that year and 1986 and 1987, the public response was basically constant, and negative. The proportion expressing trust in government most or all of the time ranged between thirty-eight and forty-four percent; those saying they trusted the government only some of the time, or never, ranged from fifty-six to sixty-two percent.

What is most telling about those *Post/ABC News* findings is that they came during a period of almost unrelieved propaganda aimed at persuading Americans that they were feeling good about things, that their trust in government had been restored, that it was morning in America, that America was back, that America was standing tall, that, in the specific words Reagan used at one point in 1986, "both the spirit and material well-being of the American people have improved dramatically."

Looked at that way, the American people demonstrated sharp resistance to all the demagogic propaganda during these Reagan years. Most refused to acknowledge any improvement at all when it came to respect for government. From the seventies to the eighties the only groups showing an increase in trust were the well-to-do, most of them Republicans, and young adults, those between the ages of eighteen and twenty-four, the most impressionable segment of the population, the ones most susceptible to the incessant propaganda.

Basically, all the talk of a renewal of spirit in the early eighties, as it referred to trust in government, was fraudulent. Most people continued to be deeply upset with government. Opinion polls aside, that has been amply demonstrated by their continued massive failure to turn out to vote.

Experts cite many reasons for the low voter turnout in this country, compared to other industrialized nations. Discriminatory registration requirements, including poll taxes, literacy tests, and the like, kept blacks away from the ballot for many years. But one factor—cynicism, the belief that it does not matter who wins—accounts more for the failure to vote than any other.

When excited by a candidate, people turn out in droves. The example of black Americans in 1984 was evidence of that. In the primaries, black turnout was up in state after state by fifty percent, eighty percent, one hundred, even two hundred percent in massive shows of support for Jesse Jackson as a presidential candidate. Came the fall, with Jackson holding back rather than working hard for Walter Mondale, and black enthusiasm waned.

At one time social and economic status helped determine who voted and who did not. Almost all better-educated, well-off people voted; the habit was ingrained, a civic responsibility. Nonvoters were mainly the poorer, less-educated.

For many middle-class Americans, especially older ones, voting remains an obligation. Cynical or not, they choose a candidate and troop to the voting place, rain or shine. But for many others, cynicism has forced them out of the voting habit. Some people blame themselves for their detachment. A doctor in Detroit remarked, as she explained to a poll interviewer in 1984 why she would not be voting in the presidential election: "There's something the matter with me. I know I should, but I'm just not interested."

Between 1968 and 1980, according to a 1983 report by Harvard government professors Gary Orren and Sidney Verba, the turnout rate for white-collar workers and people earning more than $15,000 a year fell nine points. As it happened, turnout declined even more sharply for blue-collar workers and those earning less than $15,000. Americans regardless of class were becoming more cynical.

The Orren-Verba report was presented at a forum on voting in Washington, D.C., in 1983. In it, the authors wrote that "a citizen who feels bound by civic obligation, who basically trusts the government, and has some sense of efficacy—the feeling that he/she can influence the government, and that officials will respond—is more likely to vote. Similarly—and quite obviously—a citizen is more likely to vote if he/she feels more positively about one of the candidates up for election. There has been a general erosion over the last twenty years of each of these attitudes conducive to voting."

Nowhere is it written that Americans must lag when it comes to voting. Sooner or later there will be a presidential election, I am sure, when turnout shows a smashing increase. When that happens, it will be because of what Orren and Verba considered obvious: a widespread, positive feeling about one of the candidates. The question is whether that candidate will be deserving of such warmth, or whether it is merely the result of a genius for marketing.

THE PUBLIC'S AGENDA

Americans express a sharp dichotomy between views about their personal lives, which have remained uniformly positive and essentially unchanged over the years since 1959, and their far more somber view of the state of the nation.

—William Watts and Lloyd A. Free
in *State of the Nation*, 1978

THE POLITICAL PORTRAIT OF AMERICANS THAT emerges from opinion polls, from the popularity of Rambo-type entertainment, and from voting patterns is largely one of a people that is uninvolved, suspicious, and ignorant when it comes to public affairs, showing signs of life only when poked with a stick. But that is only the political portrait. It leaves out much of the story.

People often have active lives in their own spheres; they may be extremely outgoing, successful at what they do, and engaged to the hilt in a variety of avocations. The country is filled with enthusiasts of all kinds: kids who create computer

programs at age ten, blue-collar philosophers, self-taught scientists, mechanics, and bridge masters, go-getter entrepre-
neurs and athletes rising to undreamed-of riches through
talent and drive, hikers, bikers, motorcyclists, hunters, ama-
teur actors, strummers of all kinds, do-it-yourselfers, eccen-
trics, and inventors.

Fitness spas, school gymnasiums, church halls, classrooms
of all sorts overflow during lunch hours and evenings; self-
improvement is the theme. Volunteerism is rampant: in hos-
pitals, schools, rescue squads, libraries, churches. In homes
in every city and suburban neighborhood some lights burn
late or go on early; hard at work are woodcrafters, stitchers,
writers, investors. On farms, untrained youths teach themselves techniques of crop improvement, fence-making, irri-
gation, mechanics, veterinary medicine.

There is, too, an enormous social transformation occurring.
Driven by economic need and a new sense of themselves,
masses of women have entered the workplace, many of them
seeking careers, not just jobs. Downtown business sections
and restaurants that twenty years ago were the domain of
white men today present a rich and colorful panorama. The
white men are still there, to be sure. But so are those many
women, and blacks, Chinese, Japanese, Vietnamese, Latins,
Arabs, Iranians.

Not long after Reagan took over the presidency, a European sociologist came to my office at the *Washington
Post*, wanting to discuss the move toward conservatism
in America. I asked if he had ever been to this country
before. Yes, he said, many years ago, when it was more
liberal. He had even been to the *Washington Post* on that
occasion.

Had he seen as many women at the *Post* then, or as many
blacks? I asked. By my recollection, at the time of his first
visit there was one black reporter at the *Post;* now there were
about fifty. Where there had been perhaps two dozen
women, now there were nearly two hundred. Had he noticed
any changes in who dines in the restaurants, who stays in the
hotels? I asked. Where was the conservatism in that?

These changes, so dramatic in retrospect, have occurred without a great deal of notice. Blacks want more in the way of gains; their approach to progress, quite understandably, is not to focus on advances already made but on what they do not have. The same is true for women.

In my quiet suburban neighborhood of single-family homes outside the nation's capital, an Afghan family lives next door to me, a Japanese family across the street, Latin Americans, Indians, other Japanese a few houses down; some blacks have come and gone. On the nearby streets live Chinese, Israelis, other blacks, Arabs.

This, you should understand, is generally considered a Jewish neighborhood, complete with a Jewish delicatessen, a rarity in the Washington suburbs. The deli, however, with its knishes, matzoh-ball soup, challah, and all the rest, is now owned and run by Koreans. Such change would be mind-boggling if it occurred quickly. The Washington area may be more progressive than most places. But the same kind of thing is happening all over.

Let it not be said that apathy or malaise defines the American condition. The level of culture may not be highbrow, yet many people manage to lead full lives, with no shortages of activities or interests.

But not when it comes to public affairs.

Hardly any Americans pay attention to public affairs at all, other than to complain or ridicule or lament. Like an interest in literature, art, or classical music, concern over politics is an acquired taste. If more people vote than go to the opera or museums, it is only because politics intrudes in their lives a good bit more.

Americans, proud of their lowbrow ways, like to make such statements as "I may not know much about art, but I know what I like." In politics and government the same sentiment applies. People know very well what they want from their leaders. On a broad array of issues, that is, there is a consensus, a system of beliefs, goals, and concerns that are particular to this country at this time, something that may be referred to as a citizens' agenda.

Foremost, in my view, is one that has arisen in recent years as a national first commandment:

There shall be no more Vietnams.

In January, 1987, the *Washington Post/ABC News* poll asked a random sample of Americans whether, among other things, the United States should be involved in trying to overthrow the Sandinista government in Nicaragua. The question referred to any involvement, failing to specify whether that would be support for the contra rebels, other subversion, or military action. Only sixteen percent of the people interviewed said yes and seventy-seven percent said no, a stunning repudiation for President Reagan.

Only a small part of this sentiment could be laid to the two months of revelations that National Security Council aides had been arming the contra rebels in Nicaragua despite a congressional ban on government aid.

In seven *Washington Post/ABC News* surveys from August, 1983, through March, 1986, only once did as many as thirty percent of the people interviewed favor U.S. efforts to topple the Sandinistas. And that aberration occurred in late 1983, after the U.S. invasion of Grenada, celebrated as it was by the nation's leaders, had touched a taste for militarism. On the average for those surveys, only twenty-two percent backed the Reagan position.

Reagan, never short of euphemisms, gave the contra rebels in Nicaragua a heroic name, Freedom Fighters. Sometimes he called them the "democratic resistance," and likened them to the leaders of the American revolution. Congress went one way and then another, alternately submitting to Reagan's requests for aid to the contras, or cutting them some, or ruling out aid altogether, or restoring it. But the public was never wishy-washy. In proportions of usually three to one or greater, and rising to four to one by the beginning of 1987, Americans showed in polls that they wanted no part in overthrowing the Sandinistas.

When that many Americans agree on anything, we are talking about a consensus. Groups in the population that often oppose each other are brought together in an expression of unity.

There was, to begin with, uniformity across the country. In the South, where militarism is not a dirty word and backing for Reagan was usually strongest, seventy-six percent in the January, 1987, poll opposed U.S. involvement in overthrowing the Sandinistas. In the Northeast, seventy-eight percent were opposed; in the Midwest, seventy-seven percent; in the West, seventy-six percent.

Among groups who were often the most at odds—liberals and conservatives, Democrats and Republicans—the variations also were small. What stood out were the similarities in outlook, not the differences. Eighty-three percent of those who called themselves liberals opposed Reagan's policy; among conservatives, sixty-six percent were opposed. That is about as close as those two groups ever get on any policy matter. The same was true by party affiliation: eighty-five percent of the Democrats and sixty-four percent of the Republicans interviewed opposed U.S. involvement in overthrowing the Sandinistas.

There were no differences to speak of by age, by education, by income, by race or by social class. Among the youngest people interviewed, seventy-seven percent were opposed; among the oldest, seventy-five percent. Among the least educated, seventy-nine percent were opposed, among the most educated, seventy-six percent; among those with incomes of less than $12,000 a year, eighty-two percent; among those with incomes of more than $50,000 a year, seventy-two percent; among whites, seventy-five percent, among blacks, eighty-five percent; among the middle class, seventy-seven percent; among the working class, seventy-six percent.

With numbers so one-sided, there was, obviously, agreement between those who follow public affairs and those who do not; between those who are skeptical about government and those who think the establishment acts in good faith; between those who vote and those who stay home; between born-again Christians and conservative Catholics, church-goers and nonchurchgoers; between welfare mothers and the country-club set.

It was in recognition of such sentiment that the nation's number-one military officer, Admiral William Crowe, the chairman of the Joint Chiefs of Staff, said in February, 1987, that the administration must reconsider its commitment to the contras. "If it's not paying off, if it doesn't have the benefit, if it doesn't do the kind of thing the American public wants it to do, then we back out from under the commitment," the admiral said.

Two other items in the public agenda bear directly on foreign policy; they could be called the second and third commandments:

This nation shall have a strong military defense,

AND

There shall be a reduction in nuclear weaponry.

These last precepts are simple in concept, a mix of tough-mindedness and idealism. The same holds for the other values or commandments, all of which center more on domestic concerns.

Skeptics often scoff at poll results that depict such values or goals on the grounds that people are unrealistic, unwilling to pay for what they want. There is a good deal of sense in that complaint. The public's agenda is not one that makes hard choices. Nevertheless, the objectives are clear and the agenda is consistent from year to year.

Some of the other basic citizens' goals are these:

Don't trifle with the Social Security system or Medicare.
Give the poor a fair chance at joining the mainstream of Americans.
Let government spend what it takes to reduce crime and illegal drug usage.

Restore cleanliness to the nation's air and water.
Strive for fairness and equity in government and taxation.

Above all, except in moments when foreign affairs are extremely threatening, there is one main request the people make of their leaders:

Give us a decent, stable economy.

By definition, there is consensus on each of these items. On the question of a strong national defense, for example, the well-to-do have much the same views as the poor, blacks the same as whites, rank-and-file Republicans the same as Democrats.

Great majorities in each of these groups want the United States to be as strong militarily as the Soviet Union, regardless of the cost.

The argument is often made that the two superpowers are in a status of overkill when it comes to weaponry—that each country could wipe out the other fourteen times over with current nuclear stockpiles and that there is no need for further development. Nevertheless, no serious candidate for high office dares hold that we can stop military research and development, or that, even given our capability, maintaining parity with the Russians is unimportant. It would be politically unacceptable.

Each item on the public's agenda is important enough so that at any given time it may take on a certain urgency, rising to the top of the list of concerns. For a period in 1986, a series of opinion polls showed people listing illegal drug use as the nation's number-one problem. Earlier, in 1983, antinuclear groups drew a great deal of attention, and a nuclear freeze was at or near the top of the list of national concerns.

But year in and year out, no item on the agenda is nearly as important as the desire for a stable economy. It is a matter of first things first. People must have jobs and a steady income to get by. Presidential elections turn more on the state of the economy, or its perceived state, than on any other factor.

If analysts were to determine a public agenda based on election results alone, they might never arrive at anything like the one I have presented. Two issues would dominate: the economy, and war and peace. All others would be shifted to the side; some, such as the goal of bringing the poor into the mainstream, might be lost sight of altogether.

People may question just how strong a commitment the public has to the poor, or to the environment, or to equal justice, given the record of the Reagan years. From a war on poverty in the sixties, the theme changed to a war on the poor under Reagan. Unemployment levels were higher in his first term than at any time since the Great Depression, yet he carried forty-nine states in his landslide reelection.

During his first term, Reagan cabinet members tried to sell federal parkland to private interests at bargain rates; his appointee in charge of protecting the environment was forced to resign for dereliction of duty. More high Reagan appointees resigned under a legal taint or came under investigation than in any previous administration, with the exception of Nixon's.

All that suggests that the public doesn't care about the poor or the environment or the law. Nothing could be more wrong.

The fact is, there is a great deal of slack in public opinion. It is seldom ready to spring. Expecting so little from government, people are satisfied with the most basic achievements. There will be no revolution over the plight of the poor, or the abandonment of the environment, or legal favoritism. These are definitely secondary issues on the public's agenda, not because people don't care about them, but because the primary ones are so much more important.

We know what we do about the public's agenda because of the public opinion polls, not election results. Public opinion surveys examine people's views issue by issue. They are, therefore, much better than elections at exploring and defining citizens' thinking. The abundance of frequent, nonpartisan, generally respected public polling provides the clearest available look at trends in what Americans think on the issues confronting them.

Elections, on the other hand, center on the candidates' overall performance or on overriding concerns, not the general run of issues. In voting, people make a determination that, all in all, one candidate is a better risk than another. Victors in elections, by having won, will claim a public mandate for their own programs and policies. But it is the opinion polls, not the elections, that reveal the true mandates.

PAYING THE PRICE FOR TRIFLING WITH PUBLIC OPINION
Gerald Ford's Approval Ratings, 1974

[Percentages saying they approve Ford's handling of the presidency.]

Gerald Ford began his presidency with a typically high approval rating. His fall came almost immediately, after his pardon of Richard Nixon. Ford at first suggested there was public support for a pardon; then, when polls showed otherwise, he said, "I cannot rely on public opinion polls to tell me what is right." National leaders often take that tack—they say that public opinion is on their side whether it is or not; then, when events make it too embarrassing to make such assertions, they say their job is to lead, not follow.

[Gallup Polls]

THE PUBLIC FORCES AN EARLY REAGAN RETREAT
First Assault on Social Security, 1981

Q. Generally speaking, do you approve or disapprove of the Reagan administration's plans to change the Social Security program?

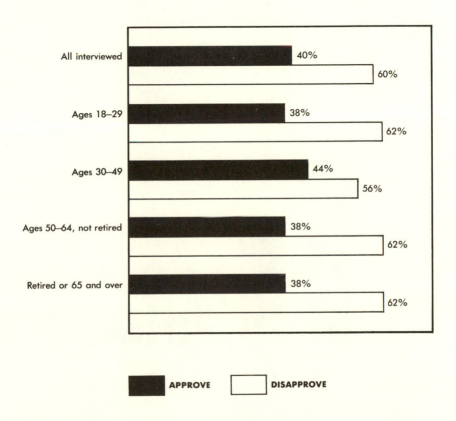

For years, political observers considered Reagan's attempt in May, 1981, to cut Social Security benefits to be his worst blunder as president. It met with sharp opposition from all age groups and on Capitol Hill, forcing Reagan to back down, and making him more wary of public opinion in the future.

[From a *Washington Post/ABC News* opinion poll of 1,003 people, May 14, 1981. Figures shown do not include those who offered no opinion, amounting to 18% of the people interviewed.]

A DOUBTING PUBLIC
The Marines in Lebanon, 1984

In early 1984, when Reagan removed the U.S. Marines from Beirut, a majority of Americans thought he did so for political reasons and not because events in Lebanon dictated their withdrawal, as he had claimed. There are many similar instances of public distrust of Reagan at all points in his tenure; Reagan never was a "Teflon president"—he was popular mostly in comparison to his Democratic opponents.

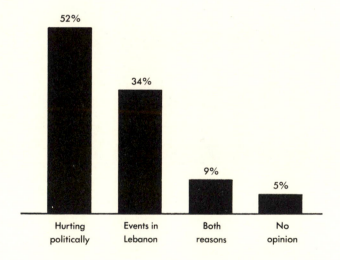

52%	34%	9%	5%
Hurting politically	Events in Lebanon	Both reasons	No opinion

Q. Do you think Reagan decided to move the Marines from land onto the ships more because of what has been happening in Lebanon, or more because keeping them there was hurting him politically at home?

[From a *Washington Post/ABC News* poll, February, 1984.]

MORNING IN AMERICA
Distrust of Government, 1964-86

Q. How much of the time do you trust the government in Washington to do what is right: just about always, most of the time, or only some of the time?

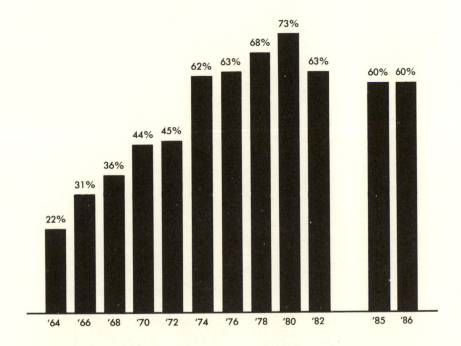

[Bars show the percentage of people who said they "trust the government in Washington to do what is right" no more than "some of the time."]

The Vietnam War ushered in an age of distrust in the United States that has not yet ended. The slight increase in trust in government during the Reagan years came during a steady stream of "morning in America" propaganda, and reflects a change in views expressed almost entirely among well-to-do people, mostly Republicans, and the young, who make up the most impressionable segment of the population.

[Findings from 1964 through 1982 are from the Institute for Social Research at the University of Michigan; those for 1985 and 1986 are from *Washington Post/ABC News* polls.]

THE GREAT COMMUNICATOR
Reagan after Grenada, 1983

Reagan was falling in public esteem immediately after the deaths of 241 Marines in Beirut on October 23, 1983, and the invasion of the Caribbean island of Grenada on October 25. His response, on October 27, came in the form of a masterful television address to the nation that immediately boosted his ratings and had a chilling effect on critics.

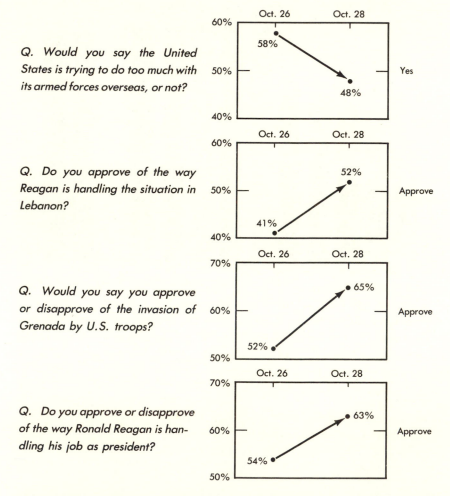

Q. Would you say the United States is trying to do too much with its armed forces overseas, or not?

Q. Do you approve of the way Reagan is handling the situation in Lebanon?

Q. Would you say you approve or disapprove of the invasion of Grenada by U.S. troops?

Q. Do you approve or disapprove of the way Ronald Reagan is handling his job as president?

[These findings are from national *Washington Post/ABC News* opinion polls the evening before and the evening after the address.]

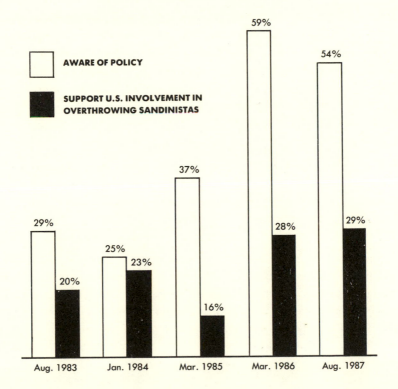

REAGAN POLICY TOWARD NICARAGUA
Public Awareness v. Support, 1983-87

AWARE OF POLICY

SUPPORT U.S. INVOLVEMENT IN
OVERTHROWING SANDINISTAS

| Aug. 1983 | Jan. 1984 | Mar. 1985 | Mar. 1986 | Aug. 1987 |

It was not until 1986 that as many as half the people interviewed in *Washington Post/ABC News* opinion polls were able to state that the Reagan administration was supporting the contra rebels, not the Sandinista government, in Nicaragua. At no time did more than 30% in those polls say they favored U.S. involvement in trying to overthrow the Sandinistas. The strong public opposition was rooted in a concern that there be no more Vietnams.

Q. Do you happen to know which side the United States is backing in Nicaragua, the rebels or the government?

Q. Should the United States be involved in trying to overthrow the government in Nicaragua, or not?

[*Washington Post/ABC News* polls, 1983–87]

THE PUBLIC'S AGENDA
NORC Spending Series, 1973—87

While people generally know little of the *details* of public affairs, they do know what they want from government. Year after year, Americans have called for a basically consistent, somewhat idealistic spending program, as shown in these findings in the General Social Survey done by the National Opinion Research Center. The one exception to the pattern of consistency is the sharp burst of support for increased military spending in 1980, which just as sharply abated the next year, and continued to decline.

Q. We are faced with many problems in this country, none of which can be solved easily or inexpensively. I'm going to name some of these problems, and for each one I'd like you to tell me whether we're spending too much money on it, too little money, or about the right amount.

[The lines across the top in each chart stand for the people saying "too little" is being spent in an individual area; lines across the bottom stand for those saying "too much" is being spent. To calculate the number saying "about the right amount" is being spent, add the top and bottom figures and subtract the total from 100. In the case of protecting the environment, for example, 51% said in 1980 that too little was being spent, and 16% said too much. Thus, the 33% that are left said about the right amount was being spent.]

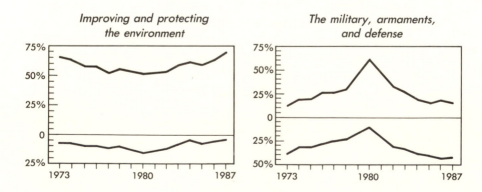

Improving and protecting the environment

The military, armaments, and defense

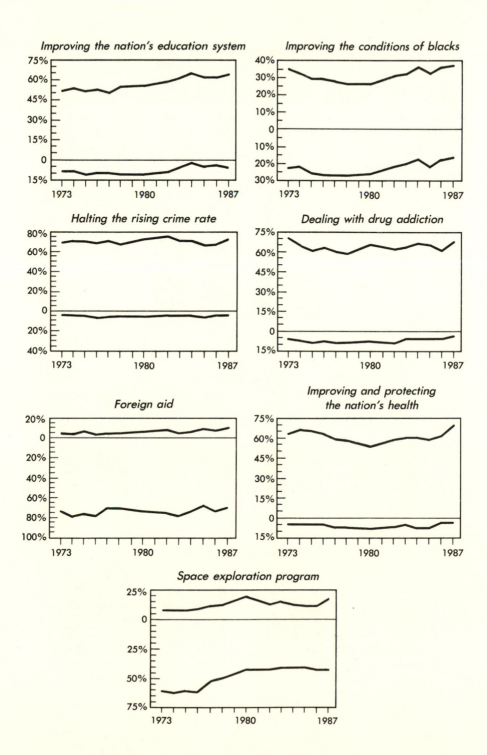

Improving the nation's education system

Improving the conditions of blacks

Halting the rising crime rate

Dealing with drug addiction

Foreign aid

Improving and protecting the nation's health

Space exploration program

THE KNOWLEDGE GAP
Lack of Public Awareness, 1987

On most public-affairs questions there is a pronounced gap in the attention paid by men and women and by whites and blacks. The gap generally exists on all educational levels, but is greatest among those with less schooling. These figures show the proportions able to state that it is the rebels, not the government, that the Reagan administration supported in Nicaragua.

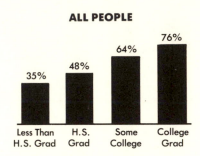

ALL PEOPLE

Less Than H.S. Grad	H.S. Grad	Some College	College Grad
35%	48%	64%	76%

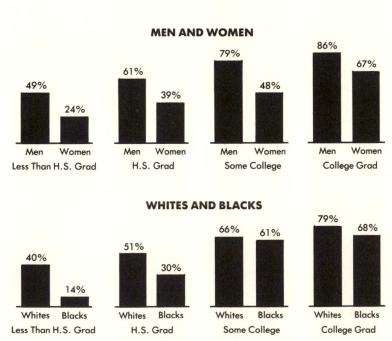

MEN AND WOMEN

	Less Than H.S. Grad		H.S. Grad		Some College		College Grad
Men	Women	Men	Women	Men	Women	Men	Women
49%	24%	61%	39%	79%	48%	86%	67%

WHITES AND BLACKS

	Less Than H.S. Grad		H.S. Grad		Some College		College Grad
Whites	Blacks	Whites	Blacks	Whites	Blacks	Whites	Blacks
40%	14%	51%	30%	66%	61%	79%	68%

[From a *Washington Post/ABC News* poll, August, 1987.]

PART TWO

THE OPINION POLLS

Not only must the citizen have the information brought to him, so that he may know what is happening and what the issues before him are, but he must have a way to make his wishes known to government. It is here that students of our government have found the weakest rib of its framework.

—George Gallup, 1935

MAKING THEIR WISHES KNOWN

It is the most stupid job you can ever take up, no matter how hard you try to find a worse one. If you get the election results right, everyone takes it for granted. If you get it wrong, you stand naked and utterly ashamed, and there is nothing you can do about it.

—Dr. Henry Durant, as quoted by George Gallup

I DID MY FIRST OPINION POLLS IN 1971. IT WAS the Vietnam war that drew me. I became city editor of the *Washington Post* at the beginning of the year. Coverage of local events that had a bearing on the war, including the enormous antiwar rallies, was under my charge.

Almost all that winter, as I recall it, activists were preparing for a huge protest in Washington to be held in April. A wide spectrum of groups was involved in the planning: labor and civil-rights organizations, feminists, government workers, socialists, communists, senior citizens, students, Vietnam veterans. As the weeks passed, it became clear that this rally would dwarf almost all previous ones, and that activists would make up only a small part of the protesters. So many buses had been chartered from cities in the East and the heartlands that it seemed certain there would be several hundred thousand people taking part.

The Nixon administration maintained that antiwar leaders were treasonous supporters of Hanoi. They tarred Daniel Ellsberg, Jane Fonda, Rennie Davis, and others with that brush, and said that ordinary people—the "silent majority" —supported the government's conduct of the war.

I decided to put the administration's position to a small test. With the aid of opinion-poll consultants, we did a telephone survey of Washington-area residents, completing it nine days before the rally. I won't forget the reaction of Eugene Patterson, the *Post*'s managing editor at the time, when the results came in on a Saturday morning. Patterson had been a World War II tank commander under General George S. Patton. He was a tough-minded southerner, who, I felt, tended until then to accept the stated Nixon view of people's attitudes toward the war.

"Look at that," Patterson said in clear surprise, "three out of five think Rennie Davis is a loyal American. That's got to be the lead."

On the day of the rally, we did another survey, this time of demonstrators themselves. The protest was to assemble at the Ellipse, between the Washington Monument and the White House, followed by a march along Pennsylvania Avenue to the Capitol. On instructions from the consultants, I had seventeen *Post* reporters and copy aides scattered about with clipboards and brief questionnaires, seeking to interview every fourth passerby.

The day was warm and clear and the rally was more successful than anyone had anticipated. People poured into downtown Washington in a constant flow, not just in the morning. Many latecomers went directly to the Capitol; tens of thousands of early arrivals could not even get near the starting point.

I posted a young clerk in the middle of the march route on

Pennsylvania Avenue with a hand counter that he would click as a file of marchers went by, each click standing for eleven people. He told me he had counted 110,000 people with no end in sight when he found out that an alternate route had been opened along Constitution Avenue, carrying just as many people. He gave up at that point.

My guess was that there were half a million demonstrators, probably making for the largest rally of the war and perhaps in the history of the nation. The Washington police chief, a Nixon favorite, issued an absurdly low estimate of 125,000.

Our poll turned out to be somewhat crude. Nevertheless, as far as I know, it was the first attempt at a scientific survey of antiwar demonstrators, and the rough profile we drew from interviews with them was quite revealing.

Two of every three we interviewed had traveled more than two hundred miles to get to Washington; more than one-third were attending an antiwar rally for the first time; men outnumbered women by more than two to one; more than eight of every ten were under the age of thirty; one of every twenty was a Vietnam war veteran.

About two weeks later I got a chance to use the polling technique again, this time in a somewhat offbeat way. On May 3, 1971, the Nixon administration swept up seven thousand people in Washington in mass arrests of unprecedented scope. Some of those arrested had been involved in blocking streets and other harassment in an attempt to shut down the government for a day. Some were less involved but sympathetic to that goal. But many just happened to be in the wrong place at the wrong time.

Over the next two days an additional five thousand were arrested. There were no holding places designed for such massive detention; fenced-in outdoor areas were used at first, then a large indoor arena.

When the administration finally began dragging the arrested people to court, judges were infuriated at the violation of due process. They berated Justice Department officials and began ordering mass releases.

It was at this stage that I got the idea for another poll, of sorts. When brought to court, those arrested had their names and home addresses listed on the docket. My assumption was that the list provided a random sample of all people who had been arrested. I had *Post* reporters copy down the information and we started calling their families at home.

Conventional wisdom at the time was that there was a generation gap when it came to sentiments toward the war, that only the young, mostly students, protested it, and that older people supported the government. It was certainly true that the most ardent antiwar activists were young. But our first survey had knocked holes in the idea that older people approved the war, and so did this one.

We reached relatives of sixty-seven of the people who had been arrested, usually their mothers or fathers. Often the call from a *Post* reporter came to them as the first word that a son or daughter had been arrested in Washington—or indeed, that their child had even been in Washington. The response, therefore, was often one of surprise, mixed with strong feelings.

"You know what you can tell Nixon," said a Flushing, New York, woman whose teenage son had been arrested: "Tell him to end the war and the kids won't get in trouble. This is what they're doing to our kids. Not what our kids are doing to them."

One young man's father, a corporation executive in Massachusetts, was at a board meeting when we called. "I'm sorry he had to get arrested," he said. "The government won again, huh?" Another father said his son was a Vietnam veteran and a Green Beret lieutenant. "He's twenty-one," the father said. "He can do what he wants."

Not every parent defended the youngsters. A suburban Washington woman was upset at hearing that her son had been arrested. "We are very staid, solid, middle-class, duty-honor-country people and this we do not approve of at all—in any way. Yet he is our son and we do love him. I hope he wasn't out all night in the cold."

■ ■ ■

Opinion Polling is rooted in a simple observation drawn from the physical sciences: that small, properly drawn samples of a substance are a microcosm of the thing in its entirety. Leo Bogart,* a noted opinion analyst, draws on a quote from Adolphe Quetelet, a nineteenth-century statistician, mathematician, and astronomer, to make the point: "Must I drink the whole bottle in order to judge the quality of the wine?"

Random sampling may be likened to the blind drawing of differently colored marbles from a container. Most opinion-poll questions give people simple choices, such as, in 1936, asking whether they were supporting Franklin Roosevelt or Alf Landon for president. The nation and its voting population of some forty-six million at the time could therefore have been thought of as an enormous vat containing marbles of two colors, let us say white for Roosevelt's backers, blue for Landon's.

Reach in, grab a bunch from here, a bunch from there, and start sorting them. They will, almost always, divide closely along the lines of the contents of the entire vat.

If only a handful, ten or twenty or fifty, are selected, the sampling will not be a reliable indicator of the entire contents. But as the numbers increase, the sample rapidly becomes quite reliable. If a hundred marbles are drawn, the margin of sampling error is, in theory, about ten percentage points, in nineteen instances out of twenty. The margin for a sampling of four hundred is five percentage points; for eight hundred, about three and a half points; for fifteen hundred, about two and a half points.

Suppose there were eight hundred white marbles and seven hundred blue ones pulled from the vat in 1936. That would mean Roosevelt, at the time of the counting, had 53.3 percent of the vote and Landon 46.7, with a 2.5 percentage-point sampling-error margin, nineteen times out of twenty.

---

* The author of an entertaining and thoroughly excellent book, *Polls and the Awareness of Public Opinion*, published by Transaction Books in 1985, and originally titled *Silent Politics*, published by John Wiley and Sons in 1972.

That would have made Roosevelt seem a sure winner had the election been held at the time of the polling. That is, there would have been a ninety-five percent certainty that he would get no less than 50.8 percent of the vote.

Luckily for pollsters, who usually care about costs, there is a rapidly diminishing return in this process. Inspection of three thousand marbles would yield a 1.8 percentage-point margin of sampling error in nineteen instances out of twenty, hardly better than a sample half the size. A sampling of six thousand reduces the error margin only to 1.3 points with the same ninety-five percent reliability.*

The beauty of the design is that it doesn't matter how many marbles are in the vat—that is to say, how many people in the population under consideration. There could be five thousand, fifty thousand, fifty million, five hundred million. As long as a genuinely random sample is drawn, the margin of sampling error remains the same.

George Gallup once told me how he used to explain the theory of sampling to promote his first syndicated newspaper column in the 1930s. One prospective client, Eugene Meyer, the industrialist who acquired the *Washington Post* in 1934, needed no prompting. "I used to mine tin in Bolivia," Meyer told Gallup; "I know all about sampling." The *Post* thus became one of the charter clients of the Gallup poll.

The Meyers of the world aside, it was, and remains, difficult for many people to grasp the idea that the views of a small sampling can represent those of the entire population. Some people never grasp it. In one variation or another, Gallup told me, people kept asking him throughout his many years as a pollster how fifteen hundred people could be expected to speak for a hundred fifty million.

Once, after he gave a speech, Gallup said, a woman remarked that she had never been polled, that she did not know anyone who had ever been polled, and that she doubted that anyone in the audience had ever been polled.

---

* Pollsters differ in the formulas they use to determine margins of sampling error, but the resulting variations turn out to be very small ones.

Gallup had a stock answer for that. "Madam," he replied, "your chances of being polled are about the same as your chances of being hit by lightning." That was not about to satisfy her. "But Dr. Gallup," she said, "I have been hit by lightning. Twice."

As noted, Gallup and the other founders of polling did not discover random sampling; the principles were long known in the physical sciences. Gallup's genius and that of his early colleagues was in understanding that those principles could be used in the social sciences.

Gallup was a student at the University of Iowa in the early 1920s when he first learned, as he later put it, that he could apply to people the same techniques employed by "government inspectors in testing wheat, or cotton, or by public health men in testing the water supply. They take a sample here, another there, and by choosing the samples properly are able to judge the quality of the whole amount from what the sample shows."

Once he came to that realization, Gallup became very brash. He knew he was onto something that would make his fortune. More than that, he felt, at least to some degree, that the innovation of scientific polling of the populace could work to improve the democratic system. In 1935, announcing his first syndicated newspaper column, Gallup wrote:

> Many political writers have said that the organized minorities in America, with their pressure organizations and their lobbyists in Washington, exert a preponderant influence on legislation. Whatever the ultimate value to the process of democratic government, this weekly poll will make it possible, for the first time, to learn what the unorganized majority thinks about the issues and laws which affect the daily lives of American citizens.

I first met Gallup shortly after the 1976 presidential election, at a conference on polling and politics at the University of

Michigan. Truth be told, I knew very little of his background at the time. I had moved into polling by accident, a natural progression in my work as an editor. When I did meet him, I was very suspicious. The Gallup firm had made several glaring errors in the 1976 election campaign, and each overstated the popularity of Gerald Ford.

Twice Gallup released partial poll results—an unusual and questionable practice—that were more favorable to Ford then the complete results. When the final results came in, the Gallup people sent out no corrections. There was one incident that especially disturbed me.

Jimmy Carter had started out with what appeared an insurmountable lead of thirty-three points after the Democratic convention in July. But Ford drew closer and closer, setting up a situation in which three scheduled television debates between the candidates could prove pivotal.

As it happened, the second debate, held on October 6 and focusing on foreign policy, was crucial. In it, Ford, not exactly the fastest thinker, blundered by saying "there is no Soviet domination of Eastern Europe and there never will be under a Ford administration." A reporter questioned Ford further, and the president said that Yugoslavia, Poland, and Romania were "independent, autonomous" countries.

Carter seized on the point. "I would like to see Mr. Ford convince the Polish-Americans and the Czech-Americans and the Hungarian-Americans in this country that those countries don't live under the domination and supervision of the Soviet Union behind the Iron Curtain," he said.

The campaign began to swirl around Ford's gaffe, with commentators picturing the president as a know-nothing.

On the morning of October 12, Ford, in a campaign appearance in New York, waved a piece of paper, saying it was a new Gallup poll showing that he had pulled within a point or two of Carter. If correct, the poll meant that all the blather had left no impression on voters.

Editors at the *Post* asked me to write a story on the poll, which had not yet arrived in our office, although our newspaper, as a Gallup subscriber, was supposed to get the report before it became public.

As I called the Gallup organization in Princeton, I had two questions in mind. I couldn't believe that Ford had made such gains after the run of bad news for him, so I suspected that the poll had been done before the second debate, not after it. I thought that, in pollsters' terminology, there had been an "intervening event"—the second debate—that made the findings obsolete. I also wanted to know how it came about that the Gallup people had lent themselves to the Ford campaign by giving him the results before providing them to clients.

The people I spoke to at the Gallup organization had no answer for the second question; they said they were mystified by how Ford had obtained the poll. They immediately wired me a copy of their release, which had a headline referring to Ford's comeback as the sharpest since the introduction of preelection polls in the thirties. I found that I had been correct in my guess about the timing. On the last page of the release the dates of the polling were mentioned, but only in a *pro forma* way, with no attention drawn to the fact that a second debate had occurred afterward.

I then made another call to the Gallup people, asking if they felt it proper to present this dated poll as though it were new. In response, I was told that the release had been worked up hurriedly, that because of my questioning they would revise it, agreeing that the dates of interviewing should be moved to the top of the report.

I also asked whether they had done any polling after the second debate. They said they had, but that they had not fully compiled the results. Their impression was that it showed Carter with a ten-point lead.

The news story I wrote appeared on the front page of the *Post* and treated the circumstances surrounding the poll, not the findings themselves, as the main story. The lead said:

Hundreds of newspapers throughout the United States today will report a Gallup organization finding, based on polling before the second televised presidential debate, that President Ford has drawn virtually even with Jimmy Carter.

The pre-debate poll gave Carter 47 percent and Ford 45 percent.

But even as the findings were released, they had been made obsolete by post-debate Gallup polling that shows Carter with a probable 10-percentage-point lead in the race for the presidency.*

I had little chance to talk to Gallup when I met him in Michigan. At age seventy-five, he was the grand old man of public opinion polling, something of a relic, the center of attention not for what he had to say but for who he was. There was always a crowd around him. We did get together briefly, and he invited me to visit him in Princeton. Early the following year I did, and after that I met with him several times before his death in 1984.

Whatever doubts I harbored he managed to dispel easily. My impression today is that Gallup probably leaned toward the Republican party personally but that he would never do the slightest thing—not even vote—that could be interpreted as a sign of partiality. He seemed totally, scrupulously dedicated to doing honest work. Through my talks with him, and through what I learned about his firm's problems in the 1976 campaign, I became convinced that the Gallup poll's flaws that year were unintentional.

More interestingly, I found in Gallup the kind of American that one associates with a previous era—indeed, his era, a child growing up at the start of the century. He saw as a youngster that opportunity was there for the grabbing. He had boundless energy and diverse interests; he was brash, energetic, charming. If Gallup had not become a pioneer in public opinion polling, he certainly would have made his mark in some other field.

"I feel sorry for the young people these days," Gallup told me once. "They have so much freedom, so many choices. How can they decide what to do with their lives? It was different in my day. I used to milk cows at 5 A.M., go to school,

---

* This time the preliminary results exaggerated Carter's lead; he was six points ahead when all the interviews were counted.

come home and go back to work on the farm. I knew exactly what I was going to do by the time I was ten years old."

"But Dr. Gallup," I said, "there were no opinion polls when you were ten."

"Polls? Who's talking about polls? I knew I was going to get the hell out of Iowa."

Gallup embarked on several careers while still a student at the University of Iowa. He used to tell associates that he went to college with six dollars in his pocket but that by the time he graduated he was earning more than the university president. He ran a towel concession at the locker room of the school's swimming pool, operated a laundry, and, as a student editor, turned the campus newspaper into a profit-making community newspaper. Obviously, since he was still a student when he seized on the idea of applying random sampling to people, he also found time to study.

From 1923 to 1932 Gallup taught journalism and worked to develop his sampling techniques by doing readership surveys for newspapers. Then, in 1932, his mother-in-law, a Democrat, ran for the position of secretary of state of Iowa, inducing Gallup to try his hand at preelection polling. He predicted that she would win, and she did.

That year a newly created New York advertising agency, Young and Rubicam, asked Gallup to create a research department and evaluate the effectiveness of advertising. Gallup remained associated with Young and Rubicam until 1947, but soon after he joined the firm he branched out into the work he became known for, polling on public issues. He formed the American Institute of Public Opinion, better known as the Gallup poll.

By 1934, he later wrote, he had developed his techniques to the point where he was able that year to predict the outcome of the congressional races "with an error of only six-tenths of one percent." If Gallup was that accurate, it was more luck than science that accounted for it. These days, with more sophisticated techniques, pollsters seldom do that well. But Gallup was never averse to promoting himself or his new way of measuring people's attitudes and opinions.

Gallup's breakthrough came in the presidential election of

1936,when he picked a fight with the *Literary Digest*, a magazine that had done straw polls of readers in presidential elections for more than twenty-five years and that had never come out on the wrong side. The *Digest* sent out ten million ballots by mail and got responses from more than two and a quarter million people, making for an enormous survey.

The main flaw in the *Digest* poll was that its sample did not represent a cross-section of voters, being skewed toward the Republicans. Gallup knew exactly what was wrong. He did ten polls from July through October and his last one showed Roosevelt ahead with fifty-six percent of the vote, and getting stronger. Making an educated guess, Gallup stated publicly that the *Digest* would show Landon getting fifty-five or fifty-six percent of the vote.

In its issue of October 31, 1936, the *Digest*, saying it was releasing "the figures received up to the hour of going to press," counted fifty-seven percent for Landon. In the election, Landon got thirty-seven percent. The *Literary Digest* folded not long afterward, and George Gallup was on his way.

His career, and polling itself, suffered a setback in 1948. To this day, the presidential election that year is regarded as proof of the unreliability of polls. Early on, Gallup and other pollsters had written off the chances of the incumbent, Harry Truman, seeing Thomas E. Dewey as a sure winner. On election night, the first editions of the *Chicago Tribune* had a banner headline, DEWEY WINS, but when day broke it was Truman who woke up victorious.

In the following weeks, Gallup was considered almost as much a loser as Dewey. Until then his polls had a fine record, coming within a few points of the actual margin in presidential elections, and never giving the lead to the wrong candidate. This time he was humiliated.

The mistake Gallup made, though, had nothing to do with his polls, which seem to have been accurate. What happened was that Gallup stopped sampling voters in the middle of October. In the last survey, Dewey held a five-point lead, which Gallup considered insurmountable. His earlier presidential polls had all been taken with Franklin Roosevelt on the ballot, in 1936, 1940, and 1944. In those elections, there was little change in voter sentiment during the life of a campaign. If Roosevelt had a five-point lead in October, he could be expected to win by five points. Gallup's error was in thinking that all presidential elections were equally undynamic.

In retrospect, it was clear that Truman was making a surge when Gallup stopped polling. He was behind by thirteen points in a Gallup poll in early September, eleven points later that month, and seven points early in October, before whittling Dewey's lead to five points in the final survey. Today any pollster would look at such a trend with excitement and continue interviewing until the final days; Gallup should have known better then, too. But that is easy to say with hindsight.

Once Gallup understood the nature of his mistake, his typical brashness came out. "I have the greatest admiration for President Truman because he fights for what he believes," Gallup said. "I propose to do the same thing."

Gallup was highly regarded for his seriousness of purpose and for paying strict attention to scientific method. He was dedicated to the promulgation of polling for the advancement of democracy, education, and betterment of the species. In the forties, when polio was rampant, Gallup experimented at epidemiology, interviewing polio victims, trying to find some commonality in background or recent experience to account for their having acquired the crippling disease. He stopped, he told me, when a polio vaccine was introduced.

In his mid-seventies, Gallup fell off a tractor at his home in Princeton and was left with an arthritic knee. One evening in Washington, as he and I crossed the street, he had to lean on me for support, and he talked about doing the same kind of polling with arthritics.

"The doctors don't know a damned thing about arthritis," he said. "They tell you to take aspirin. Maybe I can find out something."

The last time I talked to Gallup was by telephone, more

than a year before he died. Making small talk, I asked why he was in his office on such a nice day. He was, after all, more than eighty years old at the time. "We're making plans for polling in the year 2000," he boomed at me. "You've got to keep up with things."

At the time of his death in 1984, the Gallup column was syndicated in about a hundred and ten American newspapers, the Gallup organization had affiliates in thirty-five nations and a staff of a hundred and ten full-time employees and two hundred to three hundred part-timers in Princeton, not including field workers. It was not one of the top revenue-making polling firms, not even one of the top ten; more commercially oriented marketing companies made much more money. But for many years, in countries across the world when people referred to opinion polls they often called them "Gallups," or "Gallup polls," regardless of who conducted them.

SOME OF THE PITFALLS

BETWEEN THE THIRTIES AND TODAY THERE have been many developments in the art and science of public opinion polling. A great deal of effort has been expended in refining principles of sampling. Obtaining a representative sample of the population is not as easy as shaking white and blue marbles in a vat, not in 1936 or any time since.

Some marbles may be thought of as fakes—they may look white or blue but really aren't. That is, some people, out of shame or for other reasons, may say they are going to vote for one candidate or the other when they have no intention of voting at all. Others, small in number but enough to throw things off, cannot be symbolized by white or blue marbles because they are intending to vote for an independent candidate. And another color is needed as well to signify the many who are not registered to vote but who come to the door and answer the phone when the poll interviewer calls.

Difficulties in sampling are perplexing; arguments abound on every aspect. Most pollsters feel it necessary to make a number of "callbacks" to interview people who were not available the first time. At least five such callbacks are often made in polling for the U.S. government, which is expensive and time-consuming. But President Reagan's pollster, Richard Wirthlin, often did polls with no callbacks, as have other well-known polling organizations on occasion.

Polling is a nitpicky kind of work. Questionnaires must be carefully constructed to avoid "question-order bias," that is, a situation in which the answer to one question may be dictated, for many respondents, by the nature of the questions preceding it. Questions also must be phrased lucidly, as it makes no sense to have a phrase with one meaning for some respondents, different meanings for others. But obtaining clarity is not always easy.

There is also the problem of nuance. I worked on two polls on the subject of homosexuality within a period of one year, and got alarmingly different results.

In the first of those polls, in May, 1981, we asked: "Do you think homosexual relations between consenting adults should or should not be made legal?" In response, thirty-nine percent of the people we interviewed said yes, fifty percent no, and eleven percent offered no opinion.

A year later we asked a very similar question: "Should adults be allowed to have homosexual relationships if they want to without being prosecuted?" Fifty-seven percent said yes, thirty-two percent said no, and, again, eleven percent offered no opinion.

There was no reason to think any major switch in favor of homosexuality was taking place, yet in twelve months, tolerance for homosexuals seemed to have gone up eighteen points and intolerance down eighteen, for a thirty-six-point swing.

Clearly, what we tapped, by accident, was a fairly obvious distinction: There are many people who do not want to sanction homosexuality under the law but who, at the same time, have a live-and-let-live spirit.

There are many other problems that may occur in polling. Annoying bugs may creep in as a result of what is termed "interviewer bias."

Some interviewers may lead people toward one response rather than another by the inflection of their voice. When blacks are interviewed by white people, even over the telephone, some give substantially different answers to racially sensitive questions than they would if interviewed by a black. Further, the answers they give a matronly black interviewer are likely to be different than those given to a younger, more aggressive black.

The same is true for whites when they are asked racially sensitive questions. The answers many give may vary according to the complexion and demeanor of the interviewer. Monographs have been written on the subject of interviewer bias.

There was one incident, involving a *Washington Post* effort in Maryland in 1976, shortly after I had begun doing polling on my own, that stands as a classic illustration of interviewer bias. Early on, well before the Democratic presidential primary in that state, the *Post*'s editor for Maryland news at the time, Herbert Denton, wanted to use polling techniques for a story about voters along the Eastern Shore, a largely rural, southern-oriented section of the state.

Denton homed in on one precinct there and asked my help in selecting a sample and working up a brief questionnaire. I recommended that he acquire a Democratic voter registration list, publicly available where election records were kept, draw a random sample by selecting every nth name, and send his people out.

As ideas go, Denton's was not a bad one, except for one thing. One of his reporters was Jean Fugett, a black whose name may be familiar to professional-football fans. Fugett was then trying his hand at journalism while between seasons as a tight end for first the Dallas Cowboys, then the Washington Redskins. He not only was a tight end, he looked like a tight end. He was big.

I told Denton that if it was an experiment on interviewer bias he wanted, it would be fine to send Fugett out with the other reporters, all of whom were white, but that if he wanted valid results, he might just as well find something else for Fugett to do. Denton didn't like that; he said this was 1976, after all. So along went Fugett.

One of the questions in the brief survey asked people how they had voted in the 1972 Democratic primary in Maryland, when the winner, with thirty-nine percent of the vote statewide, had been George Wallace, the Alabama governor who had made his reputation as a segregationist. George McGovern, who eventually won the party's nomination, did poorly in the Maryland primary, drawing twenty-two percent and placing third in the eleven-candidate field.

On the Eastern Shore, the results were even more lopsided, with Wallace winning two of every three votes and McGovern only one in eight.

When the reporters were through, almost all the people interviewed said they had supported Wallace in 1972, as indeed they must have. Except for Fugett's sampling. Fugett "found" more people who voted for candidates other than Wallace than did any other interviewer. Not only that, he also "found" more McGovern supporters from 1972 than did all the other reporters combined.

In one instance, the man of the house couldn't contain himself when Fugett asked which candidate he had supported in the 1972 election. "Only the *Washington Post*," he said, "would send somebody like you around to ask people if they voted for or against George Wallace."

This case was a little extreme, and the newspaper story, when written, did not purport to contain the results of a scientific survey. Nevertheless, it underscored a serious problem in polling on sensitive issues. One procedure for dealing with polls in which racial matters are of concern is to have whites interview whites, and blacks blacks. But that is not always possible. And, as noted, the interviewer's demeanor as well as his or her race can create a bias.

There are other pitfalls as well. Certain subjects are just too personal for accurate polling. It is popular on and off to do polls regarding people's sexual activities; best-sellers and provocative magazine pieces are written from such surveys.

Most are without much value; there is evidence that people who limit their sex lives to traditional relationships, or who have no sex life to speak of, tend more than others to refuse such interviews. Thus, poll findings may be skewed toward the sexually active, making it appear that more people are cheating on their spouses, or more young people engaged in premarital sex, than is actually the case. How far off are these surveys? There is no way of knowing.

Some other subjects do not lend themselves to accurate polling for exactly the opposite reason: Instead of being too personal, they are too far removed from people's experience. In the field of foreign affairs, for example, many people have no views at all on a wide variety of matters. It makes little sense to ask Americans which side they favor in a dispute between Pakistan and India. That seems obvious, and pollsters tend to avoid such questions. But many issues of the day fall into the same category—disinvestment in South Africa, views on American military strength compared with that of the Soviet Union, whether certain tax reforms will result in a fairer system, the merits of Reagan's planned space shield against nuclear weaponry, a West Bank homeland for Palestinians, a national trade policy for this country, developmental aid to the Third World—all these are complicated matters that are generally unsuitable for ordinary polling.

Most Americans have no thought-out opinions on such issues, but that does not stop pollsters from asking about them. Often pollsters are hired by lobbies with agendas of their own, such as groups promoting particular weapons systems, or opposing tax legislation, or the like. It is easy in such instances to "find" whatever the lobbying group is seeking through a little creative question-wording.

Finally, there are often problems in analyzing poll results.

Data are rarely straightforward. A poll in Trenton, New Jersey, done for the *Trenton Times* some years ago, had half the people interviewed saying they would move away if they could. That seemed to suggest that many residents did not exactly think of Trenton as a garden spot. The *Times* took an opposing view, noting that half the people would stay in Trenton, even if they had the opportunity to move. "You could look at the cup as half empty," the newspaper editor told me. "I saw it as half full."

The half-empty, half-full argument recurs frequently. One of my first polling mentors liked to say that a person could have his legs in a heated oven and his head in a freezer—and, under these extreme conditions, still register an overall body temperature that is exactly normal. Reporting only the overall temperature in that instance would be misleading and incomplete. But poll reports in the media frequently do just that by focusing on the average result for all people interviewed—the marginals, as they are called—and neglecting the hot and cold extremes.

Sometimes, as when polling stopped too early in 1948, events having nothing to do with polls themselves help give the practice a bad name.

In 1968, for example, the interpretation of polls done by Gallup and Louis Harris may well have obstructed the democratic process, proving instrumental in Richard Nixon's edging Hubert H. Humphrey for the presidency. Again, there was nothing wrong with the polls, at least nothing technically wrong. Before the Republican and Democratic nominating conventions that summer, Gallup trial heats showed Nixon with a two-point lead over Humphrey, forty percent to thirty-eight percent, with George Wallace running as an independent and getting sixteen percent.

After the Republican convention in July, which saw Nixon fight off a bid by Nelson Rockefeller for the nomination, the lead spurted to sixteen points. It was a routine progression. With TV devoting full coverage to convention events and none to the Democrats, and with the convention marked by flag-waving, dramatic speeches, and colorful rhetoric, voters were naturally drawn to the Republican side.

Normally, it would have been expected that public opinion would adjust soon after the Democratic convention in August. But 1968 was not a normal year. The Democratic convention setting was raucous, to say the least, with Chicago police clubbing antiwar demonstrators in nightly battles. Contentiousness stopping just short of violence was the general mood on the convention floor.

Voters saw all that on TV as it occurred, and then saw it again, in text and bloody pictures, in newspapers and magazines. Thus, in polls after the convention, Nixon continued to hold a commanding lead: twelve points in early September and fifteen points in the middle of the month, according to Gallup.

Humphrey was a strong politician, certain to rebound eventually. While the surveys may have been valid when taken, it seemed sure the mood would change as the election approached and recollections of the convention faded. The mood did change, but too little and too late for Humphrey.

In his book *Lies, Damn Lies, and Statistics*, author Michael Wheeler noted that Humphrey's finances were so bad that one of his pollsters demanded cash before giving the candidate his findings. A worse problem was that TV stations were demanding payment in advance for advertising, preventing Humphrey from buying a full schedule of commercials.

By the end of the campaign, Humphrey almost caught Nixon, losing by less than one percentage point in the popular vote. While it cannot be proven, there is reason to believe that without those early polls Humphrey would have had the money to buy more TV ads at the end, and the ads would have carried him to victory, helping turn around one voter in a hundred, which was all he needed to win.

"It was sort of like we had a disease," Humphrey said later on. "The polls were like water in the gas tank; we just didn't have that forward thrust. If I could have come out of the convention a few points, maybe even a little further behind, I think we could have won." *

---

* Michael Wheeler, *Lies, Damn Lies, and Statistics*, Liveright, 1976.

▪ ▪ ▪

There are pitfalls all along the way in public opinion polling. Pollsters often spend days, weeks, even months preparing their questionnaires, only to find, when it is too late, that they forgot to ask a crucial question. It took me six drafts to work up my first poll questionnaire for the *Washington Post*. After each draft, I was pleased at the improvements I had made, and I wondered how I could have been so stupid in my previous efforts.

One recurring problem is a certain pretentiousness in many poll reports, brought on by some analysts' fixation on precision. A poll that gives Candidate A fifty-two percent of the vote and Candidate B forty-eight percent has the appearance of being precise. Sometimes it is, sometimes it isn't, and luck, as much as anything else, may be the determining factor. Most often, however, polls need not be exactly on the money to be valuable political and sociological tools. As denoters of trend, as portrayers of division or unity in the community, as early-warning systems for decision-makers and ordinary citizens alike, the best polls often present only a rough measure of what Americans really think. But it is a measure that can be obtained through no other means.

Despite inherent weaknesses and frequently flawed execution, the polls in general have made a worthy contribution in exactly the way Gallup had in mind. They keep putting before the people and the government a genuine citizens' agenda. They certainly are not perfect, but we are far better off with them than without them.

POLLS ABOUT POLLS
What People Think about Polls, 1944 and 1985

From time to time, pollsters measure their own approval ratings. These findings are from Gallup polls in 1944, when scientific polling was still new, and 1985.

Q. What is your general impression of how well [the public opinion polls] do?

IMPRESSIONS OF POLLS' ACCURACY

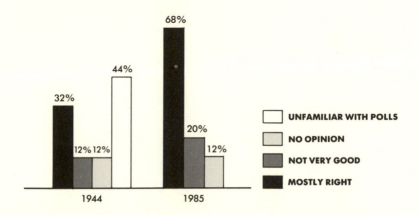

Q. *In general, would you say that polls of the opinions of the public are a good thing or a bad thing in our country?*

ARE POLLS A GOOD THING IN OUR COUNTRY?

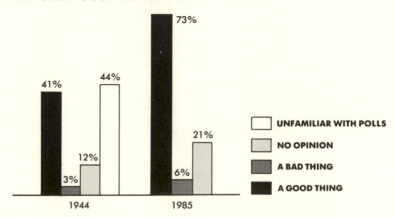

THE WORDING MAKES THE DIFFERENCE
"Welfare" v. "Assistance to the Poor," 1985

In a 1985 nationwide public opinion poll, the National Opinion Research Center (NORC) asked if too little money, too much, or about the right amount was being spent on welfare in the United States. Only 19% said too little was being spent. At the same time NORC asked another national sampling if too little, too much, or about the right amount was being spent on assistance to the poor, and 63% said "too little." These astonishing differences in response underscore the importance of nuance in the wording of pollsters' questions. By 1985, the word *welfare* had negative connotations for many, but *assistance to the poor* had positive ones. Most pollsters try to be alert to such nuance; some, looking to manipulate their findings, take advantage of them.

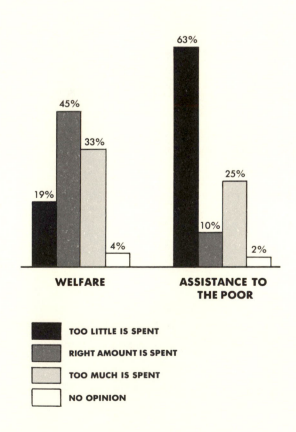

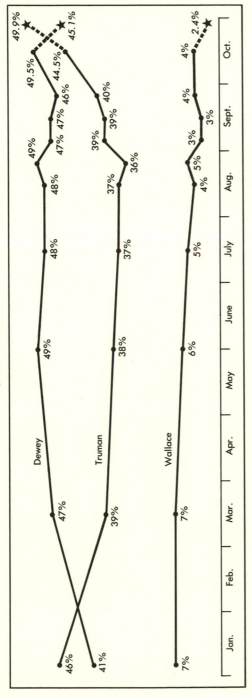

SOME OF THE PITFALLS OF POLLING
Dewey v. Truman, 1948

Dewey

49.9%
49.5%
44.5%
45.1%
49%
47%
47%
46%
48%
48%
49%
47%
46%

Truman

40%
39%
39%
37%
36%
37%
38%
39%
41%

Wallace

4%
4%
2.4%
3%
5%
4%
5%
6%
7%
7%

Jan. Feb. Mar. Apr. May June July Aug. Sept. Oct.

Election polls and the practice of polling itself came under sharp attack after the election of 1948, when Harry S. Truman won the presidency with 49.9% of the vote, after pollsters virtually gave the election to his opponent, Thomas E. Dewey. This record of the Gallup poll that year, however, shows that it was the pollsters, not the polls themselves, that were in error. Gallup simply stopped polling in mid-October, thinking a five-point lead was too much to overcome and failing to anticipate that the Truman momentum, which the polls had shown, would continue.

[This chart is based on one provided by the Gallup organization; actual election percentages are shown by the stars.]

PART THREE

WHAT AMERICANS REALLY THINK

About race relations and blacks, the news media, taxes, Israel, and other public affairs

BLACKS AND RACE RELATIONS

O NE OF THE MOST PERPLEXING ASPECTS OF American life has to do with white attitudes toward black people. In no area do ideals and practice come into greater conflict. On the one hand, opinion surveys since World War II show a major softening of white views toward blacks. A once-prevalent belief in white superiority has virtually disappeared, and the change in thinking has been accompanied by spectacular gains for blacks in many areas.

On the other hand, black leaders and some whites today maintain that conditions for most blacks are as bad now as after the race riots of the sixties, when a presidentially ordered study, the Kerner Commission report, said that blacks and whites live in two different worlds and that the black world is getting worse. In addition, these leaders charge, the concern that existed in the sixties has eroded; whites feel that blacks have been given equal opportunity and that further gains must be brought about by blacks themselves, without special assistance.

Some of the most important studies on racial attitudes have been conducted by the University of Chicago's National Opinion Research Center. Each year since 1972, the center, known as NORC, has conducted the General Social Survey, a government-financed opinion-and-attitude survey that presents the most authoritative look at the state of mind of Americans on a wide range of social issues. NORC repeats many of its questions almost every year, enabling its social scientists to describe trends or breakthroughs in public thought.

One such breakthrough was uncovered in NORC's 1984 report. For the first time, the researchers found, a majority of white Americans said they supported open-housing laws. The finding came in response to this question:

Suppose there is a community-wide vote on the general housing issue. There are two possible laws to vote on: One law says that a homeowner can decide for himself whom to sell his house to, even if he prefers not to sell to blacks. . . . The second law says that a homeowner cannot refuse to sell to someone because of their race or color. Which law would you vote for?

Racial discrimination in home sales has been forbidden explicitly in the United States since 1968. Nevertheless, in the NORC surveys from 1972 through 1982, an average of sixty percent of the whites interviewed said they would vote for the first option, and only thirty-seven percent for open housing. Year by year, however, receptivity to open housing was growing. Finally, in 1984, fifty-two percent of the people interviewed said they would vote for the second option, and forty-five percent for the first. Opposition to open-housing laws had become the minority view.

Largely accounting for the dramatic change, it seems clear, was a sharp increase in neighborhood racial integration. Whites were getting to know blacks a little better, and felt less threatened by them. From 1972 to 1982, only forty-one percent of the whites interviewed by NORC said at least one black family lived on their block. By 1984, that figure had risen to fifty-four percent.

Other NORC findings showed similar but less striking trends, all of them suggesting growing acceptance of racial integration as more black families moved to previously white neighborhoods. Overall, thirty-three percent of the whites interviewed by NORC between 1972 and 1982 said they would support laws against racial intermarriage. But that group too was constantly diminishing, and in the 1984 General Social Survey, only twenty-four percent supported such laws.

On the average in the surveys from 1972 through 1982, seventy-two percent of the whites interviewed said they would have no objections if a family member brought a black home to dinner. Twenty-five percent said blacks had been to their house for dinner. In the 1984 survey, eighty-two percent of the whites interviewed said they would not mind, and thirty-one percent said blacks had eaten dinner in their homes.

Between 1972 and 1982, seventy-eight percent of the whites interviewed said they would vote for a black for president if their party nominated one. In 1984, eighty-two percent said they would. In both instances, this hypothetical support for a black candidate was probably exaggerated by some nine or ten points, judging from my own experience in preelection polling of white voters where a black was seeking office. Some whites are just ashamed to state their true feelings. They respond to questions like this by giving what they know to be the socially acceptable answer.

But that too is a sign of growing racial tolerance. People are less likely to practice discrimination if they believe they will be criticized for it. In total, what the opinion polls are showing, therefore, is both a growing acceptance of the principles of integration and equality, as well as a growing acceptance of blacks by whites.

Since 1972, NORC has asked people if they feel whites and blacks should attend the same schools, or if there should be separate schools for each race. That battle was essentially won before the Chicago interviewers began the General Social Survey; support for integrated schools bumped the ceiling almost from the start. From 1972 to 1982, eighty-six percent of the whites interviewed said that the two races should attend the same schools. By 1984, support for integrated schools had reached ninety-one percent. Most of the NORC battery of questions on race relations was not repeated in 1985, but that one was, and ninety-two percent that year favored school integration.

On first glance, therefore, white Americans appear to have almost totally overcome whatever resistance they had thirty years earlier when the Supreme Court, in *Brown vs. Board of Education,* ruled that separate facilities were not equal and made school desegregation the law of the land. That, however, presents much too simplistic a picture. The fact is, whites continue to have many reservations about integration, including integration of the schools. They tend to welcome blacks in small numbers only.

The General Social Survey usually has three follow-ups to its school-integration question, asking whites whether they have any objection to sending their children to schools which have a few blacks enrolled, to those which are half black, or to ones where blacks make up the majority.

Hardly any whites—only six percent in the surveys from 1972 to 1982—objected to schools with a few black students. But twenty-four percent objected to schools where half the students were black, and a majority, fifty-four percent, objected to schools where most were black. Those follow-up questions were not asked in 1984 but they were repeated in 1985, and the change was minimal: fifty-two percent of the whites still objected to sending their children to a majority-black school.

Is it racial prejudice, fear of the unknown, or only common sense (in that majority-black schools are often academically inferior) that makes many whites accept integration in little doses only? Many whites no doubt think it is common sense; many blacks think it fear or prejudice. The rift between the races is extreme. Whites see some prejudice and racial discrimination remaining. Blacks think things have gotten better but they still see a great deal of racial hostility and bias.

In 1981, the *Washington Post/ABC News* poll, as one of its first efforts, conducted an extensive survey on race relations, interviewing random samples of 1,426 whites and 446 blacks nationwide. One question sought to find how much extreme racial prejudice people thought still existed in the United States: "Just your best guess," it asked:

> *How many white Americans would you say personally share the attitudes of groups like the Ku Klux Klan toward blacks? Would you say only a few Americans share that attitude, about ten percent, less than a quarter, less than half, or that over half share that attitude?*

From their response, white people showed they still considered virulent anti-black racism a national problem, with two in ten saying that at least a quarter of all white Americans harbored Klan-type feelings toward blacks. But that was nothing compared to the sentiments of blacks. Among them, four in ten thought white hatred toward them existed on that broad a level.

The survey also compared the views of blacks and whites on matters of more everyday racism, asking whether, where they lived, people felt that blacks were generally discriminated against in getting an education, getting decent housing, in wages, and in work generally. The pattern again showed whites thinking there was some but not much discrimination against blacks, and blacks seeing large-scale discrimination:

Percentage in 1981 saying antiblack bias exists in . . .

	(of whites interviewed)	(of blacks interviewed)
. . . getting a quality education	6%	28%
. . . getting decent housing	17%	44%
. . . getting unskilled-labor jobs	11%	45%
. . . getting skilled-labor jobs	21%	60%
. . . getting managerial jobs	25%	65%
. . . wages paid in most jobs	13%	57%

In January, 1986, the *Post* and *ABC News* returned to the subject, doing a poll of blacks exclusively, with 1,022 interviews. On each of the same questions, there was a six- to nine-point increase in the belief that discrimination existed. In only one area, education, did fewer than half the blacks feel there was no racial discrimination in their own cities and towns. By then, more than seven in ten perceived discrimination in the skilled-labor market and in the awarding of managerial jobs.

The first poll, of course, was taken at the outset of the Reagan administration; the second five years into it. The interim, as seen by blacks, was a period of reversals across the board.

Views on employment were of particular significance. These surveys revealed enormous discomfort for a great many blacks as they sought to acquire, hold, and advance in employment. It is as though they saw the workplace as enemy territory. In the 1986 survey, four blacks in ten said they themselves had been discriminated against in getting a job and in wages paid.

It is largely immaterial whether it is the black view or the white view that is correct, or whether the truth about discrimination in employment lies somewhere in between. The fact is, many blacks face, or think they face, a major, additional obstacle in making a living. It would seem to be more than coincidence that while one person in every seven nationally lives in poverty, the figure for blacks is one in every three. Relatively few whites express any appreciation of that.

The problem is especially acute for black men, whose unemployment levels were more than double those of white men throughout the Reagan years.* And the plight of black men spills over to all blacks, creating much of the social turmoil that so degrades American life.

Indeed, exploration of the 1986 survey of blacks strongly suggests that the employment situation of black men is the single most important factor in determining living conditions for black people in the United States. There has been wide lamentation over the decline of the black family in the United States, but not enough, in my view, over the link between employment and a stable family life.

Where black men hold full-time jobs, the profile of the black family is hardly distinguishable from that of whites. But the lack of full-time jobs for so many black men explains a great deal of the rampant crime, drug usage, illegitimacy, and instability that are associated with the black underclass.

The idea behind this line of thinking is ancient: Put a man to work and you keep him out of trouble. No one has ever doubted that; it is a truism. Nevertheless, instead of seeing work for men as a solution to the ills of black society, what we have heard from the Reagan administration, from revisionist social theoreticians, and from much of the news media has been criticism of welfare programs (or dull acceptance of criticism), lamentation of what Reagan himself called "horri-

---

* Unemployment figures from the Bureau of Labor Statistics make the point:

Average percentage unemployed each year among . . .

	1981	1982	1983	1984	1985	1986	1987 (Jan–Jun)
. . . black men	15.7%	20.1%	20.3%	16.4%	15.3%	14.8%	16.8%
. . . white men	6.5%	8.8%	8.8%	6.4%	6.1%	6.0%	7.0%

ble crimes" perpetrated by blacks, and excoriation of the black underclass for the calamity of widespread, unwed teenage black motherhood. The impression cast is that something is wrong with blacks themselves that no amount of social assistance can cure.

Democrats in Congress have been hardly distinguishable from Reagan. If not as critical, they have not been helpful in any discernible way. They generally submitted to his repeated attacks on welfare with no vocal response, refraining, as in so many other areas, from engaging in a leadership debate. Thus, the Reagan view has gone far toward being nationally accepted, by default. The best that can be said about most Democrats is that they did not allow Reagan to cut as much in social spending as he would have liked, and that, toward the end of his tenure, in 1986, they finally began what appeared to be serious discussion of job programs and a revamping of the welfare system.

In the *Post/ABC News* 1986 survey of blacks, there was an almost total link between a man's possession or lack of a full-time job and his chances of having a stable family life. Full-time work turned out to be much more important than a man's level of education, or whether he grew up in a home with both parents, or in one where most of the money came from a government dole. Poverty and deprivation were often overcome. Failure to have a job was not.

Where there was no job for a black man, the poll found, the chances were extremely great that there either was a family in crisis or, more frequently, no family at all. Only one unemployed black man in six among those surveyed was married and living with his wife. Another one in four had been married but was separated or divorced at the time of the survey.

More than half the unemployed black men in the survey said they had never been married. Marriage means more financial responsibility than the average unemployed black man can accept. That is one reason, quite possibly the main reason, for all those unmarried black girls having children out of wedlock: there are just too few men available for marriage, and there will be too few until the job market opens up for them.

If black girls put off having children until their boyfriends had regular work and could marry them, they might wait forever, the way things have been going. Thus, many of them have chosen to have babies without matrimony, and let the government pay for their upbringing.

The fathers of these babies, quite often, just happen to be those same unemployed black men. Of unemployed black men surveyed, four in every ten admitted to having fathered at least one child. Common sense suggests that the figure may in truth be considerably higher; it is hard enough to own up to an interviewer on the telephone that you are without work; harder still to admit being an unmarried father.

There is no doubt that poverty, idleness, and frustration lead to the street crime, drug use, alcoholism, and violence that plague the black community; no survey is needed to demonstrate that. But what this particular *Post/ABC News* poll showed, along with one of whites the following month, was the extent to which the opposite was true: how much the holding down of a full-time job changed the picture.

Black men with full-time work lead very different lives from those with no jobs. Their social profile is hardly distinguishable from that of whites with jobs or careers. In the surveys, about three-fourths of all men with full-time jobs, blacks and whites, got married at one time or another; about one-quarter were single. Marriage was somewhat more unstable for blacks with jobs: one in every five ended in divorce, compared to one in eight for whites who worked full time. Part of the difference, perhaps most of it, may be that a good many more of the blacks interviewed were on the edge of full-time employment—the last hired, first fired.

Indeed, having a job is for a man virtually a necessary condition for the maintenance of marriage and family life, regardless of race. Among white men who were married and living with their wives, eighty-six percent, according to another *Post/ABC News* poll, had full-time jobs, four percent were unemployed, and the rest were either retired or otherwise not in the job market. Among black men who were married and living with their wives, seventy-eight percent had full-time jobs, six percent were unemployed, and the rest not in the job market. That shows hardly any difference.

Having a job makes for a different outlook on life. Unemployed black men were substantially more likely than other blacks to view white people as racists, to blame their own problems on discrimination, and to be down on themselves —thinking, for example, that blacks lack an inborn ability to learn.

No one says it is easy to find regular work for many of the black unemployed. That doesn't mean it can't or shouldn't be done, or that it should not be a leading national priority.

But cold facts show just the opposite trend. A Michican State University study in 1987 pictured terrible deterioration in one key city, Detroit, over a twenty-year period. The study found 9.8 percent of blacks, compared to 2.9 percent of whites, to have been unemployed in 1967. Twenty years later, the jobless rate, according to the study, was 13.3 percent for whites, 30.7 percent for blacks.

Often the most exciting polls for an opinion analyst are those that are counterintuitive, in which research yields quite unexpected findings. That was the case with a *Washington Post/ ABC News* poll's examination of school busing.

During the 1984 election campaign, President Reagan, on a visit to Charlotte, North Carolina, launched into a diatribe on school busing programs, which his administration had striven to abolish. "Busing," Reagan said, "takes innocent children out of the neighborhood school and makes them pawns in a social experiment that nobody wants. And we've found out that it failed."

Reagan may have felt he was on safe ground, especially in Charlotte, which has the most extensive system of busing for school integration in the nation. School busing has caused enormous strife; speaking out against it was viewed by political conservatives as a sure vote-getter, in the South and the rest of the country as well. By 1984 it was widely assumed that most Americans, including most blacks, were opposed to busing, viewing it as another social program that had failed.

The president, therefore, must have been at least a little shocked at the local reaction. "You were wrong, Mr. President," said a headline over an editorial in the *Charlotte Observer* the following day. "Charlotte's greatest achievement is its fully integrated public school system," the editorial went on to say. Community leaders, including white Republicans, had the same reaction.

When it comes to busing, as in so many matters dealing with the sensitive issue of race relations, what Americans really think is fairly complex. In any opinion poll, most whites, probably sixty percent, perhaps more, will come out opposed to busing. In a *Post/ABC News* poll in February, 1986, we asked people whether they favored or opposed "busing of black and white students as a last resort for school integration." The phrasing was chosen to put busing in its realistic setting: not as a sought-after end in itself but as an alternative, when no other one is found, to segregation.

In response, sixty percent of the whites interviewed came out opposed; thirty-six percent said they favored busing in such circumstances, and four percent offered no opinion. So, while we found a significant minority supporting busing as a last resort, their numbers, nevertheless, were buried under the opposition.

Hidden in those overall figures, however, were other findings that relayed a different impression. The younger a person was, the more the resistance to busing began to fade. That was especially true for young people who had some personal experience with school busing.

Among whites between the ages of eighteen and thirty, support was about equal to opposition: forty-seven percent favored school busing, fifty percent opposed it. In a follow-up question, the poll asked people whether someone in their home had attended a school where there had been busing for purposes of integration. Among these younger whites, one of every five said yes, there had been. And among them, fifty-four percent said they favored busing, while forty-six percent opposed it.

Numbers like those do not evoke images of huge popularity, but fifty-four percent is, after all, a majority. Suddenly, like some medicine, the taste seemed not as bad as the thought of it. Something must have happened to whites in recent years. Either busing is better implemented these days, or students are getting used to it, or younger whites care more about integration than their elders do. Perhaps it is a combination of all three.

What is true for young whites holds even more for young blacks, as shown in the *Post/ABC News* poll of more than a thousand blacks a month earlier. In the eighteen-to-thirty age group, thirty percent of the blacks interviewed said someone in their home had attended a school where there was busing for integration. Among them, sixty-five percent supported busing, twenty-nine percent opposed it.

These *Post/ABC News* findings on school busing presented only snapshots in time, two surveys done in early 1986. But other studies show them to have been no flukes. Annually, the American Council on Education, through research at the University of California at Los Angeles, sponsors a wide-ranging attitude survey of college freshmen. Since 1976 this survey has been asking students whether they agree or disagree with the statement that "busing is okay if it helps achieve racial balance in the schools." The first year only thirty-seven percent agreed. Each year after that, except for one, the survey showed increasing support for busing. In 1986, in interviews with 192,000 students, fifty-four percent agreed.

In Washington in the eighties there never has been any talk of improving or widening school-busing plans, or even a study of the effect of busing. As in certain other important areas, the Reagan administration has set the tone, for Democrats as well as Republicans. Reagan's aim always was to abandon busing; it was part of his litany, and the Justice Department under him worked toward that end.

It seems generally accepted, without any examination to

speak of, that the American people have repudiated school busing. But during the years when opposition to busing hardened in Washington, it was softening across the country, especially among the people who were experiencing it directly.

COMPLAINTS ABOUT THE
NEWS MEDIA

---

*Newspapers are unable, seemingly, to discriminate
between a bicycle accident and the collapse of civili-
zation.*

—G.B. Shaw

*You cannot hope to bribe or twist
Thank God! the British journalist.
But seeing what the man will do
Unbribed, there's no occasion to.*

—Humbert Wolfe

A NYONE WHO HAS WORKED FOR A LARGE NEWS
organization is used to getting complaints. Praise
comes but rarely; it is through complaints that editors
know people are paying attention. How much attention? A great deal, it would seem.

A former managing editor at the *Washington Post* used to
put it much like this: "Blacks say we're insensitive to them
and whites say we are partial to blacks. Arabs say we're run
by Jews and Jews say we are anti-Israel. Conservatives say
we have a liberal bias; liberals write us off altogether. Old
people? Don't ask. There's no group that thinks we do a good

job when we write about them. We must be doing something right."

A key word in the above is *group.* Everyone who pays fifteen cents or a quarter or more for a daily newspaper has complaints of one kind or another; it is organized groups, however, that apply the most pressure. And their complaints are almost totally different from those of ordinary citizens.

On any given day in almost every metropolitan area, as sure as there is a bulldog edition, some group is in touch with reporters or newspaper editors or TV station managers, complaining about coverage, demanding corrections, charging inaccuracy, misquotation, bias.

The complaints are often outlandish, and requests extreme. In February and March of 1987, in my position as managing editor for national affairs at United Press International, I got letters from associates of the political extremist Lyndon Larouche, demanding that UPI stop referring to Larouche as a political extremist.

In 1982, a group working out of the Israeli embassy in Washington kept track of stories on Israel run by forty-eight American newspapers, categorizing them as positive, negative, or neutral. In all, more than thirty newspapers were given negative ratings. Included were the *New York Times,* the *Los Angeles Times,* the *Chicago Sun-Times,* the *Philadelphia Inquirer,* the *Boston Globe.*

The *Washington Post* was at the bottom. Israeli ambassador Moshe Arens complained to *Post* editors that of 201 articles on the Middle East between May 3 and October 31, 1982, 35 had been positive toward Israel, 100 had been negative, and 66 were neutral.

One item cited as negative was a headline, "Begin Again Rejects U.S. Plan," after Israeli prime minister Menachem Begin had, indeed, rejected President Reagan's plan for the Middle East. Reporting exactly what had happened, which is not an easy accomplishment in a headline, was deemed negative.

I can cite dozens of similar complaints from my own experience; so can every editor who has been around awhile.

Sometimes the aim of such organized activity is to obtain favorable coverage. More often it is to impose a chilling effect, turning editors away from lines of inquiry by making them wonder whether they really need the headache that stories on a particular issue will bring.

Success for these critics seems less related to the validity of the complaint than to the perceived power of the complaining group. The most notorious drive on the media was that undertaken in the late sixties when Vice-President Spiro T. Agnew was let loose by Richard Nixon. Agnew toured the country in 1969, charging that there was a press conspiracy against Nixon, that the press was out of synch with American values and was distorting events in reporting the Vietnam war.

Agnew's aim was twofold: to pressure the news media into softer coverage and to manipulate the public into thinking that most Americans supported the war, and that there was something wrong with those who did not. Media leaders reacted angrily to Agnew and various other Nixon surrogates, saying all the right things. But many reporters and editors, myself included, felt that major news organizations did indeed bend under the attack.

By 1973, Nixon and Agnew were so weakened by the exposure of their own corruption that they no longer could launch a credible attack. Surrogates had to take on the entire job, and it was one they relished. Thus came into prominence the right-wing professional media critic.

As noted, organized groups on all sides of any issue have their problems with the press, as well they should. By its nature, the daily press issues reports that are incomplete, misleading, or inaccurate. That is true even for reporters and editors with the best of intentions. It is only reasonable and proper for groups to apply pressure when they feel they have been dealt with unfairly.

In the main, however, the right-wing media critics are not interested in more thorough reporting; what they want is a less independent, less aggressive press. Their paramount goal is the containment of communism. Virtually any media coverage that could interfere with that end—such as stories on fraud in U.S. defense spending, for example—is subject to their attack.

What these critics suggest whenever there is some exposé on American government is that the writer or news organization involved is sympathetic to the Soviets, or, at a minimum, unwittingly serving Soviet ends. The reasoning is the same as it was during the Vietnam war, when people who criticized the government's conduct were portrayed as siding with Hanoi.

The constant, unrelenting charge from professional media critics is that the news media have a liberal political agenda and are bent on tearing down establishment institutions. But what most Americans really think about the news media is another story entirely.

Instead of seeing the major media as out to get the political establishment, most people, when asked, say that reporting on public figures is too soft and that the media are in bed with the leadership in Washington. Few feel the press is more adversarial toward government than it should be. The number thinking there is too little investigative reporting far exceeds those thinking there is too much. And on those occasions when the press says one thing and the leadership in Washington another, most people have no trouble deciding whom to believe: by three or four to one, they believe the press.

In 1973, with professional critics savaging the news media for blood-lust in pursuit of the Watergate scandal, the American people as a whole expressed admiration for the press. As an editor at the *Washington Post* who handled the Watergate story, I used to get letters of congratulation from ordinary citizens, and phone calls and mail from across the country begging us to look into other scandals.

A Gallup poll in May, 1973, asked whether "the Nixon Administration is being treated fairly or unfairly by television [and] by the newspapers." Thirteen percent said TV was treating him unfairly; fifteen percent said newspapers were. Not bad scores.

Journalism schools began overflowing in that period, with young people in record numbers coming to think of reporting as honest and worthwhile work—different, that is, from most careers.

In the summer of 1981, my assistant, Kenneth John, and I did an extensive poll of people's attitudes toward the major news media for the *Washington Post*. At the outset we defined the term, "major news media," as applying to "the TV network news departments, a few nationally known newspapers, and the big news magazines." We listed several by name so that people would know exactly what we were referring to.*

Our hypothesis was that ordinary people's problems with the press would turn out to be quite different from the media critics' problems.

As always, the period in which this survey was conducted was one in which press critics were hard at work, fostering the notion that the media were antiestablishment. The public basically rejected that idea.

"Would you say the major news media are too critical of the government in Washington, or not critical enough, or what?" one question asked. Only one person in four felt the media too critical of government; four in ten said the media were not critical enough.

Another question in the survey asked people whether, "when there is a protest against the government, the major news media will always support the protesters" instead of "reporting the news impartially." By two to one, fifty-nine percent to thirty, those interviewed chose the "impartial" option.

A third question noted that "from time to time, the major news media report stories that high government officials in Washington say are not true," and went on to ask: "In such instances, who do you usually think are more truthful, the major news media, or high government officials?" By more

---

* Those we cited were *ABC News*, *CBS News*, *NBC News*, the *New York Times*, *Washington Post*, *Washington Star* [now defunct], *Los Angeles Times*, and *Time* and *Newsweek* magazines.

than three to one, fifty-seven percent to seventeen, the random sample interviewed said the media are more truthful.

In every instance, the public in that 1981 survey rejected the criticisms voiced by the professional media critics. Was the press overly aggressive in its reporting of government? Not to ordinary citizens, a majority of whom thought the press too supportive of government in that it often covered up stories that ought to have been reported.

As it happens, the public's main complaint with the news media lies in an area far removed from coverage of government. It has to do with the media's gut-wrenching penchant for riding roughshod over private citizens who, through no fault of their own, come into public view under extremely stressful situations.

Whenever there is a hostage-taking, a plane crash, a terrible fire, or some other calamity, reporters seek out and often exploit the bereaved. Looking for human-interest stories, interviewers seldom seem satisfied until a wife, husband, or other relative or friend breaks down in an emotional collapse. Such press callousness always existed. Ben Hecht described how in the 1920s he and other Chicago newspaper reporters would go to homes of the bereaved and steal photographs for publication.

But there was no television in the twenties. TV has brought this aspect of reporting into full view, and it is ugly to watch. It is bad enough when people break down under strain, worse yet when they break down on the evening news, and it is totally repulsive when the breakdown is forced by relentless interviewers persisting until they evoke that response.

The relevant finding from the 1981 *Washington Post* poll came in response to a question that asked people whether they agreed or disagreed with the statement, "The major news media frequently violate the privacy of individual citizens." The response was overwhelming. Sixty-three percent agreed; only twenty-eight percent disagreed.

A few months later, in October, 1981, *ABC News* did a

similar poll, focusing on attitudes toward TV network news coverage. My colleagues there went one step further than I had on the subject of invasion of people's privacy. They asked whether it was *acceptable* for reporters to harass people in the name of the public's right to know. Their wording, also in the form of an agree-disagree statement, was: "It's okay for TV news to invade the privacy of ordinary people while gathering the news." That notion drew even stronger public censure. Seventy-nine percent disagreed; only eighteen percent agreed.

Putting the *ABC News* and *Post* findings together shows that on the one hand, the large majority feels that reporters *are* invading people's privacy and, on the other hand, an even larger majority, a consensus, *thinks it is wrong to do so.*

Subsequently, the *Post*'s 1981 poll was replicated in part by other media pollsters and by academics in two midwestern colleges. In each instance the essential findings were confirmed: only a small portion of the people interviewed saw the news media as too aggressive when it came to reporting on government; great majorities thought they were guilty of invading the privacy of ordinary citizens.

In 1985, the Times-Mirror company, publisher of the *Los Angeles Times* and other leading newspapers, hired the Gallup organization to embark on the most extensive study of public attitudes toward the news media ever undertaken, starting out with four thousand interviews that year. It too found invasion of privacy drawing more criticism than any other press practice.

"Do you feel news organizations often invade people's privacy or do they generally respect people's privacy?" the Gallup interviewers asked. Seventy-three percent said the press often invades people's privacy; twenty-three percent said they do not.*

---

* The message that the public strongly resents invasion of privacy has gotten out to chief editors and station managers, and network TV reporters are less likely to badger the bereaved these days. It may take some time, however, for the public to notice, and for editors and reporters on smaller, independent TV stations to follow suit.

On the subject of investigative reporting, the Times-Mirror survey also reaffirmed the earlier findings, with sixty-seven percent saying that press criticism helps keep political leaders honest, and concluding that the press does not do enough in the way of aggressive coverage of government.

The Times-Mirror company made these last findings the focus of full-page ads in major newspapers. "Is the watchdog really a lapdog?" said the headline over one ad. The copy under it read:

> If you're like most Americans, the thing you value most about a free press is the watchdog role it plays. You believe a free press helps the country by keeping public officials and military leaders honest.
>
> At the same time, you may also view America's free press as too often influenced by powerful interests and institutions . . . including government and the military.
>
> You're worried that the watchdog whose vigilance and tenacity you count on may in fact be a lapdog.

Opinion polls that show Americans desirous of aggressive coverage help point reporters, editors, and publishers in the right direction. Without them, many editors, consciously or not, would be strongly inclined to take the line of least resistance. As a group, newspaper editors are not crusaders. Publishers certainly aren't. "Do we really need to get into that?" is not a question that is often asked out loud in newsrooms, but editors ask it of themselves all the time.

Throughout the Reagan presidency the polls provided ballast for the news media, showing that the public supported hardnosed reporting at times when it came under sharp attack.

In one such instance, at a White House news conference on July 26, 1983, Reagan laced into the coverage of his policies toward Nicaragua and El Salvador. In an opening statement, he said he had received a letter from a thirteen-year-old asking, "Don't you wish you could just stamp your feet and shout at the press or Senators to be quiet, sit down, and listen to what you're saying?"

"Yes, Gretchen, I sometimes do feel that way," he said. He complained that there had been too much press attention to extensive U.S. military maneuvers in Central America, "and not nearly enough to other elements of our policy."

The first questioner, Helen Thomas of United Press International, noted that the maneuvers had been unprecedented in their scope, involving two battleship groups and thousands of combat troops sent to Honduras for an extended period. "The polls show the people are not for them, and they fear it may lead to war. And my question is, remembering the lessons in Vietnam, does this bother you? And do they have any say?"

"First of all," Reagan responded, "there is no comparison with Vietnam. . . . And maybe the people are disturbed because of the confused pattern that has been presented to them and the constant drumbeat with regard to the fact of suspicion that somehow there is an ulterior purpose in this."

A few days later, the *Post/ABC News* poll put this question to a cross-section of 1,505 Americans:

> *In his news conference Reagan criticized newspaper and TV news reporting on Central America, saying it has raised undue suspicion about his major goals in the area. Generally speaking, how would you rate the major TV and newspaper reporting on Central America: Would you say that reporting is excellent, good, not so good, or poor?*

The response was strongly pro-media. Sixty-one percent rated press coverage excellent or good; thirty-two percent as not so good or poor, with seven percent expressing no opinion.

A second question sharpened the battle between Reagan and the press:

> *Sometimes what Reagan says about his policies in Central America and what the news media report seem to be in*

conflict. When that occurs, who do you tend to believe more: Reagan or the major TV and newspaper reports?

The response showed the public giving significantly more credence to the press than to the president of the United States. Of those expressing an opinion, almost six in ten said they believed the TV and newspaper accounts more than they did Reagan.

Among only one group, Republicans, was there any sharp criticism of the news media and support for the Reagan view, and even among them, most of the criticism came from people who thought of themselves as strong Republicans. The question at hand, of course, elicited that kind of partisan division. But the same pattern holds on almost all questions that bear on attitudes toward the news media. Strong Republicans tend to see the media as an enemy. "Just plain" Republicans are the second most critical, but they are never, or hardly ever, uniformly antimedia.

Some editors and reporters, like some national leaders, do not need opinion polls to encourage them to do what they should be doing on their own. But in my judgment, many do. As I will show later, I think the polls were particularly instrumental in the aggressive press coverage of the Iran-contra scandal in 1986 and 1987.

The power of TV and newspapers is often overstated. The press does not indict, it does not convict, it does not have subpoena power. As an editor, I have personally worked on many stories that cried out for follow-up action by prosecutors, other local authorities, or Congress. It was far more common for such stories to fizzle and disappear without a trace than for them to be picked up and pursued by government agencies that could act on the wrongs cited. That, pretty much, is the rule, broken though it may be by some extraordinary exceptions.

But in another sense, one that is more to the point of this book, there is no disregarding the ability of the news media

—in the main, the ability of TV—to transform public opinion almost at will. Television is simply awesome in that regard.

Take, for example, the matter of the televised debates between Reagan and Walter Mondale in the 1984 presidential campaign. The reporting of the debates had a much greater impact on voter perceptions than anything the candidates themselves said in them.

The first debate took place on October 7. In three and a half years as president until then, Reagan, a polished performer while giving speeches, never was one to round off sentences in press conferences or other stand-up situations. He often strayed from a subject and got lost in midthought. He had once dozed off in a meeting with the Pope; not long before the debate it was revealed that he sometimes fell asleep at Cabinet meetings.

Wandering in conversation and nodding off are signs of advanced age. Reagan was then seventy-three years old; if reelected he would be seventy-eight by the end of his full second term. But his age had not been a serious factor in the campaign. Not, that is, until after the first debate.

During the debate, Reagan, true to form, faltered here and there. At one point he was so confused that he said, "I'm all confused now." But he did nothing that disturbed most viewers very much, at least not until they saw or read the media reviews.

Opinion polls taken immediately afterward showed no clear winner. An *ABC News* survey showed thirty-nine percent of the viewers saying Mondale had won the debate, thirty-eight percent saying Reagan had. A *USA Today* poll had Mondale as the winner by thirty-nine to thirty-four percent; a *New York Times/CBS* poll had Mondale the winner by forty-three to thirty-four percent.

Those first-night polls showed the contenders fairly close in terms of who had won the debate. In none did Mondale get a clear majority. The suggestion was that Americans felt Mondale had made a good showing, but not much more than that. Only one of the nonpartisan overnight polls, conducted by Gallup for *Newsweek* magazine, turned out differently. That poll asked not who had won, but who had done a "better job." A change in question wording may lead to a sharp change in response, which is what occurred here. In the *Newsweek* poll, fifty-four percent said Mondale had done a better job, thirty-seven percent said Reagan had.

In thrust, what these quick polls determined was that Mondale, who had been doing so dismally earlier, had brightened his chances somewhat. But there was little reason to think that many people had suddenly concluded that their president was over the hill.

At that point, however, the news media, especially TV, began to display their power to transform public opinion. The debate was held on a Sunday evening. On TV all day Monday the early polls were cited as showing that Mondale had won the debate. Reporters and anchor people repeatedly emphasized weak spots in Reagan's performance, replaying some of his stumbling. Even then, there was no discussion of Reagan's age as a factor.

On Monday and Tuesday evenings, the *Washington Post* and *ABC News* conducted a follow-up poll, and that too revealed no sudden concern that the president might be slipping. When asked why they thought Mondale or Reagan had won, only one person of all 1,035 interviewed cited the president's age as the main factor. Not exactly a groundswell.

By the time of that poll, however, the idea that Mondale had thrashed Reagan was snowballing. Among those interviewed on Monday night, fifty-five percent said Mondale had won; nineteen percent said Reagan had. What had been a good showing for Mondale when the debate ended began to be fixed in the public mind as a rout.

On Tuesday morning the *Wall Street Journal* opened the floodgates on the age "issue," running an article with the headline: NEW QUESTION IN RACE: IS OLDEST U.S. PRESIDENT NOW SHOWING HIS AGE? The TV networks immediately seized on the idea. That night, as political writers Jack W. Germond and Jules Witcover later wrote, the coverage was devastating:

One evening news show aired footage of the President dozing off in the presence of Pope John Paul II.

Another showed a most damaging tape of Reagan trying to dodge a question from a reporter at an impromptu outdoor encounter, with Nancy Reagan at his side. The tape showed, and a microphone picked up, the President's wife whispering an answer to him—and Reagan then repeating her suggested response word for word.

The networks also trotted out doctors and psychiatrists to discuss the signs and impairments of senility. The Reagan strategists thought this exercise was such a low blow that White House chief of staff Jim Baker filed a protest with one of the "offenders," *ABC News*.*

I noted in a *Washington Post* article at the time that there were even "doctors for Reagan saying, somewhat cryptically, that the president is an alert man for his age."

Polls showed momentum for Mondale gathering. Through the vagaries of survey sampling, the people interviewed in the *Post/ABC News* poll on Tuesday evening included substantially more Republicans than Monday's, giving the group more of a pro-Reagan cast. Nevertheless, among them Mondale was depicted as the winner of the debate by a fifty-five-to-sixteen majority.

Also on Tuesday, the *New York Times* and *CBS News* conducted their second postdebate survey. In it was inserted a direct question on the age factor. The result, as reported in the *New York Times* that Thursday, was that "half the public, including twenty-seven percent of probable Reagan voters, think Mr. Reagan is 'not as sharp' as he was four years ago."

The *Times*'s account also noted that "the impression [that Mondale was the winner] of the debate was intensifying as time passed," pointing out that sixty-six percent in the new survey said the former vice-president had won, with only seventeen percent giving the debate victory to Reagan.

By midweek, another major interpreter of public opinion, Johnny Carson, began weighing in, making jokes on his *To-*

* Germond and Witcover, *Wake Us When It's Over: Presidential Politics of 1984*, Macmillan, 1985.

night show about makeup and Reagan's appearance. A producer for Carson told a reporter it might be a good idea to "Betamax" the Carson monologue from here until the election, the suggestion being that problems like Reagan's age were now fair game.

Along with the new examination of Reagan came an altered view of Mondale, at least temporarily. His image was suddenly transformed from that of a weak, ridiculed also-ran to one of a masculine, aggressive competitor who had a chance of winning. Suddenly gone from the TV accounts of Mondale's daily activities was the introduction that had become standard: "In another bad day for Mondale . . ." In its place came comments about large crowds turning out to see him.

Comparison of two *Post/ABC News* polls, before and after the debate, quantified the change in perception. In the first, completed October 2, forty-one percent of the people interviewed said they had a favorable opinion of Mondale and forty-nine percent an unfavorable one. Those were terrible results for Mondale but they were consistent with other polls. In *Post/ABC News* interviews two days after the debate, fifty-seven percent said they had a favorable opinion of Mondale and forty-three percent an unfavorable one. That was not an outstanding score for a man who wanted to be president, but it was not bad, either, and it represented a world of improvement in just a few days, one that could be accounted for only by the favorable reviews from the news media.

This period was the highlight of the general election campaign for Walter Mondale. He began creeping back in the horse-race polls, cutting into Reagan's lead little by little. Polls that had shown him eighteen or twenty points behind now had him trailing by nine, ten, thirteen. Just about none of these gains were attributable to the candidate himself, or to Reagan. Both had behaved in the debate, and in their politicking afterward, pretty much as they had for months. In my judgment, all the change, every bit of it, came as a result of the treatment of the campaign by the media.

Mondale's gains were short-lived. On Thursday, October

11, the vice-presidential candidates, George Bush and Geraldine Ferraro, went on TV for their own debate. Neither did well. Bush seemed in a frenzy at the start. Ferraro throughout kept looking down instead of at the camera, as though unused to public speaking and referring to notes for her answers. (Three chief aides to Ferraro told me they were stunned at that aspect of her performance; she had never looked down in rehearsals.)

It was a debate after which pollsters might have asked not "Who won?" but "Where did these two come from?" After it, Mondale made no further gains, suggesting that Bush was on the right track in saying later on that he had "stopped the bleeding." The bleeding did stop, but it was hard to see why Bush deserved any credit.

The second Reagan-Mondale debate came on October 21, also a Sunday night. As always, I tried to watch with what I hoped was an impartial eye, attempting to assess the debate's impact on voters, paying equal attention to content and form.

I left it with two main impressions: that Mondale looked haggard, which could hurt him, and that the dynamic had been much the same as the first debate two weeks earlier. Mondale tended to be sharp in his answers; Reagan strayed. Reagan wandered so badly in his closing statement and went on at such length that he was cut off by the moderator, Edwin Newman—a terrible embarrassment.

In the course of the discussion, however, Reagan had made a small joke. In a reference to his age, one interviewer asked whether the president "would be able to function" in a situation such as the Cuban missile crisis of 1962. Reagan responded, "I will not make age an issue in this campaign. I am not going to exploit, for political purposes, my opponent's youth and inexperience."

In their book on the election, Germond and Witcover wrote that "to millions of viewers around the country, the one-liner likely told them that, like America itself, the Gipper was back—back in form; the easygoing, take-it-in-stride confident leader they liked. Never mind that the answer was a dodge and as empty of content as an air bubble. It signaled the answer they wanted to hear: the old man wasn't slipping after all." *

The remark could have pleased millions of viewers; it certainly did not hurt. But from the looks of things it had no immediate effect on them one way or the other. With one exception, the overnight polls showed results similar to those after the first debate: a *New York Times/CBS News* poll and an *ABC News* poll had Mondale slightly ahead; the exception was Gallup, which, in another poll for *Newsweek,* had Reagan slightly ahead.

But the press corps in Louisville seized on the joke, and in newspapers Monday morning and in press accounts and TV in subsequent days reporters and commentators *told* Americans that "the Gipper was back"—that through this one-liner (which had been written for him in advance)—he had discounted concerns about his age.

After the first debate, the news media exaggerated Reagan's weaknesses, giving Mondale a new opportunity. After the second one, they took back what they had given, and did their best to shut the door on the challenger. There was neither rhyme nor reason either time. Reagan did as poorly in the second debate as in the first, perhaps worse. Mondale, his appearance notwithstanding, showed little change and was perhaps a shade sharper. In both instances the reviewers in the news media would have served the nation better had they spent more energy reporting what was said and interpreting its significance, rather than determining for the people who "had won."

Strong politicians overcome such adversity and most often have themselves to blame if they cannot. Mondale had enough time for a comeback. His own weaknesses, and campaign problems brought on by his running mate Ferraro and her husband's financial dealings, seriously damaged him. But that does not make the offending media outlets and individuals less culpable.

---

* Germond and Witcover, *Wake Us When It's Over.*

TAXES: TURNING HONEST PEOPLE INTO CHEATS

I N ONE OF THEIR MAIN DEALINGS WITH GOVERN-
ment, Americans have become so upset that they have
taken things into their own hands and rebelled, breaking
the law as a matter of routine. I am talking about the way
people fudge on income taxes. Aside from those with no re-
course and a diminishing number of rigidly honest souls, it
is only the timid, it seems, who have been paying their taxes
in full in recent years. Prisons couldn't begin to hold the
nation's petty tax cheats. If the penalty were house arrest, the
country would have ground to a halt by now; perhaps a third
of all Americans would have to stay home.

The money does add up. Roscoe L. Egger, Jr., the first commissioner of internal revenue under Reagan, told Congress that by 1985 he anticipated a "tax gap" in the "legal sector" of nearly $120 billion, and in the "illegal sector" of $13 billion.

Egger defined the legal sector as income from legal activities that "take place in informal settings." The illegal sector, he said, is income "derived from organizing, financing, producing and delivering illegal goods or services related to drugs, gambling, prostitution, and so on." This is somewhat mind-boggling. Egger was saying that for every one dollar organized-crime figures and other criminals stole from the government, the rest of us stole nine. It was not just the criminals the IRS had to worry about, it was the good guys.

There is no way of knowing how many people actually cheat on taxes. More than half the people interviewed in a poll I worked on in 1985 agreed with the statement that "nearly everyone who has the chance cheats somewhat on income taxes these days." What is generally known, though, are the reasons for cheating. Greed, need, and the belief that everyone does it are no doubt important factors.

Contributing in large degree has been the belief that a person has to be a sucker to pay at his or her full rate when the tax statutes have been riddled with loopholes so that the rich have not had to pay at their full rate. An opinion poll done for the Internal Revenue Service in 1984 was typical. In it, eighty percent of the people interviewed agreed with the statement that "the present tax system benefits the rich and is unfair to the ordinary working man or woman."

If taxes are unfair, it is, of course, the federal government's fault. It makes the rules and decides how to enforce them. So it is the government that has made petty thieves out of millions, and made many of the strictly law-abiding feel like fools if they do not cheat. It is a situation that has to tear at the fabric of society, creating class resentment as well as adding to the distrust of Washington.

By the mid-eighties many opinion analysts and people like Egger had come to believe that perceived inequities were the number-one reason for cheating on taxes. After a year and a half of great hullaballoo in Washington and massive national confusion, Congress in 1986 enacted sweeping tax reforms aimed in large part at making people think the fairness problem had been eliminated.

The changes were to be "revenue neutral," meaning there would be no overall increase or decrease in the amount raised. But arguably the single most significant reform was to reduce the tax rates for wealthy people by more than one-third (and by more than *half* compared to the rates when Reagan took office), so that they would have less reason to look for legal loopholes. The public's first response was, as usual, one of distrust, according to opinion polls.

Americans were not always so repulsed by the government's tax laws. In fact, it took quite a while for the system to become despised at all. It may come as a surprise, but there was a time when the Gallup polling organization could find hardly anyone who thought taxes were unfair.

That period came around the time of World War II. In the war years of 1943, 1944, and 1945, the Gallup poll asked this question: "Do you regard the income tax which you pay this year as unfair?" There may have been a special reason for Gallup to phrase the question that way. At the time there was extremely steep progressivity in the rate of taxation, with the wealthiest people assessed at a rate of more than ninety percent. In two of those years, 1943 and 1945, eighty-five percent of the people interviewed said their taxes were fair. In 1944, ninety percent said their taxes were fair.

Even after the war, with taxes at the same high rates, large majorities had no complaints. Gallup asked the same question again in 1946, and sixty-two percent said their taxes were fair. These are strong indications, at least inferentially, that the problem of inequity in taxes did not emerge until recent decades.

Gallup, the leading tracker of social trends from the 1930s to the 1960s, stopped asking about equity in taxes after 1946;

apparently it was not an issue as far as he and his colleagues were concerned. Instead, from 1948 through 1969, the Gallup poll asked this question, on fourteen occasions: "Do you consider the amount of federal income tax which you pay too high, about right, or too low?"

The change in nuance brought about a change in meaning. Where the wartime inquiry dealt directly with the fairness of the tax system, its replacement dealt with the matter of fairness only indirectly. Many people, of course, did think their taxes were too high; people generally do. Given the opportunity, the public almost always will seek lower taxes.

Only once, in 1949, did Gallup find more people saying their taxes were "about right" rather than "too high." Only three other times, all after President John F. Kennedy had instituted tax cuts, were the numbers even close. On the average during the twenty-one-year period, fifty-five percent of the people interviewed told Gallup pollsters their taxes were too high.

At any rate, disgust with taxes clearly increased along with the growing distrust of government. By the mid-seventies the tax system was riddled with loopholes and special exemptions; the phrase "tax shelter" had come into the language. Running for president in 1976, Jimmy Carter shocked no one when he called the income-tax system a disgrace.

In 1977, a poll by the Roper organization found only three percent saying the federal income tax was "quite fair" to most people, twenty-seven percent saying it was "reasonably fair," and sixty-four percent saying it was "somewhat unfair" or "quite unfair." In repeat polls by Roper the following two years, the numbers hardly changed.

"In the view of the American public," Roper wrote in highlighting his 1978 findings, "the major problem with the federal income-tax system in this country is its unfairness." The public, he said, places "a high priority on tax reform."

There is a cynical expression about people's preferences in taxes: "Don't tax you, don't tax me; tax that fellow behind the tree." Roper took issue with that, saying his surveys showed a genuine desire for fairness in tax reform. "People do not hear the term and think their personal taxes will go up or down," he said.

The year 1978 was the year of Proposition Thirteen in California and, nationally, that of the alleged great tax revolt. Proposition Thirteen was a referendum item, endorsed by sixty-five percent of the voters, that resulted in a thirty percent decrease in tax revenues for the state and local governments in California. Afterward, similar referendum items or ones that tied taxation and spending to growth in state personal income were introduced in a number of other states.

Conservative politicians, including Ronald Reagan, maintained that the vote in California was proof that Americans were turning to the right and wanted smaller government, providing fewer services. But a number of the similar referendum items in other states were defeated, suggesting otherwise. The tax revolt, limited as it was, seemed to have little to do with large government and a great deal to do with resentment of government. Massive distrust was taking its toll.

In September, 1978, I conducted a national poll for the *Washington Post* aimed at finding to what degree people felt taxes were just too high, and to what degree their concern over taxes related to government deficiencies. In addition to the poll itself, the *Post* sent reporters to interview ordinary people in various parts of the country. What we found was the same old widespread distrust of government and, to no one's surprise, a keen concern over bureaucratic waste and inefficiency.

"Which is a greater problem," one of the first questions in the survey asked, "the amount of local, state, and federal taxes you pay, or the way the local, state, and federal governments use your money?"

In response, only eleven percent said the amount they were taxed was the greater problem. More than six times as many, seventy-three percent, said that what the governments did with the money was the greater problem. Another twelve percent said both were problems of about equal dimension.

I had expected such a result; indeed, the promoters of

Proposition Thirteen themselves seemed as interested in sending a message to government about government as in cutting taxes. On the night the measure passed, Howard Jarvis, regarded as the father of Proposition Thirteen, said, "We have a new revolution. We are telling the government, 'Screw you.' "

Some analysts at the time felt that what people disliked most was the amount government spent on social programs, especially welfare. Many had interpreted an antiwelfare mood as the explanation for the success of Proposition Thirteen. I found hardly any such sentiment. In response to one question, four of every five people rejected cutting welfare assistance to those who were eligible, preferring instead to focus on abusers of the system only.

A second question asked people whether they agreed with the statement, "All except the old and the handicapped should have to take care of themselves without social welfare benefits." Only thirty-six percent agreed; sixty-one percent disagreed.

Part of the resentment of government had to do with impressions of the government work force, which was seen as bloated, inefficient, and overpaid.

A year earlier, the Gallup Poll asked people whether the "federal government employs too many or too few people to do the work that must be done." Sixty-seven percent said "too many." I repeated that question in our poll, and eighty percent said "too many," with sixty-three percent saying "far too many."

Civil service workers have always complained that their pay was low, but by 1978 such cries were falling on deaf ears: only eight percent in our survey thought government workers were paid less than people holding similar jobs outside the government; fifty-six percent thought they were paid more.

Asked what areas they would trim if spending had to be reduced, one-quarter of the people interviewed focused on government, calling for cuts in the number of government employees, in government pay and pensions, or in other aspects of government that they considered wasteful. Twice as many people sought belt-tightening in the administration of government as in any other potential area of savings.

People hoped, in other words, that tax cuts would force government to be more efficient. They were not nearly as interested in reducing government services.

"This city here, it's probably typical," a retired farmer in the small town of Olney in southeastern Illinois told a *Post* reporter. "They're raising a hellacious amount of money in taxes. . . . You can see them down on Cricket Street down there. They dug it up first, then they repaved it, and then damn if they don't dig it up again because they done it all wrong. That's just wasting tax money."

The survey also asked people to compare public employees they had dealt with to sales people and office clerks outside government. By two to one, public employees were seen as less courteous; by three to one they were seen as less responsive and less hard-working.

Government workers themselves felt that way. About eighteen percent in the survey said they or someone in their household were employed by government on the local, state, or federal level. They too viewed public workers as being paid more and working less, and they gave only marginally better ratings to public employees than had nongovernment workers in the comparisons with clerks and sales people.

In Los Angeles, a school janitor told a *Post* reporter why he voted in favor of Proposition Thirteen despite the concern that reduced revenues might lead to the loss of his job. "Jarvis talked a lot about waste in government," he said, "but those on the outside can't even really see it. Those of us on the inside see it all the time. It's enough to make you sick."

The poll also addressed the Reagan view of things, asking people whether, all other things being equal, they would vote for a congressional candidate who says "we should cut spending on government programs and reduce taxes," or for one who says "we should keep taxes the same but make government programs more efficient so that they do what they are supposed to do." By more than two to one, sixty-four to thirty-one percent, those interviewed said they would vote for efficiency, not tax reduction.

Then, as in subsequent years, some lawmakers maintained that what really upset the public was the complicated nature of the income-tax system. Simplification was what was needed, they said. Roper, however, asked people which "should be the first priority—changing the tax laws so that more people pay their fair share of taxes, or simplifying the tax return forms and instructions so that they are easier to understand and fill out?" Only about ten percent chose simplification; more than half chose fairness, and the remainder, about a third, said both were of equal importance.

These Roper surveys also put before the public a list of fifteen national objectives, such as controlling inflation, improving the nation's energy supply, lowering the crime rate, improving defense capabilities, and the like, and asked people to list them in their order of importance. Four items on taxes were included: making the system fairer, lowering income taxes, simplifying income tax returns, and lowering Social Security taxes.

The first order of business for the public in 1979, according to that and other surveys, was controlling inflation, selected by fifty-one percent of the people interviewed in the Roper poll. Second was improving the energy supply (there were gas lines in 1979); third was lowering the crime rate, and fourth, placed ahead of improving education and improving defense, was "making the tax system fairer," selected by nineteen percent. Simplifying returns placed fourteenth, selected by three percent, and lowering Social Security taxes last, chosen by two percent.

In the 1980 presidential campaign, Reagan played cleverly on the public's feelings about taxes and government. Knowing that most people always preferred lower taxes, he pledged to cut them, never indicating, of course, that under his plans it was mainly the rich who would benefit. He also promised to cut spending, reduce inflation, strengthen defense, cut the size of the federal work force by five percent except for defense workers, increase employment, and produce a balanced federal budget.

One of his opponents in the Republican primaries, George Bush, called such promises "voodoo ecomonics." Another, John Anderson, referred to Reagan's economic platform as one composed of "blue smoke and mirrors."

Reagan did not exactly emphasize tax cuts as a major theme. Instead, he made his point early and spent the final months focusing on the more important economic issues of inflation and high interest rates, and, in foreign affairs, on the need for a strengthened military and a tough stance *vis-à-vis* the Soviet Union and Iran, whose holding of more than fifty Americans as hostages had been a main concern all year.

Reagan used tax cuts in the campaign much as he used the issues of abortion and prayer in the schools. At the outset, he took very strong positions on each matter, insuring that he drew early notice as the one candidate who most stood for reducing income taxes, outlawing abortion, and restoring school prayer. People who cared about each of those items could line up behind him early, and spread the word to others like them who might not have been paying attention.

As is so often the case, the election in 1980 was mostly a judgment on the previous four years. Interest rates and inflation were worse than they had been in a century; unemployment, approaching seven percent, was a major problem; the move of Russian troops into Afghanistan; the inability to deal with Iran—all worked to Reagan's advantage. People voted, as they generally do, on the record of the incumbent and threw out Jimmy Carter.

Reagan's pledges on taxes had little to do with the election, nor did his promise of a balanced budget or any other position he took. He won because the country had turned against Carter. Nevertheless, Reagan and his supporters took the opportunity to claim a mandate for every item on the Reagan agenda.

One of the new president's first orders of business was to substantially reduce the tax burden for wealthy Americans.

To get away with that, he also offered lesser cuts to other taxpayers, and packaged the proposal in attractive wrapping, as part of a supply-side economic program. Theoretically, cutting taxes would give people more money to spend, benefiting industry and increasing employment. In actuality, according to Reagan's first budget director, David Stockman, tax reductions for most people were "always a Trojan horse to bring down the top rate."

Stockman told Washington writer William Greider at the time that "the hard part of the supply-side tax cut is dropping the top rate from seventy to fifty percent—the rest of it is a secondary matter. The original argument was that the top bracket was too high, and that's having the most devastating effect on the economy. Then, the general argument was that, in order to make this palatable as a political matter, you had to bring down all the brackets." *

It took the public a few months to catch on. The first *Washington Post/ABC News* opinion poll coincided with Reagan's inauguration, and in our initial survey, with the proposed tax cuts in mind, I drew up a question aimed at finding out whether people considered Reagan a rich person's president. We asked:

> *Would you say Reagan cares more about serving poor and lower income people, middle income people, upper income people . . . or would you say he cares equally about serving all people?*

Showing a traditional optimism about a new president, two of every three in the survey said Reagan cared about serving all people equally; fewer than one in four said he cared mostly about upper-income people. By September of that year, however, a majority of Americans had decided that Reagan cared the most about serving upper-income Americans, and that belief never changed.

It was not until 1984 that equity in taxes became a leading

---

* *Atlantic Monthly*, December, 1981.

political issue. Early in the presidential campaign that year, Walter Mondale proposed a tax increase for high-income people, pledging to use it to reduce the federal budget deficit by half. Americans always like the idea of taxing the rich, and Mondale was effective in making an issue of the deficits early in the campaign, so he could have had a good thing going. But he ran a muddled campaign and apparently changed his tax-raising theme, to his detriment, later on.

By the middle of September, Mondale was talking about raising taxes for all people with annual family incomes of more than $25,000. Upper-income people would have borne the brunt of the increases, but the message that stuck was that Mondale intended to raise taxes, period.

Not knowing that Mondale would shoot himself in the foot, Reagan meanwhile had set his secretary of the treasury, Donald Regan, to work on a tax proposal. Had Mondale been able to use his tax-increase plan effectively—as he might have by underscoring repeatedly that he intended it only to overcome the peril of grotesque budget deficits—Reagan would have been able to say that he himself was preparing tax reform, to be unveiled after the election.

Thus it was that in November 1984, around Thanksgiving time, the Treasury Department introduced sweeping tax proposals that amazed and exhilarated some reformers, sent all of establishment Washington into a shock that lasted almost two years, and led to changes in income tax laws that totally confounded ordinary Americans.

Regan's proposal called for individuals to be taxed at fifteen, twenty-five, or thirty-five percent of their income. It would have allowed homeowners to continue to deduct interest on their mortgages but closed other loopholes for the well-to-do, and it would to some degree have restored corporate taxes that had been largely eliminated under Reagan. It also aimed at simplifying the filing of tax returns, so that people could figure out what they owed without becoming bookkeepers or having to hire accountants.

In one regard the plan had a frightening Big Brother aspect: many taxpayers would not have had to fill out tax forms

at all. By 1990, according to Internal Revenue Service commissioner Egger, the elimination of deductions and credits
would have made it possible for the IRS to do the tax work
for two of every three taxpayers.

Two simple principles shaped Treasury One: almost all
income, whether earned or unearned, was to be taxed the
same, and people of like means would pay like taxes.

The first response was largely one of derision. A wide array
of pressure groups—the U.S. Chamber of Commerce, real-
estate and oil lobbyists, other business interests, big labor,
state governments, Wall Street—were opposed. Treasury
One had so many high-placed enemies that it had little
chance of passage as it stood. But it also had its supporters,
including consumer advocate Ralph Nader, who seldom
backed any Reagan administration proposal, and a number of
tax experts across the ideological spectrum.

Egger, in a speech in Boston on November 30, 1984, based
the case for reform on public disgust with the existing system. Citing a public opinion poll done for the IRS earlier in
the year, he said that four of every five taxpayers believed
the tax system benefited the rich and was unfair to ordinary
people; that almost one person in five (nineteen percent)
admitted to cheating on taxes, that "experts tell us that the
incidence of reported tax cheating is probably understated,"
and that the main reason for cheating was that people consider the system unfair.

The survey Egger referred to contained a luscious finding:
that most Americans would rather tolerate tax cheats than
inform on them. Most of the survey dealt with ways to find
out how many people cheat, and how to cut down on cheating. Deep into the poll, as question number fifty-seven, this
formulation was put to the more than 2,200 people interviewed:

*Mr. X says that the whole idea of rewarding informers
who tell on people who cheat on their taxes is sort of un-
American. Mr. Y. disagrees. He says that it is un-American
NOT* [emphasis in the original] *to report people who you*

know are cheating our country—and besides, it's unfair for those people to get away with cheating. Do you strongly support Mr. X, lean to Mr. X, strongly support Mr. Y, or lean to Mr. Y?

This was not the most balanced poll question ever asked, being weighted toward Mr. Y's side. On the one hand, it is true, the idea of being an informer is not popular, and that tended to work for Mr. X. But working for Mr. Y were three factors, not just one: (A) the proposition that tax-shavers are "cheating our country"; (B) the idea that they are profiting unfairly; and (C) a subliminal effect known to survey researchers in which, when people are asked to make a difficult choice, some tend to be pulled toward the last option expressed.

These subtleties, one would think, must have inflated the number who sympathized with Mr. Y. I read the question to a colleague at the *Washington Post,* and asked how he thought the public divided. "For Mr. Y, heavily," he said.

He was wrong. Only nine percent supported Mr. Y strongly; only twenty percent supported him somewhat. Fifty percent supported Mr. X: twenty-four percent took his side strongly, and twenty-six somewhat. Twenty-one percent offered no opinion; had they been omitted from the calculations, the verdict would have been sixty-three percent against informing, thirty-seven percent in favor. In other words, landslide support for tolerating tax cheats.

"This survey clearly indicates," Egger said, "that our system is in real trouble. The system is responding to people in similar circumstances in quite dissimilar ways. And people resent a system which gives special privileges to a few, making it more costly and tougher on everybody else."

Regan's report and Egger's speech both focused on the grotesque use of loopholes, citing how a sample of eighty-eight high-income people reduced their tax obligations through legal tax shelters. As a group, these people had a gross income of $17,000,000, or an average of $193,000 each. But by taking legal deductions, they ended up reporting a gross income of only $1,900,000, and their taxable income was even further reduced by adjustments and itemized deductions.

Nineteen of the people had gross annual incomes of about $250,000, but through their use of shelters paid less than $500 in taxes. Thirty-seven others, with an average gross income of $172,000, paid $6,000 or less in federal income tax, about the same as paid by a family of four with a household income of $45,000.

Regan's report also noted that in 1983, by Treasury estimates, 9,000 people with "incomes of $250,000 or more paid no tax as a direct result" of tax shelters. An additional 59,000 at the same income levels were able to reduce their tax payments by at least half.

Donald Regan did not devise the modified flat-tax proposals that he introduced to the public; experts at Treasury did. But at the outset Regan stood by them in eloquent and admirable fashion.

The report, released over his signature, charged that "fundamental reform of the tax system is required to correct the problems. . . .The tax system must be made simpler, more economically neutral, fairer, and more conducive to economic growth." Repeatedly, the report referred to deterioration of taxpayer morale, and Regan said all the right things:

> These proposals are bold, and they will be controversial. Those who benefit from the current tax preferences that distort the use of our nation's resources, that complicate paying taxes for all of us, and that create inequities and undermine taxpayer morale will complain loudly and seek support from every quarter. But a far greater number of Americans will benefit from the suggested rate reduction and simplification.

Regan's introduction of Treasury One and his early support for it were to be his personal high point as a public servant. His strong language seemed sincere; his reading of the public mood was accurate. But in a matter of weeks, after a decidedly lukewarm reception by the president and sniping from many quarters, Regan lost heart for the fight, saying that Treasury One, after all, was written on a word processor and could be changed.

The president certainly was not happy with the plan that had been drawn up in his name. Unfamiliar with its details, he complained when he heard that one deduction to be eliminated would be country-club dues. "That is unfair," he reportedly said; "many doctors get new clients at country clubs." Reagan seemed surprised when he was told at a meeting with staff members of the *Wall Street Journal* that Treasury One would bring about an increase in corporate taxes, although that feature of the plan had been widely advertised.

The public, on the other hand, while a good bit more uninformed than the president, took to Treasury One with enthusiasm. People wanted anything that would bring fairness. In a *Washington Post/ABC News* opinion poll done in January, 1985, just over half the people interviewed said they had heard or read about the proposal. Among them, sixty-three percent favored it; only twenty-seven percent were opposed. Among all people interviewed, including those who said they were totally unfamiliar with the plan, it was backed by fifty-three percent, opposed by twenty-six percent.

Hardly any of the people interviewed—only one in seven —felt they would end up paying less in taxes; one in three thought they would pay more. That is clear evidence for the view that what drew people to Treasury One was the promise of a fairer system, and confirmation of Burns Roper's finding that fairness does not mean taxing only the "fellow behind the tree."

In our survey, a large majority, sixty-one percent, said their taxes were too high. But of that group, eighty-four percent agreed with the statement, "I wouldn't complain about the amount I pay in taxes if I thought the rich were paying their fair share."

Another poll, by the *Los Angeles Times*, asked people whether they "were angry" about the amount they paid in taxes the previous year. Seventy percent said they were not. Nevertheless, the majority in that survey, fifty-six percent, said the tax system was unfair and needed changing.

As 1985 began, then, the move toward tax reform was a swirl of confusion. Reagan's Treasury Department had presented sweeping reform proposals. Reagan himself and many special-interest lobbies opposed parts of them; some liberal leaders, like Governor Mario Cuomo of New York, opposed other parts. Experts seemed to agree that, all in all, the new plan would be better than the existing tax system.

During the first months of 1985, talk of tax reform abated and it seemed that strong opposition groups had succeeded in killing it. Then a funny thing happened. For totally unrelated reasons, Reagan's approval ratings began to drop. In January, at the time of his second inaugural, his score was around seventy percent, about as high as at any previous time. Political observers marveled at his popularity. By April, the ratings were down to just over fifty percent nationally and below that treading-water mark in a number of states. There was talk, not all of it from his opponents, that the president had prematurely reached the status of lame duck.

In early May, Reagan took a battering on Capitol Hill. Senate Republicans had pretty much ignored his budget proposals, going easier on social cuts than Reagan had requested and limiting his proposed spending increase for the military to only the cost of inflation. The House of Representatives went further, eliminating the inflation factor. The House also rebuffed Reagan's plea for $14 million in nonmilitary aid to the contras in Nicaragua, and the Senate approved only half the number of MX missiles Reagan had sought.

These defeats were compounded by a month-long controversy over Reagan's visit in early May to the Bitburg military cemetery in West Germany, where a number of World War II Nazi stormtroopers had been buried, and by discouraging economic reports.

All in all, things were suddenly going very badly for the image-conscious Reagan. For him, a high approval rating was more important than for most presidents in that he could point to it and claim public support even as he tried to implement unpopular policies.

It was in such circumstances that, on May 28, 1985, Reagan put himself foursquare behind tax reform, announcing in a prime-time televised address to the nation what he called "America's tax plan," a revised version of Treasury One.

Appearing on TV as soon as Reagan finished was Democrat Daniel Rostenkowski of Chicago, chairman of the tax-writing House Ways and Means Committee. As had other Democrats in crucial moments, Rostenkowski gave Reagan a big boost, saying the president was "bucking his party's tradition as protectors of big business and the wealthy," and that Reagan's "words and feelings go back to Roosevelt and Truman and Kennedy, but the commitment comes from Ronald Reagan. And that's so important and so welcome."

In the following weeks Reagan went on tour, promoting the tax plan in carefully selected sites and avoiding states, such as New York, where there was criticism of it. The drive served to shift the focus from such issues as the budget, military spending and Central America. When people saw Reagan on TV, he was talking about America's tax plan.

What the country was witnessing, once again, was the force of public opinion exerting enormous pressure on a president. There were aspects of tax reform Reagan liked, such as reducing the maximum rates from fifty percent to thirty-five percent. But other parts of it, such as increasing corporate taxes by twenty-two percent, were anathema to him. "There really isn't a justification" for taxing corporations, Reagan had said in his first term. But there he was on the hustings, promoting just such a tax.

Reagan's drive for tax reform was a thinly veiled attempt to regain a high approval rating, an orchestrated maneuver. By early June he rebounded sharply, probably due more to other events and the fading of Bitburg as an issue than to his drive on taxes.* The Gallup poll, the *Washington Post/ABC News*

---

* Figuring most importantly, in my judgment, were two weeks of crisis after terrorists hijacked a TWA plane, killed an American passenger, and

poll, the *New York Times/CBS News* poll, all showed gains. Reagan's pollster, Wirthlin, said the president's popularity was level with that of his first months in office, the halcyon days.

So the country's president was back in fine fettle, and its people were headed for tax reform in 1986. It may well have been that the changes enacted, for better or worse, were due to the bumbling advance work of one of Reagan's closest associates, Michael Deaver, who had set up the trip to Bitburg with which his earlier approval-rating slide began.

Still, there were many hurdles along the way. Suddenly another element in the formation of public opinion came into play: the introduction of a genuine leadership debate. Governor Cuomo, speaking out regularly in New York and making repeated visits to Washington to draw national attention, repeatedly attacked one aspect of the propsals, which would have eliminated as a deduction the amount that people paid in state taxes. House speaker Tip O'Neill termed the overall Reagan plan unfair and unsound.

With the debate came public uncertainty. Poll findings released by the Democratic Study Group of Congress showed strong majority opposition to lowering the top tax rate. So did another Roper poll. In addition, despite administration disclaimers, majorities or pluralities in most surveys continued to feel that their own taxes would rise, not go down, under the president's plan. People who regarded Reagan as a rich man's president doubted that they could trust him to come up with a fair tax plan.

Reagan stressed two elements in his proposal: its simplicity, and the lowered rates for many Americans. But simplicity continued to be of low priority with the public, and people just did not believe the president when he said their tax rates would be cut in a plan that was supposed, after all, to be revenue-neutral.

In September, 1985, a *Washington Post/ABC News* poll

---

held others hostage. People generally rally around a president in such crises, and did so then.

showed a majority, fifty-seven percent, so uncertain about the Reagan plan that they expressed neither approval nor disapproval; they said instead that they did not know enough to have an opinion. The rest of the people interviewed were sharply divided along party lines, with rank-and-file Democrats opposing the plan by more than two to one and Republicans favoring it by almost three to one.

In Washington, pollster Wirthlin and others began saying that the public was no longer interested in tax reform. Senate and House members said they were not getting much mail on the subject. After Labor Day, Reagan promoted his proposals in seven cities in what was called a "fall offensive." But the drive seemed to be losing steam.

Analysts said the public was concerned more with federal budget deficits, the trade imbalance, and unemployment. No doubt that was true; these were severe national problems. But because people cared about them was no reason to think they were no longer interested in tax reform.

In subsequent months, Reagan, along with both Democrats and Republicans on Capitol Hill, went in so many directions over taxes that there was no way for the citizenry to keep up with the developments. Some in Congress insisted that reform be put aside until the government dealt with the budget deficits—reasoning, apparently, that it was impossible to take up two important pieces of legislation at the same time.

Through his highly publicized stumping in 1985, Reagan managed to alter the discussion of tax reform. Treasury One, which had drawn so much public support, was based on a promise that tough actions had to be taken to make taxes fairer, not to reduce them. Reagan spoke about fairness but his emphasis was on additional tax cuts. The "revenue-neutral" plan he described was one, he said, in which eighty percent of taxpayers would end up paying less. The more he spoke about new cuts, the more ordinary Americans began to think, once again, that their taxes were too high and that cuts, not necessarily fairness, were what was needed.

In January, 1985, shortly after Treasury One was introduced, fewer than half the people interviewed in a *Washington Post/ABC News* poll thought they were paying too much in taxes. But in the period of a few months, by May of 1985, with Reagan focusing on reform as a means of bringing taxes down, seven in ten said their taxes were too high. So did six in ten in succeeding polls in June, 1985, and May, 1986.

Tax reform wound its way through both the House and Senate, and the final product reduced the tax rate for the highest-income Americans even more than Treasury One would have. Two rates were to be in effect by 1988: fifteen percent for most people, twenty-eight percent for the rest. (For many upper-income people, however, the rate, through a "hidden" or "phantom" provision, was to be fixed at thirty-three percent.)

In October, 1986, with fifteen hundred people on the White House lawn and the U.S. Marine band playing patriotic tunes, Reagan signed the measure, referring to it, as he had many times, as a revolution. "I feel like we just played the World Series of tax reform and the American people won."

As far as the public was concerned, however, the best that could be said was that the landmark legislation was confusing. In a poll done for *Money* magazine that month,* only nineteen percent of the people interviewed said they favored the legislation; sixteen percent said they opposed it. The rest, two of every three people interviewed, had formed no opinion despite the glowing reviews from Washington.

By almost two to one among those expressing an opinion, the reform was seen as making lower- and higher-income people "better off," but by more than two to one it was seen as making middle-income people "worse off." There was an even split on views as to why Reagan favored a new tax formula: forty-two percent said he wanted it because it would be better for the country; forty-one percent said he wanted it primarily for political reasons.

In its conclusions, *Money* magazine noted that "only thirty-

---

* The poll consisted of interviews with 511 people nationwide who were described as those "responsible for deciding the financial decisions in their households."

five percent think that, in the long run, the new program will result in fewer tax loopholes than the old program." By contrast, a plurality, forty-seven percent, thought there would be the same amount of loopholes or more. Twenty-six percent felt the change would cut down on tax cheating, but the other seventy-four percent thought there would be as much cheating as in the past or more.

There was hardly any change in thinking as time passed. In April, 1987, a *Washington Post/ABC News* poll asked people if they agreed or disagreed with the statement, "Many rich people pay hardly any taxes at all." Seventy-four percent said they agreed, a condemnation of the system, although not quite as lopsided as the result the *Post* and *ABC News* obtained in June, 1985, when the same question met with agreement from eighty-one percent of those interviewed.

It may take years to determine whether the changes wrought by the tax reforms of 1986 will make for a fairer system. What is clear at this point is that, despite the enthusiasm in Washington, the public was left cold at the outset.

The Republicans under Reagan got no credit for making things fairer. In elections in November, 1986, they got wiped out in Senate races, losing eight seats, and giving the Democrats a fifty-five-to-forty-five majority. If there is insufficient evidence to conclude that anger over the tax bill accounted for the Republican losses, the vote nevertheless demonstrated that there was too little satisfaction with it to turn it into a successful political issue for them.

SOCIAL SECURITY AND
SMOKED SALMON

There has been lots of discussion about the financial condition of the Social Security system. Do you think Social Security will exist or not when you retire?

ONE OF POLLING'S MAIN DISCOVERIES IN RE-cent years has been the degree to which ordinary Americans have come to cherish the Social Security program. It was never a secret that Social Security was popular. But only since 1981, when Ronald Reagan was forced to back off after proposing cuts, has it become clear that the public's commitment to the program for the elderly is virtually total.

There are other consensus issues but hardly any with such salience. In New York, as elsewhere, about eighty percent of voters favor the death penalty. Nonetheless, in 1986 they reelected Mario Cuomo, an opponent of the death penalty, with the largest majority in the history of the state. But let him plump for cuts in Social Security and see what happens.

In a sociological test some years ago, many children said they would sooner give up their fathers than their TVs, if they had to choose. Well, from the looks of things, many parents would sooner give up their children than their Social Security, and probably throw in a TV to boot.

There are valid complaints about Social Security. The tax for it is regressive, with moderately paid workers putting in a much higher proportion of their income and taking out less than the more highly paid. For many years after its inception in the thirties, withholding for the program was so small as to be almost invisible, so its regressivity was not very noticeable. From 1937 to 1959, one percent of a worker's first $3,000 in salary was deducted.

It rose to 3 percent of the first $4,800 in 1960, 5.2 percent on incomes up to $7,800 in 1971, 6.7 percent on incomes up to $32,400 in 1982, and it will be 7.65 percent on salaries up to $57,000 in 1990. The maximum withheld will have gone from $30 a year in the fifties to $4,360.50.

For all workers, that is a change from next to nothing to a substantial bite. The tax remains sharply regressive: while most workers will be paying at the maximum 7.65 percent rate, people with salaries of $100,000 a year will have 4.36 percent withheld and people with higher salaries even less than that. As a proportion of their pay, such people will be putting in less than three-fifths of what lower-paid people do, and receiving much more in benefits.

Some Democrats and many Republicans would fix that if they could by applying a stronger means test than now exists, cutting into the old-age funds of middle-class people as well as the wealthy. Some would drop the system altogether, encouraging people to save on their own, and pointing out that they would get a great deal more in return if they did. But since Reagan's blundering efforts to cut benefits in 1981, most politicians have been loath to go near the program.

It was only by creating a bipartisan commission, with considerable help from House Speaker Tip O'Neill, that Reagan was able, in 1983, to effect any changes. Republicans and Democrats in power congratulated themselves for that, claiming to have rescued the program and stating that their actions had proved that government can work. But poll data at the time showed the public to be miffed, not happy. A June, 1983, *Post/ABC News* survey found only eighteen percent of the people interviewed saying Reagan and Democratic leaders in Congress had worked well together "in the handling of problems in the Social Security system." The largest single group, thirty-seven percent, felt the Democrats had given in too much to Reagan.

The more the politicians get into public opinion data, the more likely they are to bite their tongues rather than talk about changing Social Security through means tests or other methods. Most Americans simply do not care if some older people get benefits they do not need. The public takes a broader view. Sooner or later, Social Security brings money into just about every household. One person out of seven is receiving benefits at this moment.

The program has brought dignity to the nation's elderly, making life easier for them and for their children and grandchildren. The great majority are not about to put that dignity at risk by any fine-tuning.

What many Americans are worried about, though, is the durability of the program, and that of its younger sister, Medicare, the government health plan for older people that was begun in 1965.

In January, 1982, a *Washington Post* reporter, Dan Balz, then working out of Texas, made what seemed to me a strange request. He wanted the *Post/ABC News* poll to ask people if they thought the Social Security system would exist when it came time for them to retire. Balz was not interested in any namby-pamby questions about whether people thought benefits should be reduced, or witholdings increased, or whether the program was in financial trouble. He wanted to go whole hog: Did people think they would ever see a dime from Social Security or didn't they?

What he was hearing from Texans, Balz said, was that there would be no benefits at all for them. And if that was hard for some of us back in Washington to believe, there seemed to be a lot of people in Texas who felt that way.

That month we put Balz's question before the public, asking:

> *There has been lots of discussion about the financial condition of the Social Security system. Do you think Social Security will exist or not when you retire?*

The result was an even split: forty-seven percent felt the program would still be around, forty-seven percent felt it would be abandoned before they stood to benefit. But the overall average did not begin to tell the story.

Among people near retirement age, hardly any expressed concern. The younger a person was, the greater the fear that the system would collapse. About one-third of those between ages forty-five and sixty thought Social Security would be defunct when they retired. And among those between thirty-one and forty-four, fifty-six percent felt the program would not exist for them. Among those aged eighteen to thirty, three of every four said they would never get old-age benefits.

I had not expected findings like these. Social Security was the crowning New Deal achievement. To doubt the future of Social Security seemed to me to doubt the future of the government altogether. As our poll findings came in, I did an informal survey around the office, asking people the same question we had put to our random sample.

Older colleagues thought the question was stupid: of course there would be Social Security. Younger ones were not at all surprised by the inquiry. It seemed to be something they had thought about, and, like the young in our scientific survey, they were skeptical.

One poll at an isolated moment does not prove very much, so the following January the *Post* and *ABC News* repeated the question. In the interim, Reagan's bipartisan commission was drawing a lot of attention, and its efforts seemed to have had a slight effect. In the new survey forty-nine percent took the optimistic view, forty-four percent the pessimistic one. But doubts persisted among the young. By about two to one, people under the age of forty-five felt the program would be abandoned before they retired.

Two years later, in January, 1985, we asked the question again. What we found was continued uncertainty and lack of optimism, with forty-three percent saying Social Security would exist and forty-five percent saying it would not. Age forty-five continued to be the cutoff point, with a heavy majority of older people expressing no doubts about the program's survival, and a big majority of younger ones expecting its demise.

When politicians in Washington talk about Social Security, they often seem to regard it as an older person's concern. Poll findings should make them take another look. Not only are the young fearful that Social Security will be abandoned; they, at least as much as the elderly, want it kept intact.

In May, 1985, Congress was discussing plans to give Social Security recipients smaller cost-of-living adjustments, or COLAs, then they were scheduled to receive. The cuts were part of proposals aimed at reducing the federal budget deficits, a goal very much supported by the public.

Reagan, playing at semantics, said cuts in the COLAs were not reductions in benefits. Others who favored the cuts made no such pretense but argued instead that it was only fair for all groups in society, including the elderly, to share the pain of dealing with the deficits.

In a *Post/ABC News* poll that month, four of every five people opposed limiting the COLAs. That overall figure probably surprised no one; most Americans simply did not want any tampering with Social Security. What might have come as a surprise, however, was the almost uniform rejection voiced in all age groups. There was no generation gap whatsoever. If anything, younger people were more opposed to curtailing benefits than older ones:

Percentage in 1985 favoring cuts in COLAs . . .

---

among those . . .

. . . ages 18 to 30	18%
. . . ages 31 to 44	20%
. . . ages 45 to 60	17%
. . . ages 61 and older	24%

In that survey, some young people may have wanted to protect the COLAs because their parents got benefits or soon would; others perhaps because they felt reductions would have meant a lower floor for themselves in years to come, when they retire. But whatever the reason, it is apparent that when leaders talk about Social Security, and Medicare too, the young as well as the elderly tend, for once, to be listening.

That has been true throughout the Reagan presidency. Early on, at a time when budget-cutting was drawing substantial public approval, the *Post/ABC News* poll asked people whether they would support cuts in Medicare. Eighty-seven percent said no. In 1985 the survey asked about cuts in Social Security and ninety-four percent said no. No other programs have drawn support on such levels. In both instances, the young were as much in opposition to cuts as the elderly.

Nevertheless, critics keep coming back to these two giant programs when they look for ways of reducing government spending.

In recent years a new, intriguing rationale for cutting Social Security has been developed: the program, it is argued, has been too successful. Older Americans are being taken care of so nicely that it is unfair to the rest of the population, especially children.

In December, 1985, the *Wall Street Journal* noted that "perceptions have begun changing among what political scientists call the elite media. Articles in serious journals and influential newspapers are attacking the common view that the elderly are feeble, vulnerable and financially strapped. Supporters of this revisionist line say the articles mark the beginning of an overhaul of how the nation looks at the elderly."

The *Journal* cited reports in *Scientific American* magazine, the *New Republic*, the *New York Times*, and *American Demographics* magazine. (Lagging slightly behind was the *Washington Post*, which had a lengthy piece along the same lines in January, 1986.) The articles tended to focus on the lack of a means test for Social Security; typically, the one in *New Republic* castigated the East Side widow in a luxury apartment for getting "what amounts to welfare at the expense of the low-wage earner in the South Bronx."

Actually, the *Journal* and these other organs were late in coming to the story. One of the first findings I made as a pollster for the *Washington Post* in the mid-1970s was that people of retirement age were somewhat less concerned about inflation than younger ones. That surprised me at the time but it was old-hat even then to experts in the field, who attributed it both to Social Security and to the COLAs that kept recipients from having to live on fixed incomes as prices rose.

I expect the new attack on Social Security to continue; every couple of months I see some item noting how well the elderly are doing in comparison to other people, and questions as to whether the nation can afford such luxury. Little by little, Americans are being asked to look at the aged much the way Sigmund Freud, in *Jokes and Their Relation to the Unconscious*, spoke about a poor soul with a taste for luxury. A wealthy man, Freud wrote, lent twenty-five florins to an impoverished acquaintance, only to see him in a restaurant the same day, dining on smoked salmon.

"What? You borrow from me and that's how you spend the money?"

"I don't understand you," the poor man replied. "If I haven't any money I can't eat smoked salmon, and if I have some money I mustn't eat smoked salmon? Well, when am I going to eat smoked salmon?"

The benefactor was not reproaching the borrower for having smoked salmon that day, but for eating it at any time. "He is reminding him," Freud wrote, "that in his circumstances he has no right to think of such delicacies at all."

In thrust, the new assault on Social Security and Freud's humor, too, are much like the decades-old criticism of public welfare, focusing on abuses as a means of discrediting the entire program. Such charges are essentially unsound, as well as mean-spirited. Government figures portray the elderly in a much different light, showing hardly any of them able to afford East Side apartments or dine on smoked salmon.

According to Census Bureau statistics, the median income for a man between the ages of twenty-five and sixty-four in 1984 was $20,934; for one sixty-five or older it was $10,450. Take away Social Security and the older man was well below the poverty line.

For women between twenty-five and sixty-four, the median income in 1984 was $8,886; for women older than that, $6,020. The relatively slight decrease in income for older women understates their problem. Four in ten of the older women lived by themselves. Less than one in ten of the younger ones did, giving almost all the younger women the benefit of additional incomes in their households. Thus, for aging women even more than men, Social Security made the difference between getting by decently and not getting by at all.

A report by the Urban Institute in 1987 told the same story in a somewhat different manner. It noted that two of every ten elderly women who live alone had incomes below the poverty line, that the same held for three of every ten elderly blacks, and, all in all, that thirteen percent of the elderly were needy.

"Many older people are subsisting on meager incomes

even as the average senior citizen has reached a state of rough equivalence with nonelderly adults in terms of per capita income," the report said, according to an account in the *New York Times.*

There is no denying the inequities and other problems in the Social Security program. The tax is high and getting higher. It is reasonable to resent the inclusion of the well-to-do in such a program. Perhaps those are good reasons to alter the system. But don't tell that to the people.

The universal support for Social Security and Medicare does not make it impossible for government to reduce benefits. Through bipartisan efforts such as that employed by Reagan in 1982 and 1983, government can do what it wants. A little hysteria will once again allow many Republicans and some Democrats to take the position that, distasteful as it may be, the only responsible course is to reduce benefits. One approach that will not work would be a renewed assertion that the program is on the verge of insolvency. By January, 1987, the Social Security old-age and disability fund had a balance of $50 billion; by 1991 it was expected to be almost five times as large, and to continue escalating for the next twenty years, enabling it to handle the needs of the baby-boom generation.

There is little doubt, however, that there will be new attempts to do in Social Security. They may be rationalized by charges that the program is too costly or that it is unfair, or even by further use of the peculiar assertion that it works too well.

HOME HEATING AND NUCLEAR POWER

SOMETIME AFTER THE START OF THE ARAB OIL embargo of 1973, a councilwoman in Prince George's County, Maryland, a suburb of the nation's capital, complained that for many people the cost of home heating and other utilities came to more each month than their mortgage payments. It was getting almost impossible for many young people to buy a home, she said.

Since then, rising housing costs and interest rates have pushed mortgages way up, so that the point she made, so striking at the time, is no longer technically correct. Utilities generally do not cost more than home mortgages. They simply cost a great deal more than they used to, both in constant dollars and in proportion to people's incomes.

The price of oil, natural gas, and electricity in general soared so much in the seventies that household budgets became severely strained and living standards often were reduced substantially. Many people shut off rooms in their homes to keep from having to heat or cool them; they would go without heat during the night, sleep in long johns, do anything to keep the bills down.

Jimmy Carter appeared on TV wearing a sweater to reinforce the theme of energy conservation and sacrifice. At night, he turned off the exterior lights that helped make the White House and other Washington government buildings and monuments so attractive.

What government is doing about energy costs and availability is probably a blur of confusion to most people. Policies undergo sweeping change from administration to administration. Under Carter there was a synthetic-fuels program, with government-sponsored research on solar power, gasohol, and other energy sources. When Reagan took office, he turned the capital lights back on and shut off the synthetic-fuels program.

What has remained constant is the high cost of energy to consumers, compared to earlier years. Prices and availability of oil were better in the eighties than in the late seventies, but for many they were still hardly affordable, forcing difficult choices for those of moderate means. In a number of public opinion polls, some people told interviewers they often had to decide whether to eat or heat their homes.

In three special surveys of individual communities that Kenneth John and I did for the *Washington Post* in 1983, eight of every ten people in Rockford, Illinois, and three of every four in Manchester, New Hampshire, and Waterloo, Iowa, told interviewers that the cost of heating oil, gas, and electricity was a serious or very serious problem in their communities.

In Rockford and Waterloo, only unemployment drew more concern from among a battery of problems listed. In Manchester, more people cited utility bills as a serious problem than any other issue mentioned, including unemployment.

Nationally, a *Post/ABC News* poll that year found seventy-four percent of the people interviewed referring to utility bills as a serious or very serious problem, with concern somewhat lower than that in the South and West, higher in the East and Midwest.

In 1982, a poll done for Honeywell, Inc., found forty percent saying "they would like to cut back more on energy but can't," and ninety-two percent saying the cost of energy and fuels is a serious "threat to the American standard of living." That survey and the ones by the *Washington Post* were ones in which some people told interviewers they faced a choice between eating and paying their utility bills.

The great majority at the time felt that rates were so high as to be unconscionable. A 1983 poll by the University of Maryland's Survey Research Center, for example, found that eighty-one percent of the people in that state felt that the price of gas and oil for heating was too high "given its cost to produce."

Such a situation provides a golden opportunity for politicians. Huey Long of Louisiana may have been a demagogue for his attacks on the utilities, but voters still respond to the beat of that populist drum.

A good example came in Mississippi not long ago. There a political outsider, William Allain, was elected attorney general in 1979. He became the first high state official ever to fight the utility companies, representing the people against the Mississippi public service commission. Allain won rate reductions and sent rebate checks to citizens through his attorney general's office. As one Mississippi reporter put it, "It was the magic formula for Allain. He became the first state official to stand with the consumer and protect his pocketbook."

In 1983, Allain ran for governor. He won the Democratic primary and looked like a shoo-in for the general election. But at the end of the campaign he was accused of being a homosexual, the result of allegations made after an investigation financed by oil interests.

Allain responded by denying that he was a homosexual, saying that "not since the days of Sen. Joseph McCarthy and Adolf Hitler has the big-lie technique been used with such reckless abandon." He also pointed out that the oil men behind the investigation were among those who fought an oil-and-gas-tax increase to finance public kindergartens. He ended up winning easily.

Looking at the opinion poll data late in 1983, it seemed to me there should be many Allains across the country, but I had heard of very few. At that moment, all eight of the Democratic candidates for the following year's presidential election had spent months in the field but only one, Alan Cranston of California, had picked up on the subject of utility rates, and he had mentioned it only infrequently.

Unable to understand why so potent an issue drew so little comment, I began asking political consultants about it.

One of those I talked to was Robert Squier, a consultant to Democratic candidates. It was Squier who alerted me to Allain's success. He also told me that a stand against the utilities had helped propel to victory two other southern governors, Mark White of Texas in 1981, and William Clinton of Arkansas in 1982.

It was his view, Squier said, that any of the Democrats who were lagging behind, stuck at the bottom of the presidential pack, could spurt forward by focusing on the problem of high energy costs. But, he added, the candidates might have been unaware of the strength of the issue, in that it just about never surfaced in national polls.

I talked also with Peter Hart, the pollster for Walter Mondale, and William Hamilton, John Glenn's pollster. Hart said much the same thing: he had found utility rates to be a major concern in polls for state and local campaigns but not in his national polls. He acknowledged that it was a lively issue— "populist in nature," as he put it, "and one that doesn't fit into an ideological scale." Populist or not, utility rates were one matter Mondale did not focus on during the campaign.

Hamilton offered a different reason for avoidance of the

subject. Candidates "have only so many message units," he told me, noting that at that early stage of the campaign "they are trying to establish the fact that they understand the big picture first." Glenn clearly was a candidate who might have profited from taking on the utilities. His campaign was stifled in part because he did not give the appearance of being a Democrat; utility costs were tailor-made for him. But like Mondale, he never did turn to it.

All in all, I would have to conclude that the absence of national poll data and a limited number of "message units" had little if anything to do with the decision of Democrats to avoid the subject of utility rates. The candidates did not need polls in 1983 or 1984 to tell them what a local officeholder in Prince George's County had discovered on her own a decade earlier.

The problem with taking on the utilities is in large part a big-money, special-interest problem. Oil and utility political-action committees contribute millions in election campaigns; they also lend key staff members to work on behalf of candidates they can get along with. In other words, they strive to coopt candidates.

Top Democrats may avoid the issue for another reason, as well. They and their advisers are so well off themselves that they simply may not understand how serious a problem utility rates are for ordinary people. The candidates have no problems in paying their own utility bills; some may never even see them. Years in high position have tended to insulate them from the circumstances of the average citizen.

Thus, in 1984, Democratic candidates for president lingered repeatedly in televised debates over such matters as whether Jerusalem or Tel Aviv should be recognized as the capital of Israel, a subject of not much importance to any voters, including almost all American Jews. But they were content to pay no attention at all to the question of utility rates, a matter that three of every four Americans regarded as a serious problem.

■ ■ ■

The contrast between William Allain in Mississippi and the Democrats (and the Republicans) who ran for President in 1984 is a stark one. It illustrates the rewards and perils that may come to political figures who fight moneyed interests to focus public discussion on matters of universal concern. Allain was elected, but the personal attack on him took its toll. After a few months in office he said, "I'll never run for public office again. I'll never put myself through that again." When the time came, in 1987, he made good on his promise.

For the presidential candidates, especially the Democrats, the contrast reveals a haughty disregard at the highest level for issues of importance to the many.

Democrats should be talking about utility rates; it is their kind of issue, or should be. A Washington activist, Robert Brandon, who was executive director of the Citizen/Labor Energy Coalition in 1983, told me that a year earlier his organization worked for candidates in thirty-five congressional campaigns in which utility rates were made an important focus of discussion. Those candidates won in thirty of the contests. Brandon cited races in Illinois, Ohio, and West Virginia in which, he said, opponents of decontrolling natural-gas prices won for that reason alone.

Nevertheless, there has been virtually no leadership debate or public focus on energy policy since the shortages of the 1970s. As for the news media, the basic approach is the same as that in the handling of civil rights: occasionally a good series of articles may be written, but there is no consistent attention of the kind owed a matter that eight people in ten regard as a serious or very serious national problem.

One result is that, except in isolated instances, the people are left ignorant of efforts made either on their behalf or against their interests. Many Americans would consider utility rates and overall energy policy as vital election issues, if given a chance. They seldom are. The result contributes to low voter turnout and increased cynicism.

■ ■ ■

Americans will do almost anything to ensure the availability of electrical power; in public opinion polls in 1987 and earlier years, a majority even supported military action to keep Persian Gulf shipping lanes open to oil tankers.

Nevertheless, citizens have come to reject the one source of energy that for decades was thought of as having the potential to provide a clean, inexpensive, inexhaustible supply of power.

How the public came to turn against the nuclear-power industry, making further development infeasible today, is yet one more stunning display of the enormous force of concerted public opinion.

As of this writing more than a hundred nuclear plants are generating electricity in the United States, providing about eighteen percent of the nation's power. But no new ones are in the planning stages; the last application that resulted in the start of construction came in 1974. In the following eight years there were mass cancellations of plans for new plants. In twenty-two instances plans were dropped although construction had been approved. In an additional forty-eight cases projects were terminated while permit requests were under review.

It was for reasons other than public opinion that the drive toward nuclear generation of electricity began to wind down. By the eighties, however, it was public fear, as much as other factors, that kept the industry from rebounding. As John F. Ahearne, a member of the Nuclear Regulatory Commission in 1981, put it at the time, "Nuclear power in the United States has a fatal flaw; it cannot get public acceptance."

This shaping of mass sentiment was a gradual one. In the early days the only critics of nuclear power were environmental activists who warned against the danger of accidents, problems in storing radioactive waste, and damage to the environment even in normal operation.

The activists were maligned by utility companies and disregarded by government. Often they had to fight in court simply to be heard; their first victories were rulings allowing them to testify in public hearings. If ordinary people thought of them at all, it was mainly as kooks, extremists, back-to-nature idealists.

Over the years, however, accidents did occur, including several near-catastrophes. No acceptable means of storing nuclear waste has been developed. The Arab oil embargoes of the 1970s and rising prices taught people to conserve energy, lessening the need for the nuclear option. Instead of being inexpensive, the cost of nuclear power—the expense of building nuclear plants, and the rates charged consumers—zoomed. In addition, the lame response to these problems by regulatory agencies and utility firms stoked people's distrust of government, and of authority in general.

One side effect was that many Americans, probably without being aware of it, began to hold the antinuclear activists in high esteem, as people who could be trusted, unlike many government and nuclear-industry leaders.

Utility firms are keenly aware of that. Some have taken to hiring environmentalists to help in planning and to give the appearance of concern for the common good. "Save the Manatee," said a bumper sticker distributed in the early eighties by Florida Power and Light, a utility that is particularly alert to public opinion.

Local and state elected officials also have deferred to the activists. Politicians who might have rubber-stamped proposals for nuclear plants fifteen years ago now block the opening of those same plants, and some are outspoken opponents, keenly aware that they are taking the safe and popular position, the one prescribed by people to whom no one paid attention twenty years earlier.

Americans' thinking about nuclear power has gone through three stages: from docile acceptance to growing reservations to the rejection prevalent today. The first phase came in the fifties and early sixties, when there was a general public faith both in technology and government.

For many years, despite the criticism of the activists, it was simply unthinkable to the average American that power companies would embark on unsafe projects, or that the government would let them. As late as 1976, thirty-four percent of the people in a Gallup poll thought it "very important" and thirty-seven percent "somewhat important" to build more nuclear plants to meet the nation's energy needs. Various surveys, including that one, found only one-quarter of the people opposed.

Three years later came an event that shook the nation. On March 28, 1979, there was a partial meltdown at the Three Mile Island nuclear power station outside Harrisburg, Pennsylvania. No one died, no one was injured. But for days radiation spewed from the plant, terrifying many in the area and riveting public attention.

The plant's operators, Metropolitan Edison Company, were not forthcoming with the public, initially holding off for hours on alerting area residents to what had occurred, then putting out comforting reports that were soon exposed as either lies or half-truths.

Three Mile Island moved public opinion to its second stage. The accident did not turn Americans into opponents of nuclear power, as is widely believed today. But it did increase skepticism, pushing people to a wait-and-see posture.

A nationwide *Washington Post* poll that I did three months after the accident showed twenty-six percent of the people interviewed saying they opposed the use of nuclear plants for generating electricity—no real change from the Gallup poll of 1976. Findings like mine were common; there was no mass increase in opposition.

But no longer did a majority consider themselves supporters, either. Instead, many people began to list themselves as undecided about the use of nuclear power to generate electricity. In my 1979 survey the largest single block, thirty-eight percent, were those who said they had not made up their minds.

In effect, however, to be uncertain meant to be opposed. When asked whether they approved or disapproved the construction of new nuclear plants, the people in the middle knew exactly what they thought. Four of every five disapproved. To them, wait and see meant exactly that.

In the following years, sentiment hardened. Polls I worked on in 1983 and 1985 showed two out of three people opposed to the construction of new nuclear plants. In both those surveys, the largest single group continued to be not opponents of nuclear power but those those who said they were undecided about it.

What people were waiting for, it seemed clear, was some new technological breakthrough. Instead, in April, 1986, they got Chernobyl, which moved American public opinion to its third stage.

Clusters of polls after the meltdown in the Soviet Union showed how much the fear of nuclear power had swollen. In a *CBS News* poll, fifty-five percent said a similar accident "is likely" to occur in the United States. In the state of Washington, a *Seattle Times* poll showed fifty-seven percent agreeing with the statement that major accidents "are inevitable in the production of nuclear power, even in the United States."

In our May, 1986, *Washington Post/ABC News* poll, for the first time in any survey I had worked on, more people listed themselves as opponents of nuclear power than as undecided about it. Asked how much they trusted government statements about the risks of nuclear power, only fourteen percent said they had a great deal of trust; forty-six percent said they had some trust, and thirty-nine percent said they had very little trust.

Perhaps the most stunning finding in that poll was that forty-one of every hundred people interviewed favored phasing out existing nuclear plants. By comparison, in a local poll I did after Three Mile Island, only five of every hundred wanted to shut down existing plants.

For years the nuclear industry has been developing strategies for recovery. In June and July, 1987, I ran across full-page ads in popular magazines that aligned nuclear power with coal as protection against any new Arab-inspired oil crises. "The 1973 Arab oil crisis is a haunting reminder of the darker side of foreign oil dependence," one of those ads said. "Since then, America has turned more to electricity from nuclear energy and coal to help restore our energy security. As a result, these are now our leading sources of electricity and a strong defense against an increasing oil dependence that again threatens America's national energy security." The ads I saw had fairly lengthy texts. They focused on the problems of dependence on foreign oil. But they dealt not at all with the safety or costs of the nuclear option. Those matters were avoided.

If, someday, the nuclear industry is able to proclaim once again that atomic power can be clean and safe, it will find a receptive public. Even at this stage, many Americans who have turned away from nuclear power are reserving their right to change their minds about it.

Eight in ten in our May, 1986, survey said they wanted no new nuclear plants built. But in the same poll, half the people interviewed foresaw the possibility that nuclear power may at some time be safe. Americans have not yet given up on technology.

THE GROWTH OF CITIZEN ACTIVISM

I HAVE REFERRED TO THE ROLE OF ENVIRONMEN-
talists in changing people's attitudes toward the use of
nuclear power. These activists alone, of course, had a limited role. Their concern would not have brought the nuclear industry to its knees; it had hardly any effect in the
early years. It was events—the scores of safety violations, the
several near-catastrophes, Three Mile Island and Chernobyl,
the gradually growing concern about radioactive waste, the
escalating costs—that are in the main responsible for current
public thinking on the subject.

But for their efforts as an advance guard, as outspoken

monitors and prods to government, for being correct in their warnings, environmentalists came to be highly regarded by their fellow citizens. Once neglected, even ridiculed, they have become recognized as a force for good in the United States. The same is true for activists in various fields, such as consumerism, civil rights, feminism, and other areas.

People probably have little awareness of how much stock they put in the various activist movements; it is something that has just crept up on us, like computers.

Modern-day activism may be said to have begun with the black civil-rights movement of the late fifties. Ignored by the majority at first, blacks and whites who were committed to equal opportunity began drawing popular support because their cause was just, they themselves were persistent, their efforts dramatic and courageous. By example and at the cost of a number of lives, they set the stage for a sympathetic president, Lyndon Johnson, to enact sweeping civil-rights legislation.

The war in Vietnam gave rise to the next wave of activists, the antiwar protesters. Through their efforts, many citizens found themselves questioning government for the first time. The word "radicalized" came into being, used to describe ordinary people who sympathized with protesters or who took to protest themselves to force the government to change its course.

Around the same time, a single individual, Ralph Nader, became a national force with his spirited attack on the American automobile industry.

It was no coincidence that activism rose in the sixties and seventies as people began to expect less and less from government. Polls I have worked on show respect for activists highest among those who trust the government least. Thus, as trust declined generally, regard for activists became widespread.

Activist leaders are well aware of this relationship. Brock Evans, a member of the board of directors of the Sierra Club, a vice-president of the National Audubon Society, and one of the chief environmental lobbyists, put it like this to me in 1983: "If the government were responsible, we wouldn't need to exist."

Richard Viguerie, publisher of the *Conservative Digest* and one of the best-known right-wing activist spokesmen, told me in an interview, "There are large numbers of reasonable people who are frustrated because the establishment— Democrats, Republicans, whatever—are not responsive to citizens' needs. . . . There are problems of crime, drugs, schools that don't teach, all hopping around, and government is either powerless to deal with them or has other issues on its agenda."

Viguerie noted that "most of the effective leaders for liberal and conservative issues do not hold public office and never have: Jesse Jackson, Martin Luther King, Ralph Nader, John Gardner, George Meaney, Lane Kirkland, the feminists, Phyllis Schlafly, Jerry Falwell, Paul Weyrich."

Viguerie reserved his sharpest complaints for the Republican party but he saw his liberal counterparts as having the same frustrations with the Democrats. "If the party isn't going to take a stand, you don't look to the party to fight your battles, you form an organization."

Many in the political establishment still refer to activists as gadflies, kooks, extremists, Utopians, roadblocks to growth. They do get in the way. But by the early eighties, the average American, probably without realizing it, had come to think that activists were doing more to solve the nation's problems than were the Democrats and Republicans in Congress or the Reagan administration.

In a *Washington Post/ABC News* public opinion poll in April, 1983, only about one person in six took the view that environmentalists "generally go too far in trying to stop commercial development of federal parks and wilderness areas." Three times as many people felt the environmentalists were not going far enough, or were taking the right approach.

The same survey asked people their impressions as to whether President Reagan, the Democrats in Congress, the

Republicans in Congress, local governing bodies, business leaders, environmentalists, and the Environmental Protection Agency were or were not doing what they should to protect the environment.

The best ratings by far went to environmental groups; scoring the worst, with substantially more negative ratings than positive ones, were business leaders and Reagan:

Percentage in 1983 rating these groups . . .

	favor- ably	unfavor- ably	no opinion
environmental groups	63%	20%	17%
local government	55%	30%	15%
the Environmental Protection Agency	46%	36%	18%
Democratic leaders in Congress	41%	22%	37%
Ronald Reagan	36%	45%	19%
business leaders	33%	48%	19%
Republican leaders in Congress	31%	35%	34%

Environmentalists, of course, are only a small segment of the activist citizens. The list of groups trying to prod government (leaving aside the big lobbies whose chief interest is their own economic stake) is simply enormous.

One of the most inspired activist drives is of recent vintage, begun and carried out by handfuls of blacks who were instrumental in bringing about a dramatic reversal of American policies toward South Africa. The key to their success, as is so often the case, lay in rallying pubic opinion. Their method of operation provides a classic model of activism as a national force.

About two weeks after the 1984 presidential election, around Thanksgiving, a small group in Washington known as the Free South Africa Movement began picketing near the South African embassy, protesting that nation's jailing of a number of labor leaders. Demonstrating too near an embassy is against the law, so protesters could get themselves arrested simply by taking one extra step. Many did.

The period was one of political lull, and the protests drew a good measure of media coverage. Similar protests sprang up in other cities.

After sixteen days, the labor leaders in South Africa were released. But the picketing continued, shifting in focus to the larger issue of apartheid. By July, 1985, 2,900 people had been arrested in Washington and more than 4,000 at demonstrations in twenty-six other cities or on college campuses. Included on the list were twenty-two members of Congress and a number of mayors and union and religious leaders.

Getting arrested in Washington was an easy form of protest, bringing attention but little inconvenience. The police treated the demonstrators gently, and prosecutors refused to jail them or press charges.

The actions did not bring Pretoria to its knees. The news out of South Africa was more of blacks being killed week after week than of any move toward desegregation. But the activists' domestic success was beyond dispute. There were waves of public support, which, in turn, were followed by the introduction and enactment of antiapartheid legislation in Congress.

In January, 1985, when the protests were two months old, the *Washington Post/ABC News* poll asked a random sample of Americans if they had heard of the picketing in Washington and elsewhere. About half said they had. Among them, forty-six percent said they approved of the protests, while twenty-one percent were opposed to them.

In subsequent months there was only incidental news coverage of the protests, but the activists did manage to attract some attention from time to time. In mid-June, the *Post/ABC News* poll found that awareness of their activities had gone up ten points since January, with sympathizers continuing to outnumber opponents by more than two to one.

Before the Free South Africa Movement got involved, apartheid was a back-burner issue in Washington. For years the Reagan administration had insisted on a policy called constructive engagement, whose stated aim was to bring about reform in South Africa by persuading the Afrikaners to change, rather than pressuring them with direct action from outside.

The activists moved apartheid to the front burner. In June, 1985, the House of Representatives overwhelmingly passed a tough measure that included a ban on U.S. imports of South African gold coins, Krugerrands. The previous year, $600 million worth of Krugerrands were sold to Americans, more than half the total exported.

In July, the Republican-controlled Senate—Reagan's Senate, that is—voted, eighty to twelve, for a bill that fell short of what the House had approved but that was stronger than anything Reagan wanted. It sought a ban on new bank loans and nuclear-technology exports to South Africa and required U.S. companies with interests there to take an active role in opposing apartheid.

From that point on, American policy toward South Africa got tougher. Wrangling between Reagan and Republicans in the Senate grew heated. American corporations began withdrawing from the strife-torn country, universities and municipalities pulled out their investments. Constructive engagement was repudiated, divestiture and disinvestment took its place.

One of the leaders of the Free South Africa Movement was Randall Robinson, a spokesman for the group and executive director of a foreign-policy lobby, TransAfrica. "Before this movement started," Robinson told me in the summer of 1985, "probably fewer than ten percent knew what apartheid was, or where South Africa is.

"We realize this is the first step. But we hope we are making it clear to South Africa that this is a shot across the bow, that the United States is reversing course."

Robinson listed three factors that had transformed the idea of economic sanctions from a nonstarter to an effective force. They serve as a model for all successful activist movements.

First, he said, was consistency and dedication. "The people involved are prepared to go on as many months or years as necessary," he said.

Second was what Robinson called a consumable message. "We felt that if we could put the message before the American people, they would make the right decision. The issue is what is fair and what is unfair."

Third was hard work on Capitol Hill and elsewhere. "Congress has to be lobbied from within," he said, and protests and "other kinds of pressures are needed to make them more responsive."

Not long after the Senate vote, Senate Majority Leader Robert Dole came to the *Washington Post* for lunch with a number of editors and reporters. His view of how the government reversed its policies toward South Africa were similar to Robinson's.

Asked whether there would have been any legislation if not for the embassy protests, he said, "Well, it focused on the problem. And I think from that standpoint, those who had the responsibility [a reference to Richard G. Lugar of Indiana, the Senate Foreign Relations Committee chairman at the time] and others at the hearings made modifications. . . . Not only the focus, not being arrested and all that, but the fact that they were very actively visiting the different people on the Hill. Let's face it: some see it as a big civil-rights issue that's important down the road or whatever. All that has an impact."

In the end, Dole said, the Senate had little choice but to vote for sanctions. "I think generally, if you find people pushing an issue and you find out that there's rather broad support for it, there's certainly some obligation to bring it up."

In typical understatement, Dole said that "the administration's not too excited about what we did."

In September, 1985, Reagan issued an executive order eliminating new loans to the South African government, leading to a ban on importation of Krugerrands. His action, a slight backdown from constructive engagement, succeeded in keeping the Senate from joining the House in a stronger measure.

Pressure continued. In November, Reagan imposed new restrictions on the export of computers, software, and some computer technology to South Africa, but they were regarded as weak actions by many.

The following year the debate sharpened. In June, 1986, the House voted to force all American firms out of South Africa. Senate Republicans urged Reagan to move forcefully in dealing with the Pretoria regime. Senator Lugar reportedly urged Reagan to never again use the term "constructive engagement."

In July, Reagan made his first televised speech as president on South Africa, insisting that strong sanctions would hurt blacks there and "destroy America's flexibility, discard our diplomatic leverage, and deepen the crisis." Republican leaders disputed him, and began voicing concern that the matter had become a civil-rights issue in the United States and that failure to act strongly might damage members of their party in the fall elections.

In August, the Senate overwhelmingly voted to bar imports of steel, textiles, and agricultural goods from South Africa, to bar new American investment and to suspend air service between the two countries. Under Lugar's urging, the House went along, dropping its stronger measure. Reagan vetoed the bill in September but was overridden in the House in a 313-to-83 vote, and in the Senate by 78 to 21.

The merits of the new, tougher policies are open to question. Some maintain that no change would ever occur without them. Others in this country and in South Africa who support abolition of apartheid feel the sanctions have been counterproductive. As American corporations left, Japanese and other investors moved in.

Merits aside, it seems virtually certain that Congress was driven to act through the pressure applied by a small band of activists who knew how to catch the public's eye.

ISRAEL, THE MIDDLE EAST, FOREIGN AFFAIRS

ONE DAY IN MARCH, 1982, AN *ABC NEWS* VICE-president gummed up the works in one of our *Washington Post/ABC News* polls. His interference resulted in some personal embarrassment for me, some criticism of the *Washington Post* in the Jewish press, and a rebuke from a head of state, Menachem Begin of Israel.

The criticism and rebuke referred, oddly enough, to what the newspaper *did not* write. The incident served to underscore how much world leaders, not just those in this country, care about American public opinion.

The network vice-president was one who nominally oversaw the polling operation for ABC. Drafts of our joint polls went to his desk as a courtesy. On the day in question, he looked over a poll we had spent weeks preparing, dealing mostly with the elderly in the United States. Interviewing was to start that night.

Instead of simply approving the draft or making recommendations about particular questions, the executive said he wanted to add a section on the Middle East and Israel. To me, the request seemed improper. For once things were quiet in that part of the world, so there was no need to act in a hurry. The Israeli invasion of Lebanon was still three months off, a gleam in the eye of Ariel Sharon.

I felt we could not do a good job on such short notice. We had asked very few questions on the Middle East until then in our year-old poll. My counterpart at ABC, Jeff Alderman, was on jury duty that day, making things worse. Alderman might have been able to persuade the executive to wait a month and give us time to prepare adequately.

My concern was twofold. We obviously could not do the best possible job in framing questions on such short notice, and we were bound to get results we could not interpret well. On the matter of what Americans thought of Begin, for example, a question sure to be asked, we had no track record of any kind. Thus, while we would be able to say what proportions saw Begin in a favorable or unfavorable light, we would have no idea if his image was improving or getting worse.

Alderman's assistants worked up about ten questions; at the *Post,* Kenneth John and I made some suggestions of our own. In my mind I decided that if I had problems in interpreting the results, I would leave them unreported for the time being, go back to the subject after a few months, and have the material available as a baseline. It would not be a total loss.

When the results came in they showed thirty-nine percent of the people interviewed holding a favorable impression of Begin, twenty-two percent with an unfavorable view, and the rest with no impression of him.

Seventeen percent said President Reagan was leaning too much in favor of Israel, twenty-one percent said he was leaning too much toward the Arab countries, and the bulk, sixty-two percent, either had no opinion on the matter or felt he was not leaning in either direction.

As I had feared, I didn't know how to interpret such findings, so I put them aside. Independently, producers of ABC news programs had the same problem, and shelved that segment of the poll, reporting none of it. Told that a ranking ABC executive had requested the inquiry, a producer for *World News Tonight* said, "Then let him put it on his show."

In the first years of the *Post/ABC News* survey, ABC routinely sent out the results, question by question, to several hundred people or organizations. Included in the mailing for March, 1982, was the segment on Israel and the Middle East.

Not long afterward, I got a call at work from a reporter for the *Washington Jewish Week*, asking whether the *Post* was going to report the findings he had in his hand, and if not, why not. I explained my difficulties in making sense of the data and said I would use them later on, as a baseline, after we did a new poll. His response came in the form of an article giving some of the findings and charging that the *Post* had withheld material favorable to Israel. He also complained to the ombudsman of the *Post,* who asked me about the matter.

In June, 1982, Israel invaded Lebanon. Before long the *Post* and *ABC News* did several surveys on attitudes toward the Middle East, repeating a number of the original March questions.

All in all, there was not what I would call a lot of heat put on me or the *Post* over the incident. Late that summer, however, Bill Claiborne, the *Post*'s correspondent in Jerusalem at the time, returned to Washington for a few days, and looked me up. "Menachem Begin wants to know why you withheld a poll that was favorable to Israel," Claiborne told me.

I asked if he was kidding. He said he was not kidding at all, that Begin's chief press aide had complained to him, saying that Begin was upset about the matter.

■ ■ ■

As time passed, we did a more thorough examination of Americans' attitudes toward Israel, both in the few relatively quiet periods in the Middle East, and during times of difficulty there and in U.S.-Israeli relations. My main finding has been that most Americans, probably two of every three, have no deeply held views about Israel one way or the other.

At the height of the 1982 invasion of Lebanon, with American TV depicting the bombing of Beirut on every newscast, fewer than half the people we interviewed said they were following those events closely. Later, in 1986, some opinion analysts were surprised to find that, despite extensive front-page coverage, the case of Jonathan Pollard, convicted of stealing American military secrets for Israel, had made no discernible impression on the public in this country.

This lack of interest or concern is common in almost all areas having to do with foreign affairs. The great majority of people simply do not get involved. They may give an opinion when pressed, but it is not worth very much. There is no salience to it. Attitudes are loosely held at best, subject to quick change. Generally, it is only when events become threatening, as in situations when American troops may become involved, that the masses of people even begin to take a harder look. Nonthreatening situations seem to spark interest only if they are particularly dramatic.

There have nevertheless been swells in negative opinion toward Israel in the eighties, with the largest occurring in the fall of 1982 after Lebanese groups massacred Palestinians in the Sabra and Shatila refugee camps in Beirut. That atrocity could have been blocked by Israeli occupiers, an Israeli investigation concluded, causing a furor there that had repercussions in the United States as well. Afterward, however, negative opinion toward Israel in the U.S. quickly subsided.

In the spring of 1985, Palestinian terrorists hijacked a TWA plane on a flight from Athens, killed an American sailor, and held other Americans hostage for an extended period. One of their demands was that Israel release some twelve hundred Palestinians being held in detention camps. Once more there was heavy TV coverage, including frequent repetition of the terrorists' demands. As Israel at first refused to give in, American public opinion again began to turn sour.

Israel eventually did capitulate; the American hostages were freed, and Israel again rebounded in the polls.

My analysis of *Washington Post/ABC News* polls showed that shifts in American opinion followed a consistent pattern: the ups and downs were mainly caused by fluctuations among the large part of the population that paid the least attention to events in the Middle East. The informed public tended to side steadily with Israel in its conflicts with Arab neighbors, but for the rest, feelings rose and fell according to the poignancy of the evening news.

The natural condition, it appeared, was one of reflexive sympathy for Israel as a beleaguered nation surrounded by hostile Arabs. Since that time, sympathy for Israel has been furthered by a renewed American distrust of Arabs and Middle East Moslems in general, brought on by repeated incidents of terrorism against Americans. By 1986 most Americans' regard for Israel had reverted to the high standing that had been common in the sixties and early seventies. In between, however, largely through the efforts of one man, Anwar Sadat, there had been a period of heightened respect for Arabs and a consequent diminishing of the one-sided view that Americans had of the peoples of the Middle East.

Sadat charmed much of the world, including a great many Americans and Israelis as well. By himself, he dissipated the view of Arab leaders as uniformly hostile and belligerent. His legacy in this country, at least for a while, was to persuade Americans that Arabs, too, could be civilized, could want peace, and that there could be cooperation between the United States and nations such as Egypt.

In September, 1982, with disfavor of Israel at its height and the Sadat legacy intact, a *Post/ABC News* poll, in fact, showed more people thinking of Egypt than of Israel as a reliable ally of the United States. Such sentiment has since dissipated; it could take another Sadat to restore it.

In early 1988, Israel began facing a major crisis within its borders, brought on by almost two months of rebellion by stone-throwing, tire-burning Palestinians in the West Bank, the Gaza strip, Jerusalem, and elsewhere. In trying to repress the demonstrations, Israeli soldiers killed more than two dozen young Arabs in the first few weeks. As protests continued, and as deaths mounted, the Israeli government changed tactics. It had soldiers beat rather than shoot the more violent demonstrators, and it instituted curfews. But by the beginning of March, more than seventy Palestinians had been killed.

Press and television coverage of the incidents portrayed the squalid living conditions of much of Israel's Arab population. Many Israelis themselves found the government's behavior repugnant and held their own demonstrations in protest of it. Some American Jewish leaders, in a rare action, also condemned the repression.

Conditions became so tense, and so dramatic, that the Israeli government may have fallen into one of those rare situations in which surging public opinion forces an abrupt shift in national policy. For many of Israel's leaders, that would mean thinking the unthinkable: giving at least some form of self-determination to the Arabs in the West Bank, and moving to improve conditions for those elsewhere in the nation.

At the time of this writing, in March, 1988, it is only conjecture that points to such a conclusion; no such shift has occurred. But it is a conjecture that mounts with each passing day, and one factor that could make it a reality would be the arousing of public opinion in the United States. This, too, is problematic: dramatic as the events in Israel are, they do not threaten American lives and, hence, may fail to move the citizenry here. For Americans, the issue could simply fade away.

The first opinion polls were inconclusive. In a poll for *Time* magazine in late January, 1988, only one person in four claimed to be paying close attention; in a Gallup poll in February, three people in ten said they had a "less favorable" opinion of Israel because of its handling of the crisis.

If, however, sympathy for the downtrodden Arabs in Israel were to grow and coalesce, certain events will necessarily follow. Candidates for president will pick up on the problem. So will members of Congress. Pressure on Israel would mount substantially, and eventually could prove irresistible.

In the process, another aspect of the power of American public opinion would be revealed: that what Americans think carries enormous influence far beyond this country's borders. People and governments everywhere—not only in our own country or in a client state such as Israel—cater to American opinion, appeal to it, and study it almost endlessly.

From time to time, representatives of many foreign countries have gotten in touch with me about American public opinion, either to complain about our reports, as Begin did to Bill Claiborne, or just to make inquiries. The president of the American-Arab Affairs Council once sent me a letter complaining that an article I wrote after a *Post/ABC News* poll was "an example of the bias and slanted coverage given to the Arab world by the U.S. media."

On one occasion I got a more pleasant call from someone at the Egyptian embassy who was simply asking for further data from a survey. I have received similar inquiries from representatives of the governments of Italy, West Germany, Japan, Great Britain, France, Yugoslavia, the Soviet Union. And those are ones I recall; I'm sure I have forgotten some, and equally sure that other pollsters whose work bears more on foreign affairs have drawn a great many more inquiries.

Once I got a phone call from a high Argentine official asking if I had material on American public opinion toward his country. I told him I had never asked questions about Argentina; that Argentina, despite its dramatic move toward democracy and its searing economic problems, was not widely discussed here. I said that in my judgment, most Americans probably had no impressions one way or the other about events in Argentina, except to value any move toward democracy.

He asked if he could visit anyway, and did. In a half-hour discussion, he explained, quite emotionally, that what Americans thought was of extreme importance in Argentina. First, he said, he knew that many members of Congress paid attention to public opinion, and polls might guide them in legislation.

He also said that the Argentines themselves cared deeply about how the American people were responding to the turmoil there—that a favorable reaction by ordinary Americans to the democratic reforms might help carry the government through its many crises.

His was a most striking point of view, and, on reflection, one that seems widespread throughout the world. What ordinary Americans feel seems of immense importance almost everywhere. In Asia, Europe, the Middle East, Latin America, in industrialized countries and developing ones, people care deeply about American public opinion. They are looking to us for approval and assistance.

Governments often cater to the American press; almost every mass protest anywhere in the world shows people carrying posters written in English, an appeal for the sympathy of the citizens of the United States in the hope of forcing change.

Americans themselves are insular, paying little attention to overseas problems except when there is some crisis. That is simply the way things are; few of us speak foreign languages, only a minority can satisfactorily define the term "Third World." Abroad, most people do not know that about us. Those who discover it are often horrified.

ABORTION AND SOCIAL CHANGE

W E HEAR IT SAID FREQUENTLY THAT THE government cannot legislate morality. That is wrong. Government laws and Supreme Court rulings on social issues have helped make for massive changes in people's thinking about fundamental issues of right and wrong, about what is acceptable behavior and what is not.

That has been proven true in civil-rights issues, as demonstrated in the softening of white attitudes toward blacks after court rulings and legislation of the fifties and sixties. It has been proven equally true in the easing of attitudes toward abortion.

Polls offer conflicting views on what proportion of Americans accept abortion as simply another birth-control measure. Some surveys suggest that about forty percent of adults favor abortion on demand; others put the figure as high as sixty percent. Either way, there is no doubt that attitudes have softened, that many Americans are far more tolerant of abortion than they once were.

In large part the change is a result of the social revolution of the sixties. Easy abortion is clearly linked to increased premarital sexual activity, disregard for authority (including religious authority), and to the women's movement, which in its early years valued work and a career much more than homemaking and motherhood. But it is also due to acts of government.

Twelve times between 1972 and 1985, the National Opinion Research Center of the University of Chicago, in its annual General Social Survey, asked Americans their views on legalized abortion. Almost always, the results came out pretty much the same. They have shown about four people in ten approving abortion on demand, one in ten opposed to abortion in all circumstances, and the rest of the people, about half, approving of abortions in certain unfortunate situations.

Overall, eight in ten, for example, have said in these polls that abortion should be legal if "there is a strong chance of serious defect in the baby" or "if a woman becomes pregnant as a result of rape." Nine in ten have favored abortion "if the woman's health is seriously endangered."

By contrast, almost six in ten have said abortion should not be legal for a woman who "is married and does not want any more children," and more than half have been opposed in the instance of a single woman who is pregnant but "does not want to marry the man." The public has divided evenly in the case of a family that is poor "and cannot afford any more children."*

These attitudes have been so consistent, varying by only a

---

* It is to NORC's credit that its surveys were designed to elicit views on the propriety of abortion in these circumstances. Many polls fail to do that, and often result in simplistic findings.

few points from year to year since 1974, that on first glance they seem locked in place, a steady expression of deeply held values. In fact, however, there has been a sea change in the people's thinking about abortion, but one that occurred sometime before NORC began asking its series of questions almost every year.

The evidence for that is limited but nevertheless conclusive. It confirms what many people believe intuitively, that American society became more permissive and many citizens sharply more tolerant as part of the great social upheaval of the latter half of the sixties.

George Gallup began measuring opinion toward various issues in 1935, but he did not ask about abortion until 1962, according to the fat books that index all Gallup Poll questions. Failure by Gallup to even ask about a subject is an indication that it was either not an issue at all, or that it was too sensitive for public discussion.

Gallup's first inquiry was made after an Arizona woman, Sherri Finkbine, went to Sweden for an abortion because she could not obtain one legally in the United States. She had taken the drug Thalidomide and feared giving birth to a deformed baby.

A bare majority in 1962, fifty-two percent, said Finkbine had done the right thing, according to the Gallup poll. That is worlds apart from the eighty-two percent who have told NORC in recent years that they approve of abortion to avoid having a baby with serious birth defects.

The questions that became standard in the General Social Survey series during the seventies were composed earlier, and were included in a survey done by NORC in 1965. It was this prior test that provides documentation of how much views changed between the early sixties and the time of the Supreme Court decision legalizing abortion in 1973. In 1965, fewer than one person in five interviewed by NORC approved abortion on demand, and more than one in four opposed abortion under all circumstances.

It was about that time that social change, including the sexual revolution, began in earnest in the United States. The nation's young people were becoming more worldly than their elders, more educated, generally less concerned with religious dogma, supportive of the women's-liberation movement. In some states, legislation permitting abortion was enacted, creating a national clamor as women from across the country traveled to them in order to end unwanted pregnancies.

Each of these developments played a significant role in the shifting views on abortion. Increased educational levels may have been the most important, resulting, as they did for many, in a turning away from the religiosity of their parents and an introduction to feminism.

On the average in the General Social Surveys since 1972, fifty-four percent of the college graduates interviewed have favored legalized abortion on demand, compared to only thirty-four percent among those with less than a high-school degree. The increase in the number of college graduates in the late sixties and seventies meant more tolerance for abortion; increased worldliness was leading to more abortions as well.

People have always known of the ties between religiosity and views on abortion; the NORC polls simply quantify them. The General Social Surveys from 1972 to 1985 showed thirty-three percent of Americans saying religion should have a less important role in national life. Among them, three of every five felt a woman was entitled to an abortion regardless of the reason. On the other side were a slightly smaller twenty-nine percent who believed religion should play a greater role. Among them, only one in five supported abortion on demand.

Members of one religion in particular, Roman Catholics, have shown perhaps a more striking change than any other group. In Gallup's 1962 survey, thirty-three percent of the Catholics interviewed supported Finkbine's decision. Catholics today are radically different: seventy-seven percent of the ones interviewed by NORC since 1972 said abortion should be legal in situations like Finkbine's, where there is a strong chance of serious defect in the baby.

Similarly, the NORC surveys show that men and women who support at least one aspect of the feminist agenda, the Equal Rights Amendment, are twice as likely to support abortion on demand as those who oppose ERA. As things stand, a majority of Americans, especially the younger, better-educated ones, do support ERA.

The attitudes that began to change with the social revolution of the sixties became entrenched after the 1973 Supreme Court decision legalizing abortion and overturning restrictive laws in forty-six states. Between 1972 and 1974, the NORC surveys showed increases of six percentage points in the number of people supporting the right of a single woman to have a legal abortion. That jump in support after the court decision was sharper than in any other two-year period of polling; it signified a switch in position for some ten million adult Americans.

In addition, there was a seven-point spurt between 1972 and 1974 in support for abortion on demand for married women who do not want another child; six points for abortion on demand for the very poor; eight points in the case of rape or possible birth defects; five points (and bumping against the ceiling) for a woman whose health is endangered.

In the eighties, with President Reagan frequently speaking out against abortion, the NORC polls have shown a slight decline in support for abortion in some circumstances, such as for single women, the poor, the married women who do not want another child. Surveys done by other polling organizations, however, offered a conflicting view, occasionally showing increasing tolerance of abortion on demand and in special circumstances. Conceivably, the differences may be accounted for by variations in question wording, the location of questions in surveys, and the like.

Given the trend over the past twenty-five years, the differences are minor ones. The nation has moved far from the days when opposition to abortion on demand was the dominant view. Should a new Supreme Court reverse the 1973 ruling and restrict a woman's right to an abortion, the public outcry would be certain to make current protests by antiabortion groups seem tame in comparison.

But for many the court would once again become a moral arbiter. My best reading of public opinion suggests that such a decision would lead to a marked decrease in the numbers who believe that a woman alone has the right to determine whether to abort a pregnancy. A citizenry that distrusts the government nevertheless looks to it for guidance.

Still, it seems out of the question that the views of the many on abortion will ever revert to what they once were. The social revolution has simply gone too far, particularly in regard to sex. Filmmakers in the mid-eighties, through movies such as *Back to the Future* and *Peggy Sue Got Married,* have delighted in poking mild fun at what today appear to be the quaint mores of the fifties and early sixties.

Common living arrangements of young Americans these days, such as coed dormitories for college students and group homes with men and women sharing the rent, could hardly have been imagined three decades ago, let alone tolerated or encouraged. In stable, middle-class society it was rare for young couples to live together outside marriage; now, it seems, it is rare when they do not.

Just as the General Social Survey traces a gradual easing of attitudes toward abortion, so too does it quantify the widening acceptance during the seventies and eighties of premarital sex. "If a man and a woman have sex relations before marriage," reads a question that was asked nine times between 1972 and 1986, "do you think it is always wrong, almost always wrong, wrong only sometimes, or not wrong at all?" In 1972, thirty-seven percent of those interviewed said premarital sex is always wrong, and twenty-seven percent said it is not wrong at all. Thus, among those holding the strongest views, a strong plurality came down against premarital sex. By 1986, that was reversed: only twenty-eight percent felt premarital sex is always wrong, and forty-two percent said it is not wrong at all.

People's outlooks aside, large numbers of them either decreased their sexual activity or became more careful about it by the mid-eighties because of the scourge of AIDS (acquired immune deficiency syndrome). In a *Post/ABC News* poll in March, 1987, more than one-third of the younger, unmarried people—those most at risk—said they had altered their sexual behavior because of the fear of AIDS. (So too did fourteen percent of the married people interviewed.) A Gallup poll, also in 1987, even showed a decline in the numbers saying they approved of premarital sex. Gallup analysts linked the decline to concern over AIDS, not to any return to an earlier morality.

Interestingly, tolerance of both abortion and premarital sex has risen during a decade in which the United States also is believed by many to have witnessed a spirited religious revival. Not only proselytizers, fundamentalists, or the newly converted think religion is growing in importance; the average person, more and more, is also coming to that view, reversing an earlier pattern.

In each of twelve surveys from 1965 through 1981, the Gallup poll found a plurality or majority of people feeling that religion was declining in its influence on American life. The nadir came in 1970, when seventy percent saw religion as declining in influence and only fourteen percent thought of it as increasing. But in each of four annual Gallup reports beginning in 1983, pluralities, reaching as high as forty-eight percent in 1985, thought religion was increasing in influence on the nation.

It would be one of those inexplicable conflicts that some people love to find in public opinion surveys if religion indeed were becoming more important to Americans even as common religious strictures, such as ones against premarital sex and abortion, were becoming more widely disregarded. But a closer look at the Gallup findings suggests that it is not the case. To a large extent, people who say there is a religious revival are talking about a phenomenon they regard as occurring among others, not themselves. Many Americans are quite religious. But as a nation, several important measures show religiosity to be slightly declining, or, at best, staying constant.

Off and on, Gallup has been asking people since 1957 whether "religion can answer all or most of today's problems," or whether instead "religion is old-fashioned and out of date." In 1957, eighty-one percent said religion was the answer to all or most problems and seven percent said it was out of date. That strong expression of faith has waned some, however, so that in 1986, after a steady downward trend, fifty-seven percent told Gallup interviewers that religion was the answer to all or most problems, and twenty-three percent said religion was passé.

In another measure, since 1952 Gallup has regularly asked people whether they regard religion as very important, fairly important, or not very important in their own lives. That first year seventy-five percent said religion was very important. In 1980 only fifty-five percent took that view, and in annual polls since then the figure has held steady, at fifty-five or fifty-six percent.

One basic indicator, attendance at a church or synagogue, has remained flat for some two decades. In several surveys in 1958, forty-nine percent of the people interviewed by Gallup said they had been at a church or synagogue in the previous seven days. In the following years it declined slightly, so that in 1967 the figure was at forty-three percent. Since then, reports by Gallup show church attendance staying just below that level, ranging narrowly between forty and forty-two percent in studies issued for twelve separate years, including one in 1986.

In thrust, such findings show religion to be important for a majority of Americans—but not, despite frequent assertions, of *growing* importance.

THE GENDER GAP

I F EVER THERE WAS A POLITICAL PHENOMENON
that lent itself to wildly varying interpretations, it has
been the gender gap, the difference in voting preferences
between men and women that first came to national attention in 1980 with the election of Ronald Reagan.

According to *New York Times/CBS* election-day surveys
that year, men overwhelmingly chose Reagan over Jimmy
Carter, by fifty-four to thirty-seven percent. Women were
evenly divided, forty-five percent for Carter, forty-six percent
for Reagan. By contrast, the same pollsters had found no such
pattern four years earlier, with men and women both divid-

ing fifty percent for Carter, forty-eight percent for Gerald Ford.

Among the first interpretations was one that is still often heard: that the gender gap signified fear on the part of many women that Reagan was too bellicose, and might take the country to war. Thus, in that view, all or most of the difference in the vote was laid to women; it was believed that they, not men, were changing the way they voted. In addition, it was believed that the response was one aimed at Reagan personally, not at other Republicans.

As time passed, though, the same gender gap occurred in numerous lesser elections. My own preelection polls in the state of Virginia in 1981 showed the Democratic and Republican candidates for governor tied among men but the Democrat ahead by fifteen points among women, and, therefore, winning easily. Later, in 1982, 1984, and 1986, the women's vote was cited as decisive for the Democrats in many gubernatorial and Senate contests.

According to an analysis by the Women's Campaign Fund, the women's vote tipped the balance for the Democrats in nine Senate races in 1986. In one state, North Dakota, the Republican won by nine points among men, but lost narrowly because of the gender gap, and because more women than men turned out to vote.

At about the time of the 1981 and 1982 elections, new gender-gap theories were introduced. One was that there were attitudinal differences between working and nonworking women, that entry into the workplace, especially in inferior jobs, was pushing women away from the Republicans and toward the Democrats. My surveys in Virginia tended to confirm such a theory. But in later polls that I worked on, and in some by other agencies, just the opposite occurred: housewives leaned more heavily to the Democratic side than did working women.

Some Republicans began saying that the shifts taking place had little to do with changes among women, that what was really taking place was a shift among men, toward the Republicans. Reagan's macho image was not a weakness after all, this view had it. It had little or no effect on women but was said to be drawing millions of men toward the president. That proposition, surprising when first advanced, seemed as logical as most.

Also put forth was the idea that the gender gap had nothing to do with issues, but rather that it simply reflected men's and women's difference in party affiliation. More women than men were Democrats, thus higher proportions of women opposed Reagan and the Republicans.

The theorizing did not stop there. Another hypothesis was that Reagan's positions and those of other Republicans on so-called "women's issues" such as abortion and the Equal Rights Amendment angered feminists and other women.

In line with that came an embellishment: that the gender gap was mostly a reaction to Reagan's economic and social policies. Women as a group have been worse off than men financially and therefore hurt more by domestic budget cuts. In addition, women tend to be more compassionate, and thus more likely than men to be critical of inequities in Reagan's, and the Republicans', economic programs.

At several points I examined each of these theories through *Post/ABC News* opinion polls and a look at the historical record. My findings showed most of them to be of little worth, but some were holding up well.

THEORY NUMBER ONE: Women are more concerned than men about issues of war and peace.

Historically, women have been more fearful than men about war, more likely to oppose use of military force under any circumstances, and thus were more likely to take a harsher view of Reagan. But such factors would seem to have little bearing on candidates in Senate races, and none at all in gubernatorial elections. Logically, therefore, they could account for only a small part of the gender gap.

In two *Post/ABC News* polls at the end of 1983, a period right after the deaths of the Marines in Beirut and the invasion of Grenada, I found small differences in the views of men and women on Reagan's actions. Among Republicans, women slightly more than men—forty-three percent to thirty-nine percent—said the president's actions were increasing the chances of war. (For both sexes, that seemed a high level of concern, given Reagan's popularity among Republicans.) Among Democrats, sixty-seven percent of the men and seventy-seven percent of the women felt Reagan was increasing the chances of war. Thus, on the war-and-peace issue, there was a mild gender gap. I repeated this test in later polls, and found much the same result.

Conclusion: Perceptions of bellicosity are a factor in the gender gap, but a relatively small one. If concern over war were eliminated, the gender gap would still exist.

THEORY NUMBER TWO: The gender gap was really a movement by men toward Reagan. Women were standing still.

This view was promoted by Republicans and some independent analysts who cited Reagan's sharp vote-getting ability among men. But it is flawed—failing, for one thing, to take into account the gender gap in elections below the presidential level. In addition, Gallup poll studies from 1975 through 1984 show that it was definitely women who were moving, and men standing still.

In 1975, twenty-four percent of all men identified themselves as Republicans and thirty-nine percent Democrats in the Gallup poll. In 1984, those figures increased by two points and three points respectively, leaving men essentially unchanged in party affiliation, with a five-point decline in the number thinking of themselves as independents.

Women, however, underwent substantial change in those years. In 1975, twenty-seven percent of the women in Gallup polls listed themselves as Republicans and forty-two percent as Democrats. In 1984, only twenty-four percent said they were Republicans, forty-seven percent listed themselves as Democrats.

Conclusion: The gender gap is indeed a female phenomenon.

THEORY NUMBER THREE: The gender gap reflects nothing more than party affiliation, with men tending to be Republicans and women Democrats.

If true, this wouldn't be much of an explanation, failing to explain why the sexes differ in party identification at all. But it is not true, anyway. There are clear gender gaps within the parties—splits between Republican men and women, and Democratic men and women, on certain issues.

Conclusion: The gender gap signifies differences in views between men and women on particular issues, not only on support for Reagan, and it cuts across party lines.

THEORY NUMBER FOUR: Reagan's positions on so-called women's issues, such as abortion and the Equal Rights Amendment, have led to the gender gap.

This one does not hold up well, either. Feminists were as vocal as any group in their opposition to Reagan and, often, to other Republicans. But men have been as likely as women to take feminist positions. They have supported ERA as much as or more than women have, and there has been little difference between the sexes in views toward abortion.

Conclusion: It is not "women's issues" *per se* that have made for the gender gap.

THEORY NUMBER FIVE: The gender gap is mostly a reaction to Reagan's social policies, and those of other Republicans.

This explanation stood up better than any other. Almost all polls showed a substantial difference between men and women on Reagan's handling of the needy. The differences existed in both parties to about the same extent—showing them to be gender-related, not matters of partisanship.

I merged the data from several *Washington Post/ABC News* polls to get a larger, more reliable sample. What I found in them was that forty-six percent of Republican women, but only twenty-six percent of Republican men, felt Reagan administration cuts in social programs had created hardship for many people. Among Democrats the same kind of split existed, but to a lesser extent. Thus, in the same polls, seventy-two percent of Democratic women and sixty-four percent of Democratic men said Reagan's policies were creating hardship for the many.

In a sense, spending cuts may be defined as women's issues in that women suffer the most from them. Many feminists do take that position. From that perspective, at least some women's issues may be regarded as accounting for the gender gap.

Conclusion: While it may not be the only factor, it is social-policy differences between candidates that largely explain the gender gap. Where such differences exist between the parties or in individual election contests, women are more likely to vote for the candidate who advocates sharing. Most often, when the situation arises, that means voting for the Democrat.

One social issue—what to do about pornography—has revealed such gigantic splits between men and women as to dwarf other gender-gap differences.

In February, 1986, a *Washington Post/ABC News* poll found that men were fairly evenly divided on whether newsstand sales of all kinds of magazines should be permitted and on whether the laws dealing with pornography were strict enough. By more than two to one in the poll, men did not think pornography was damaging to adults who saw it.

The views of women could not be more different. By about three to one, women said newsstands should not be allowed to sell pornographic magazines and that laws against pornography were not strict enough. A majority of women also thought pornography was harmful to adults who saw it.

At the time of the survey, the Supreme Court was considering whether to rule on a 1984 Indianapolis statute that had banned pornography on the grounds that it discriminated against women by exploiting and degrading them, and could lead to violent crimes against them. Civil libertarians protested the statute, charging that it violated the First Amendment. A lower court agreed, ruling that the ban amounted to "thought control."

At the Supreme Court, the only woman justice, Sandra Day O'Connor, gave no indication of her views of the case, but said she wanted to hear oral arguments. Not enough other justices joined her in that, so there was no hearing.

Almost a dozen cities had been preparing statutes like Indianapolis's at the time, and the dispute created an unusual alliance, with religious conservatives and radical feminists supporting the ban on pornography. Librarians, booksellers, and civil libertarians opposed it.

The split by sex in the *Post/ABC News* poll was the largest I recall having seen on any issue. One question in the survey asked,

> *Do you think laws on pornography in this country are too strict, not strict enough, or just about right?*

Overwhelmingly, men were satisfied with things as they were, but women seemed disgusted:

Percentage in 1986 saying laws on pornography are . . .

	(of men)	(of women)
. . . too strict	10%	2%
. . . not strict enough	41%	72%
. . . about right	47%	23%
. . . no opinion	2%	2%

I checked these tables over several times, looking for errors in them, but found none.

THE ECONOMY AND POLITICS

The U.S. Economy Is Healthier Than in Decades

—Headline, *New York Times,* March 16, 1986

Gloomy Data Making Economists Uncertain on Outlook for Growth

—Headline, *New York Times,* March 17, 1986

SOME ECONOMISTS MAINTAIN THAT THE NA-tional debt has grown so huge that it will surely reduce the standard of living for generations of Americans as bills come due. Others say the debt, when viewed in proportion to the gross national product, is not all that high and can be gradually eliminated through growth in the economy, inflation, increased taxes, or a deliberate reduction in government spending.

The economists are not only in conflict, they are also in the dark. Like pollsters, they are better at explaining what already happened than at looking ahead. With good reason it is said that an economist is someone who has predicted one hundred of the last three recessions, and one hundred and three of the last three recoveries.

Since the experts have such problems, it goes without saying that ordinary people simply cannot understand the complexities of the national debt, or international trade imbalances, or the gamut of economic issues that are so important to us all.

Yet it is the status of the economy, or the perception of its status, that dominates the thoughts of the many about public affairs. A belief that the economy is in good shape, or heading upward, leads people to give the president a favorable approval rating, to have a higher regard for his political party, to think the nation is headed in the right direction. Perceptions of a downturn result in just the opposite conclusions. It is taken as a given by many analysts that the main political decision people make, which candidate to select for president, is largely an estimate of how he will handle the economy, or how he did handle it in his first term. Only one other concern, the threat of war, is potent enough to compete with the economy as a voting issue in most presidential contests.

Logic suggests that the economy may fade some as an electoral issue in periods of expansion and confidence (we don't worry much about our health when we feel fine), and that other matters will rise in prominence. Not every presidential election, therefore, has to be one centering on inflation, interest rates, unemployment, deficits, and the like. But the late seventies and eighties have mostly been years of economic fragility, with high unemployment, excruciating problems in farming, the auto industry, and other areas, and a national and personal debt climbing to unprecedented levels. Such conditions make the economy more important than ever in people's choice for a president.

Growing distrust of government has had the same effect. Being told almost incessantly that social programs have been a failure and an enormous waste, seeing almost daily instances of deceit, incompetence, and personal corruption in

Washington, persuaded that elected officials do not care about them, people quite understandably stop looking for frills and select the candidate who offers the best hope of being a capable money manager.

From all this, one question arises: can ordinary people really use the economy as the basis of their vote for president if they have an extremely limited understanding of economic issues? The answer is yes, they can and do, for better or worse. First and foremost, they judge the economy by their own experience with it. By that standard, at any given time there are three national economies: one for the well-to-do, one for the poor, and one for those in between.

Opinion surveys show how strongly people's own circumstances affect their political views. A *Washington Post/ABC News* poll done in February, 1986, was typical. In it, the main economic question, asked almost every time we did a survey, was, "Do you think the nation's economy is getting better, getting worse, or staying about the same?"

Overall, almost three people in ten in that survey thought the economy was getting better, and a like proportion thought it was getting worse. More than four in ten thought things were staying the same. Beneath the symmetrical distribution, however, were extreme differences in outlook based on individual circumstances. The better off a person was, the rosier the economy appeared. The relationship was very direct:

Among the thirteen percent of the people interviewed with household incomes of more than $50,000 a year, optimism outpaced pessimism by four to one. For those with household incomes below $30,000 (six of every ten people interviewed), pessimists outnumbered optimists slightly. And among the one person in five at the bottom, with household incomes below $12,000, there were twice as many pessimists as optimists.

In each income group except the highest one, the largest single block consisted of those who said the economy was neither improving nor getting worse. My interpretation, based on responses to other questions in the survey, was that "staying the same" tended to be a favorable comment when it came from those at the top, an unfavorable one from those toward the bottom. That would mean that among people at the top, as many as six out of seven were satisfied with the state of the economy; at the bottom, four of every five were dissatisfied. Comparisons between the two groups gave weight to such reasoning.

At the top, unemployment was a blip, measuring two percent. At the bottom, twenty-three percent were unemployed, and of those working, more than four in ten had only part-time jobs. At the top, seven of every ten had spouses with full-time jobs, a major financial benefit; at the bottom, fewer than three in ten.

There were nine times as many college graduates in the $50,000-and-up income range as in the $12,000-and-below category. Those better off tended to be younger, with only five percent being of retirement age. By comparison, forty percent in the lowest income category were retired.

These people at the top and bottom income levels account for one third of all adult Americans. For them, personal experience—their income level—is often all they need to know about the economy. For most at these economic extremes it also determined their politics.

In the top income group, among those who felt the economy was improving, more than eight in ten who voted in 1984 had supported Reagan, and more than seven in ten said they planned to vote Republican in the 1986 congressional elections.

In the bottom group, among those who thought the economy was getting worse, more than half had voted for Mondale in 1984, and seven in ten said they were backing Democrats in the 1986 congressional races.

This *Post/ABC News* poll of February, 1986, was typical, not an exception. There are wealthy Democrats and poor Republicans, of course. But cumulatively, what we see is that personal experience with the economy strongly determines partisanship and voting behavior for both groups. The correlation is about as total as may be found in politics.

But there is an ebb and flow in thinking about the economy. A month later, in March, 1986, optimism took a sharp upswing; in subsequent months it declined radically. Movement like that has enormous political consequences.

The financially comfortable as well as the poor take note of recessions, periods of high unemployment, national deficits. One group is always more optimistic, the other more skeptical, but both respond to current events. It is among the broad range of people in between, however, those of moderate to middle incomes, where the main buffeting occurs. They are the ones who are most optimistic that good times will push them up a level on the economic plateau, most fearful that setbacks will find them unable to keep up.

It was this broad middle, making up two-thirds of all Americans, that determined the swing in mood from uncertainty over the economy in 1981, to gloom during the recession of 1982, to general optimism through most of 1983 and 1984, to another downturn—mostly uncertainty once again—beginning in mid-1985.

Electorally, their high economic spirits in 1984 led to the easy triumph for Reagan over Mondale; their subsequent worries in 1986 to the gain of eight U.S. Senate seats for the Democrats. From one period to the next, there had been a substantial souring among the broad middle.

In September, 1984, in response to the standard question on the state of the economy, forty-five percent of the people in a *Post/ABC News* national survey said the economy was improving and only twenty-four percent said it was getting worse, an overall ratio of almost two to one. In the broad middle, those with household incomes between $12,000 and $50,000, the ratio was five to two. It was such a circumstance that led to Reagan's sweeping victory.

Two years later, in September, 1986, the number of optimists in the *Post/ABC News* poll was down by one-third and pessimism up substantially: only thirty percent said the economy was improving, thirty-four percent said it was getting worse. The stage was set for the shellacking the Republicans took in the U.S. Senate.

■   ■   ■

The 1984 Reagan landslide serves as a classic case of the dominance of the economy in voting. Reagan was seen as less capable than Mondale in many important ways, and less in tune with deeply important American values. But he was judged better able to handle the economy, and especially better able to protect people's own stake in it. That was all he needed.

Our September, 1984, poll provided ample illustration. In it, Reagan led Mondale by sixteen points overall. More than coincidentally, he also came out sixteen points ahead when people were asked, "Under which one, Reagan or Mondale, do you think you personally will be better off financially?"

Many people in the survey saw Mondale as preferable at reducing the threat of nuclear war, felt that Mondale was more likely to keep the country out of any kind of war, that Mondale more than Reagan sided with the average citizen and not special interests, that Mondale's programs would be fairer to all people, and that black Americans had been hurt, not helped, by Reagan during his first term. A good number also disapproved of the way Reagan had handled the nation's economy.

These were all reasons to support Mondale. But each paled as a factor for voters who thought they themselves would be better off under Reagan. In some instances, the pattern was startling. On the matter of reducing the threat of nuclear war, for example, Mondale was seen as the better choice by forty-five percent of the people interviewed. But those in that group who felt they themselves would be better off financially under Reagan came out in support of the president's reelection by more than two to one, sixty-eight to thirty-one percent.

The pattern was pervasive:

- *Almost four in ten said they had the same views as the Democrats on most issues. But those who also felt that they personally would do better under Reagan sup-*

ported the president by four to one, seventy-nine to nineteen percent—giving him a margin equivalent to about 8 million votes.

- *Sixty-two percent of the people interviewed felt Reagan sided with special interests, not the average person. Among such people, those who felt they would be better off under Reagan backed him by five to one.*
- *Similarly, fifty-three percent felt Mondale's programs would be fairer to all people. But among them, those who also felt they themselves would be better off under Reagan told our poll interviewers that they supported his reelection by almost three to one.*
- *More than a third of the people interviewed felt taxes should be increased to cope with the mounting federal budget deficits, as Mondale had recommended. But if these people also felt they themselves would be better off under Reagan, they supported the president by five to one.*

That survey was taken early in the election campaign, but there was no sign that feelings ever changed. Reagan eventually won by fifty-nine to forty-one percent, very close to the sixteen-point margin found in September.

I do not want to make too much of these numbers. Many of those who felt Mondale would be better than Reagan at preventing nuclear war, or better in some other way, probably felt he would be only slightly better. There was no widespread sentiment that Reagan, for example, was about to bring about a nuclear holocaust. Had the threat of nuclear war become a key campaign issue, perhaps people would not have been as likely to vote their pocketbook.

The essential finding nevertheless remains crystal clear: perceptions of the economy and of financial self-interest tended to dominate people's thinking in 1984. It was not that other issues were unimportant to people. They were, and always will be, very important. It is just that the economy is most often much more important.

THE MEDIA EFFECT
Presidential Debates, 1984

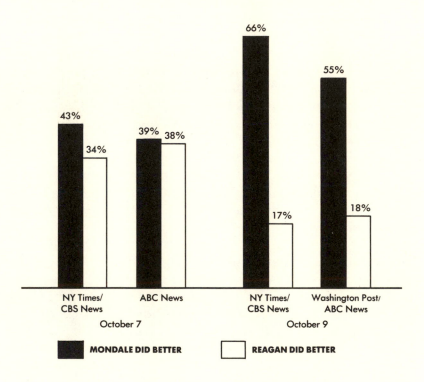

Any doubts as to the power of the news media to alter public thinking should be dispelled by the progression depicted here, in the days following the first campaign debate between Ronald Reagan and Walter Mondale. On October 7, 1984, the night of the debate, a *New York Times/CBS News* poll and an *ABC News* poll showed narrow pluralities picking Mondale as having done better. Immediately afterward, TV and print accounts focused on Reagan's poor performance and raised questions as to whether he was too old to be president. Subsequent polls, taken only two days later, showed how dramatically such coverage had affected the public: suddenly Mondale was seen as the debate winner by enormous majorities.

CONCERN OVER SOCIAL SECURITY
Will It Survive? 1985

Q. Do you think Social Security will or will not exist when it is time for you to retire?

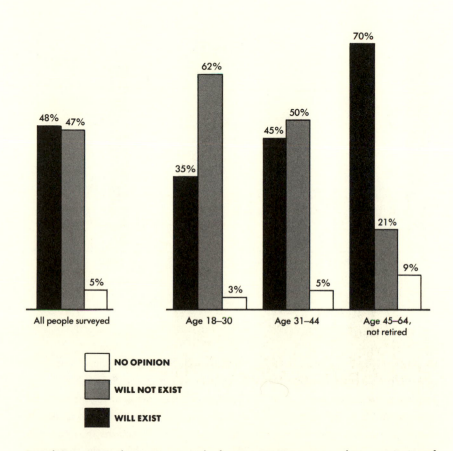

Social Security is the most revered of government programs, but a majority of Americans under age forty-five, including an enormous majority age thirty or under, have been concerned for years that the system will be defunct before they reach retirement age. *Washington Post/ABC News* polls in 1982, 1983, and 1984 showed even slightly more pessimism in the younger age groups than did this 1985 survey.

[From an October, 1985, *Washington Post/ABC News* poll.]

SHIFTING VIEWS OF ISRAEL AND EGYPT
Are They Reliable Allies? 1981—86

Q. . . . Would you say that [Israel . . . Egypt] is a reliable ally of the United States or not?

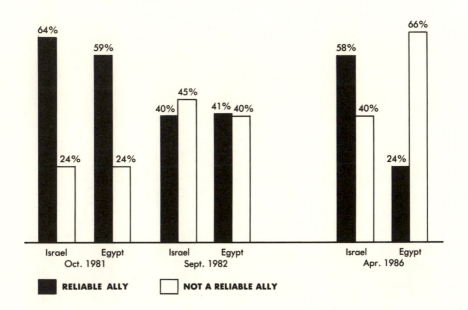

Regard for Israel as a reliable ally of the United States declined among Americans after the invasion of Lebanon in 1982, and was at a low in September of that year after the massacre of Palestinians (by Lebanese). After that, regard for Israel rebounded. As for Egypt, one aspect of the legacy of Anwar Sadat was to elevate that nation in the eyes of Americans, so that in 1981 it too was thought of by most Americans as a reliable ally. By 1986, however, much of that feeling was gone.

[From *Washington Post/ABC News* polls on dates given. The full question asked was: *I'm going to mention the names of some foreign countries. For each, I'd like you to tell me whether you think that country is a reliable ally of the United States—one that can be trusted to cooperate with the United States in almost any circumstance—or not. Would you say that [Israel . . . Egypt] is a reliable ally of the United States or not?* Other countries were mentioned; results are given here only for Israel and Egypt.]

THE SOCIAL REVOLUTION AND ABORTION
Changing Attitudes, 1965–87

Q. Please tell me whether or not you think it should be possible for a pregnant woman to obtain a legal abortion in the following circumstances (percentages show those favoring legal abortion in each instance):

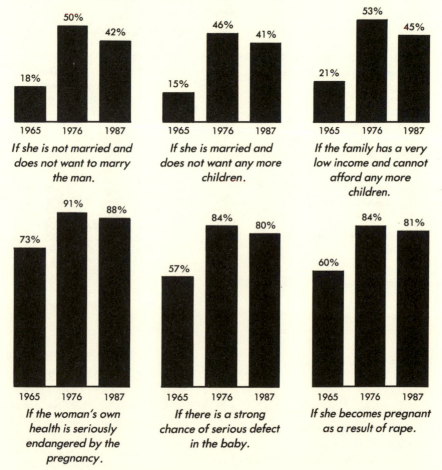

If she is not married and does not want to marry the man.
1965: 18% · 1976: 50% · 1987: 42%

If she is married and does not want any more children.
1965: 15% · 1976: 46% · 1987: 41%

If the family has a very low income and cannot afford any more children.
1965: 21% · 1976: 53% · 1987: 45%

If the woman's own health is seriously endangered by the pregnancy.
1965: 73% · 1976: 91% · 1987: 88%

If there is a strong chance of serious defect in the baby.
1965: 57% · 1976: 84% · 1987: 80%

If she becomes pregnant as a result of rape.
1965: 60% · 1976: 84% · 1987: 81%

There has been a massive easing in public thinking about abortion since the social revolution of the 1960s, as these findings show. The slight decline in support in the 1980s reflected here is at variance with some other surveys showing recent increases in support for abortion on demand, not decreases. Those differences are minor ones at this stage, having no bearing on the overall pattern.

[From polls by the National Opinion Research Center (NORC), University of Chicago.]

ECONOMIC SELF-INTEREST AND PRESIDENTIAL CAMPAIGNS
The Pocketbook Gets the Votes, 1984

If 1988 turns out to be like 1984, the question of pure, unadulterated economic self-interest could emerge as a dominant factor in the presidential election. On many matters, large numbers of people thought better of Mondale than of Reagan in 1984. Even so, they tended overwhelmingly to support Reagan, as long as they felt they personally would be better off financially under him.

Voters who feel they will do better financially under Reagan, but...	SUPPORT REAGAN	SUPPORT MONDALE
	(in millions of voters*)	
Feel Reagan sides with special interests	16.5	2.3
Feel Mondale sides with the average citizen	15.6	2.2
Feel blacks have been hurt, not helped, by Reagan	11.0	3.0
Feel Mondale more likely to keep U.S. out of war	9.4	3.0
Feel Mondale programs will be fairer to all	9.2	3.5
Feel Republicans are more conservative than they themselves on most issues	8.2	2.3
Say they have the same views as Democrats on most issues	7.9	1.9
Feel Mondale more than Reagan will reduce the threat of nuclear war	6.9	3.1
Disapprove Reagan's handling of foreign affiars	6.1	2.9
Disapprove Reagan's handling of the economy	4.1	2.2

[From a *Washington Post/ABC News* poll of 1,507 registered voters in September, 1984. *Figures are based on the percentages in the poll matched against the actual election turnout of just over 92 million voters.]

A REAGAN REPORT CARD
The Public Gives Him a C Average, 1985

Through most of his presidency, the conventional wisdom was that Ronald Reagan was extremely popular with the American people. That was certainly the perception at the beginning of 1985, after his landslide reelection victory over Walter Mondale. Nevertheless, this "report card" from a *Washington Post/ABC News* poll in January, 1985, shows the public giving the Reagan administration only mediocre grades on most matters, with a median score of C.

Q. *I'm going to mention some national problems, and for each I'd like you to give the Reagan administration a grade of A, B, C, D, or F for fail, for the way it handled that problem over the past four years.*

	Median score	Percent giving grades of . . .		
		A or B	C	D or F
Bringing Inflation Under Control	2.9	62	21	16
Improving the Nation's Economy	2.8	59	22	18
Dealing with the Soviet Union	2.5	48	23	24
Reducing Unemployment	2.4	47	23	24
Establishing a Sound Foreign Policy	2.4	47	23	27
Improving the Quality of the Public Schools	2.3	41	26	24
Reducing the Chances of Nuclear War	2.2	38	25	29
Reducing Crime	2.1	31	33	27
Handling the Federal Budget Deficits	2.0	32	28	34
Reducing Poverty	1.8	28	29	39
Dealing with Toxic Wastes and Other Environmental Problems	1.8	24	31	36
OVERALL POINT AVERAGE	2.3			

[Figures are from a nationwide *Washington Post/ABC News* telephone survey January 11–16, 1985. The median score is figured on a scale of 0 to 4, with 4 = A, and 0 = F. The grade percentages do not add up to 100, because some people did not assign grades in come categories.]

UNDERSTANDING POLITICAL REALIGNMENT
Reluctant Republicans, 1985

For many Americans, voting has become a choice between one political party they regard as uninviting, the Republicans, and one they consider ineffectual, the Democrats. The findings here, taken from a poll in June, 1985, at the height of GOP gains of the 1980s, illustrate the point.

Q. Which of these statements would you say represents a greater danger for the country?

- *The Democrats in Congress will go too far in keeping costly government services that are wasteful and out of date.*

or

- *The Republicans will go too far in helping the rich and cutting needed government services that benefit average Americans as well as the poor.*

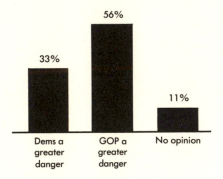

Q. Overall, which party, the Republicans or the Democrats, do you trust to do a better job with the problems the nation faces over the next few years?

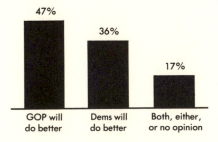

[From a *Washington Post/ABC News* poll of June, 1985.]

PART FOUR

SCANDALS AND POLITCAL REALIGNMENT

I think the Watergate tragedy is the greatest tragedy this country has ever suffered.

—Senator Sam Ervin, 1973

In many ways, Iran-contra is worse than Watergate.

—Archibald Cox, Watergate special prosecutor, 1987

NIXON'S AND REAGAN'S
ASSAULTS ON DEMOCRACY

O N NOVEMBER 13, 1986, PRESIDENT REAGAN gave his first televised address to the nation on the secret sales of arms to Iran. Americans had been confounded by the sketchy reports, first made in the Beirut magazine *Al Shiraa* ten days earlier, that for more than a year the United States had been sending weapons and spare parts to the regime of the Ayatollah Khomeini in hopes of freeing hostages taken in Lebanon.

Reagan began his talk by criticizing the press for spreading rumors from "unnamed government officials of my administration" and other unidentified sources. "Well, now you're going to hear the facts from a White House source, and you know my name," he declared.

At that early stage, with the press groping to uncover the story, it was easy for Reagan to find details in the coverage that were incomplete, technically incorrect, sometimes just plain wrong. In citing them the president tried to malign all the coverage. At one point in his talk he seized on a few details and said, "All these reports are quite exciting, but as far as we're concerned, not one of them is true."

Later, in the summer of 1987, it was revealed that the tactic of focusing on minor press errors had been carefully planned, worked up by the president and his advisers to divert attention from the actual dealings. It was an approach similar to Richard Nixon's in Watergate, when he told his aides, "I want you all to stonewall it."

Notes from a meeting between Reagan and his top cabinet members and advisers three days before his speech showed Reagan saying a statement was needed "for all of us." It was to refer to "no bargaining with terrorists," "no ransom for terrorists," and a "hope for moderate government" in Iran. "We don't talk TOWS [the missiles sent to Iran], don't talk specifics."

In his address, Reagan followed that line. But he made a number of statements of his own that were incorrect and misleading.

He said he had "authorized the transfer of small amounts of defensive weapons and spare parts for defensive systems to Iran. . . . These modest deliveries, taken together, could easily fit into a single cargo plane." In fact, the weapons that had been sent were as offensive as defensive, and they could not begin to fit in one plane.

He said that since the "contact began with Iran, there's been no evidence of Iranian government complicity in acts of terrorism against the United States." But there had been additional terrorist incidents, more hostages had been taken, and administration leaders believed that Iran was responsible.

He said emphatically, "We did not—repeat—did not trade

weapons or anything else for hostages, nor will we." It was later revealed that the first aim of the dealings with Iran was the recovery of hostages.

Reagan also said the dialogue with Iranian officials was in line with one of "America's longstanding goals in the region . . . to help preserve Iran's independence from Soviet domination." If so, that backfired. The Ayatollah had been as hostile to the Soviet Union as toward the United States, or almost as hostile. But by the summer of 1987, a Soviet delegation was in Tehran, negotiating to reopen a natural-gas pipeline that had been shut during the eight-year Khomeini regime, and for the creation of a second railroad link between the two nations.

Toward the close of his address, Reagan said, "I've always operated on the belief that, given the facts, the American people will make the right decision. I believe that to be true now. . . . As in the past, I ask you for your support."

My feeling that night, similar to that of many people, I am sure, was that Reagan had raised more questions than he had answered. It just seemed inconceivable to me that Americans would find any secret dealings with the Ayatollah to be acceptable. I noted that not even once in his talk to the people could the president bring himself to mention the name Ayatollah Khomeini.

As soon as Reagan was done speaking on Thursday evening, my polling colleagues at *ABC News* did a quick nationwide survey, asking just a few questions. We reported their findings in the *Washington Post* on Saturday morning, November 15.

The survey showed four of every five people opposed to trading arms for hostages, a majority doubting Reagan's version of what had taken place, and an even larger majority saying that, even if he was telling the truth, the policy was unsound. By two to one, the people interviewed felt that trading arms for hostages would lead to an increase in hostage-taking.

That Saturday I was out for much of the morning and early afternoon. The phone was ringing when I came home. "This is the White House switchboard. We've been trying to locate you," the caller said. "Please hold." Eventually I was connected to Richard Wirthlin, the president's pollster.

Wirthlin had seen the account of ABC's poll in the *Post* that morning but noticed no mention in it of Reagan's approval rating. Did I have anything on the approval rating? he asked. I told him I did not but that perhaps my colleague Jeff Alderman at ABC did. We talked briefly. I asked how damaging he felt the incident was to Reagan. He said it was clearly the most serious crisis of his presidency. Wirthlin then called Alderman, who was not at home. The pollster left a message, and Alderman called him back, reaching him in the office of the White House chief of staff, Donald Regan. In times of crisis, pollsters to presidents are near at hand.

Shortly afterward, Reagan took a different tack from Wirthlin, minimizing the importance of the Iran affair in an interview published in *Time* magazine. "After my speech, some eighty-four percent of those people who called in supported me," Reagan told columnist Hugh Sidey. "It was the biggest outpouring of calls they've ever had. The letters coming in are in my favor. This is a Beltway bloodletting," he said, suggesting that the story was of interest only inside the highway that encircles the nation's capital.

Again, Reagan took off after the press. "There is bitter bile in my throat these days," Sidey quoted him as saying. "I've never seen the sharks circling like they now are with blood in the water. What is driving me up the wall is that this wasn't a failure until the press got a tip from that rag in Beirut and began to play it up."

From the beginning of the Iran-contra debacle, as Wirthlin's request for the approval rating and the president's reference to calls and letters showed, a chief concern in the White House was public opinion.

As I have noted earlier, the approval rating is suspect as a gauge of what the public thinks about a president's handling of his job. But it is extremely important nevertheless. A high approval rating is often a protective wall around a president, discouraging many would-be attackers. A low rating is an open door, inviting criticism and confrontation.

That is especially true for the way the news media deal with a president. A high rating seems to restrain many reporters and editors; a low one makes him fair game. A worthwhile scholarly paper could be done, I am sure, on the correlation between the toughness of news coverage and the approval ratings during Reagan's presidency and Jimmy Carter's before him.

The same pattern exists, to a lesser degree, in the way members of Congress deal with a president. Many in Congress are too sophisticated to fear a high approval rating. Instead, they use it as a crutch, citing a high rating as a rationale for a vote or other action that they themselves favor but that might be unpopular with constituents.* But some on Capitol Hill, like so many in the press corps, do hold a high approval rating in awe, deferring to the president while he possesses it, thumbing their nose at him when he doesn't.

In those first weeks, Reagan did everything he could to shore up his ratings. With his five TV appearances in less than three weeks, he seemed almost in an election-eve mode, reaching as deeply as he could for support.

The televised appeals did not work for him this time. As revelations continued to gush, the inaccuracies of Reagan's own statements about the affair were brought out. New polls showed majorities of the public believing that he was lying, and his approval ratings plummeted. In October, a *New York Times/CBS News* poll had his rating at sixty-seven percent; a month later it had dropped twenty-one points, and it stayed below fifty percent through the end of the year.

As the scandal burgeoned, Reagan changed tactics. Except

---

* Voting on the 1981 tax cuts, which mainly benefited the wealthy, comes to mind here. Legislators who personally favored the cuts, but who feared constituent opposition, could grumble about the tax plan, then rationalize their vote of approval on the grounds that Reagan's high approval rating gave him a mandate for change, and that it would be wrong for them to stand in the way.

for cameo appearances and his State of the Union address, he stayed off TV for months. For all intents and purposes, it was not until March, 1987, that Reagan reappeared. Making a televised speech on March 4, he took note of his absence. "For the past three months, I've been silent on the revelations about Iran," he said. "You must have been thinking, 'Well, why doesn't he tell us what's happening? Why doesn't he just speak to us as he has in the past when we've faced troubles or tragedies?'

"Others of you, I guess, were thinking, 'What's he doing hiding out in the White House?' "

It was to be another two weeks before the president held a nationally televised press conference, making a full four months between such sessions with the Washington press corps.

Out of nowhere, the Iran-contra debacle had assumed the dimensions of the Watergate scandal of fourteen years earlier. It quickly threatened to destroy Reagan's presidency.

One person who did not see it that way, at least not publicly, was Richard Nixon, who rather inanely told a group of Republican governors in December, 1986, that "it is not going to be another Watergate, as long as you stay ahead of the curve." Nixon, of course, was not the best prognosticator. He never thought Watergate itself was much of a scandal either, at least not until it was too late for him.

In fact, there were many parallels between Watergate and the Iran-contra debacle.

Both were the result of presidential activities that *had to be* furtive because they were both illegal and unacceptable in a democracy. Had Congress and the American people known of them in advance, they never could have been undertaken.

In Watergate, Richard Nixon set up the "plumbers" in the White House to serve as a spying unit, tapping people's phones, including those of reporters and administration aides, and conducting break-ins. Private agents were hired to disrupt the campaigns of political opponents. He used the

CIA and the FBI where he could, but the bulk of the dirty work was kept from them.

The motives behind the various Watergate crimes were essentially political, aimed at easing the reelection of Nixon by manipulating public opinion through illegal or simply repugnant means. But in part the crimes also had to do with keeping certain governmental actions, such as the bombing of Cambodia, a neutral nation, hidden from the American people.

In the Iran-contra affair, there was more of a mix between politics and policy. Reagan turned his National Security Council, an advisory body, into an operational group and had it performing sensitive activities that ordinarily would have been done by the State Department, the Defense Department or the CIA. As in Watergate, many of the actions themselves were so odious that they could not be given over to State or Defense, and few people at the CIA, aside from its director, were let in on them. Each of these departments was to some degree drawn into abetting the scandal, but within sharply constrained limits.

In Watergate and the Iran-contra debacle, thus, a government within a government was set up and private operatives were hired to take part in illegal, undemocratic activities.

In the Iran-contra affair, election politics also figured importantly. The first to plead guilty to felonies were a Republican fundraiser and a White House aide who admitted using tax-exempt funds to help arm the contras. In addition, the fundraiser, Carl R. Channell, pumped some of that money into television ads aimed at damaging congressional incumbents who opposed the president's proposals for creation of spaced-based weaponry, the Strategic Defense Initiative.

In late 1986, one apparent aim of negotiating with Iran was the hope of giving Republican Senate candidates a boost by gaining the release of American hostages. A participant in the dealings, Albert Hakim, testified that "the subject of the elections was definitely discussed during our attempts to try to reestablish our relations with Iran." He described what he called "political pressure" applied just before the elections.

The idea that the president or his men would use the hostages for something that cold and crass lay around the edges of the scandal, hardly mentioned even in the lengthy Senate and House hearings during the summer of 1987.

In both Watergate and the Iran-contra scandal, the two presidents' first reactions were to minimize the wrongdoing and attempt to separate themselves from it. Nixon referred to Watergate as a third-rate break-in; Reagan called his scandal "a collection of rumors." Both claimed lack of first-hand knowledge, saying they were as anxious as anyone else "to get to the bottom of things"; in both instances their aides, when caught, spoke of "deniability," or prior arrangements making it difficult if not impossible to link the president to the actions undertaken.

In Watergate a main operative, Gordon Liddy, shredded papers the morning of the original arrests, and cautioned the attorney general, Richard Kleindienst, that White House aides were involved in the break-in at Democratic headquarters. Kleindienst kept the information to himself, in violation of the law. In the Iran-contra affair, Attorney General Edwin Meese saw to it that close political associates of his, not tough criminal lawyers, would be the first to examine the papers of the main operative, Marine Lt. Col. Oliver North of the National Security Council. In sending cronies to investigate, Meese disregarded pleas from William Weld, the head of the Justice Department's criminal division. Later, North testified that even as Meese's handpicked associates were going over some of his papers, he himself was shredding others.

Both Nixon and Reagan hoped to take the heat off by giving the appearance of cleaning house. Nixon fired his highest aides, chief of staff H.R. Haldeman and domestic adviser John Ehrlichman. Reagan speedily removed his national security adviser, Adm. John W. Poindexter, and North. As the furor continued, he removed his Haldeman, chief of staff Donald Regan.

Nixon and his supporters tried to make the assorted Watergate crimes appear nothing more than politics as usual, noting that Republican campaign offices, as well as those of the Democrats, had been raided. But there was no comparing the occasional dirty tricks committed against Republicans with the organized political spying and sabotage conducted by the Nixon camp.

The equivalent for Reagan and his supporters and aides was their claim that the dealings with Iran were nothing more than sensitive diplomacy that had to be conducted in secret, akin to overtures made by Nixon toward China fifteen years earlier. "Mistakes were made," Reagan admitted, but he said they were ones in procedures, not goals.

The most vociferous advocate of that position was North. In testimony before Congress in July, 1987, North was given the opportunity to press his case for six days, and he caught the fancy of many Americans as he did. At one point North said it was an "ultimate irony," a trick played on the Ayatollah, that Iranian money was made available for funding of the contra rebels.

But North's argument was perverse. To be acceptable in a democracy, covert operations must strive to achieve desirable policy goals that are in the national interest. That clearly was not the case. Instead, as an editorial writer in the *Washington Post* pointed out, the ultimate irony was that "the United States has been embarrassed in front of Arab moderates and European allies, its policy on terrorism has become a mockery, it has given palpable aid and comfort to a detested regime."

Probably no world figure since Adolf Hitler was more despised by Americans than the Ayatollah Khomeini. In December, 1979, a month after the American diplomatic staff was taken hostage at the embassy in Tehran, the *Los Angeles Times* did a poll in which the Ayatollah got an approval rating of two percent. Three years later, in a Gallup poll done for the Chicago Council on Foreign Relations, he got a score of eleven on a "feeling thermometer" in which zero stood for the coldest feeling, one hundred for the warmest. By comparison, Palestine Liberation Organization leader Yassir Arafat, not exactly an American favorite, got a twenty-eight.

There was simply no way that any covert action that helped the Ayatollah could be explained as being in the national interest. In avoiding uttering the name "Khomeini" in talking to the American people, Reagan showed that he recognized that.

The purpose of the dealings from the outset was to gain the freedom of nine Americans taken hostage in Beirut over a period of more than a year. Documents and testimony made public in 1987 made that clear, and showed that an early rationale offered by Reagan and North and others—the hope of opening a dialogue with moderate elements in Iran—was a cover story.

By committing himself to such a trade, hostages for arms, Reagan was terribly deceitful. No world leader had been as outspokenly opposed to dealing with terrorists as Reagan in his public statements; that he should be bartering with their sponsors in private came as a cruel shock.

A second shoe in the Iran scandal fell on November 25, 1986, when Attorney General Edwin Meese revealed that North had used some of the millions from the sale of arms to Iran to fund the contra rebels in Nicaragua during a period when Congress had cut off American aid to them. (In fact, very little money went to the contras. According to House and Senate investigations, of almost $17 million available, $3.5 million made its way to them, primarily in the financing of an air resupply operation.)

This time, Reagan, North, and others did their best to make it appear that the covert operation was in the national interest. North, in his six days in front of Congress, was given an opportunity to put the case in its best light, criticizing Congress for waffling by now extending aid to the contras, now pulling it back.

North made a favorable impression on many Americans, but few accepted his reasoning. More than $1 million came pouring in to an Oliver North Legal Assistance Fund during the two weeks after he began testifying. A *New York Times/*

CBS News poll done on July 9, 1987, two days after he first took the stand, found large numbers thinking of him as patriotic, sincere, honest. But a majority said he had gone too far in his actions, and a majority also felt Reagan was lying in claiming that he had not known that money from the arms sales had been diverted to the contras.

Strangely, North was a more effective lobbyist for the contra cause than Reagan ever had been. In his first four days of testimony, North was allowed to ramble on at length, with no opposing view given as he offered a rationale for violating the congressional ban on aid to the contras. The result, at least temporarily, was to present to the American people another one-sided game of tennis, with North serving the aces. Never had so much been said on behalf of the contras for so long with so many people watching. For days on end in July, 1987, with perhaps 150 million people watching bits and pieces, North made the case for the contras in dramatic terms, lambasting Congress as spineless, inconsistent, and untrustworthy.

No response came from the seventeen legislators on the panel during that time; the format of the hearings called for them to get involved only after their attorneys had completed the interrogation. Thus, there was, again, no true debate over an issue of keen importance to the American people, although so many, for once, were tuned in.

As North testified, the overnight public opinion polls began to show huge bursts of support for the contras. How ironic. In Reagan's worst moment, through the vehicle of a congressional show trial of his governance, the president suddenly seemed on the verge of winning what had always been beyond his reach—public support for overthrowing the Sandinistas.

On July 15, a *Washington Post/ABC News* poll showed forty-three percent of the people interviewed favoring the granting of military aid to the contras, an increase from twenty-nine percent six weeks earlier, and far higher than had been the norm during the Reagan presidency. A *New York Times/CBS News* poll taken July 21 and 22 showed forty percent favoring aid to the contras, substantially higher than previous *Times/CBS* polls.

Findings like these were seized on by Reagan. "The American people are waking up," he said on July 24. But the moment did not linger long. When the committees' counsel were done with their interrogation, there came a counter to North: some sharp commentary by a few of the senators and representatives on the investigative panel. It was not so much that they were critical of aid to the contras; little such opposition was offered. Instead, here and there they were tough on North, casting a good deal of doubt on his honesty and sincerity, as did news accounts and testimony by those who followed him to the witness table.

For the president personally, it soon seemed that North's testimony had provided no real benefit. In a follow-up *Post/ABC News* poll in early August, three of every five people interviewed felt Reagan would not be able to put the scandal behind him, and nine out of ten said he had made either major or minor mistakes in the Iran-contra affair. One question in the survey asked, "Do you think Ronald Reagan himself participated in an organized attempt to cover up the facts about the Iran-contra arms affair, or not?" and more than four in ten said they did think so.

In the brief period between the two *Post/ABC News* polls, public support for aid to the contras began dropping, so that in August only thirty-six percent said they favored it.

There were other important similarities between Watergate and the Iran-contra scandal.

Nixon and Reagan and their supporters tried for long periods to divert attention from their own actions by criticizing the Democrats in Congress and the press for reveling in the scandals. Both at various stages attempted to put the debacles behind them by saying the nation had to get on with its important busness. "I'm not going to wallow in Watergate," said Nixon; "I'm no lame duck," were Reagan's words as the scandal continued to envelop him.

In certain key ways, however, the relationship between Watergate and the Iran-contra scandal was less one of parallels and more one of the first scandal establishing precedents for the way the government, the news media, and Americans at large responded to the second one.

Watergate set the mold. Had there been no Watergate scandal, it seems certain that the response to the Iran-contra affair would have been far slower in forming and, in all probability, much more limp. In the main, *sans* Watergate, in my view, there would have been no lengthy House and Senate hearings at all on the Iran-contra scandal, no special prosecutor appointed, and, therefore, considerably less embarrassing scrutiny of the Reagan presidency. During his term in office, Reagan frequently consulted with Nixon and did his best to help rehabilitate the fallen president. What Nixon bequeathed him, however unintentionally, was a debasing public examination, courtesy of mechanisms that had been put in place because of Watergate.

Watergate was the political crime of the century, dwarfing earlier high governmental corruption such as the Teapot Dome scandal fifty years earlier. In essence, scandals in previous administrations had been about venal actions by greedy men who defiled the public trust for money.

Watergate was a series of crimes committed with the belief in the White House that the American people could not be trusted, that some members of Congress, the press at large, and the people themselves were, in effect, enemies of the president of the United States, obstructions to his goals. Nixon the introvert, always fearful of the public, used dirty tricks to win election, and ruled by cabal.

The Watergate crimes were so horrendous an attack on democracy itself, so without known precedent, that it took a long while for ways of dealing with them to be established. Few have given much consideration, even at this late stage, to this aspect of the scandal.

Two attorneys general, an assistant attorney general, and the head of the FBI had their reputations ruined for either taking part in the Watergate scandal or seeing to it that the investigation was narrowed in its early stages to protect Nixon. The original Justice Department prosecutors were relieved of their duties, replaced by a special prosecutor, after they appeared to have been submissive in their pursuit of the case. The FBI itself was shamed.

In the first months, a bold, clear-eyed Texas congressman, Wright Patman, sought to hold hearings but was thwarted by all the Republicans and some of the Democratic members of his committee; thus Congress did not get down to real business for some ten months after the original Watergate arrests.

With very few exceptions, the press avoided the Watergate story in its early, crucial stages. Only five news agencies— the *Washington Post,* the *New York Times,* the *Los Angeles Times, Time,* and *Newsweek*—had serious investigations. The TV network news operations ignored it entirely.

A study by media critic Ben Bagdikian, mentioned earlier, concluded that "it is possible that more man-hours of investigative journalism were put into the 1962 rumor that John F. Kennedy had been secretly married in 1947 than were assigned to investigate the Watergate affair."*

In addition, and of generally unacknowledged importance, there were no early opinion polls measuring public reaction to the Watergate scandal. The first polls I have been able to locate were done in September, 1972, and released in October, almost four months after Nixon's burglars were caught at Democratic headquarters. And those polls dealt with soft issues, such as whether Watergate was politics as usual. It was not until much later on that the public was asked its views on the severity of the scandal, whether Nixon was being truthful, and the like.

It took more than two long years for Watergate to run its course, slowly, like a tank through mud. As it did, it created deep grooves that remained in place for later use.

The Iran-contra scandal had the same root cause as Watergate: the belief in the White House that the president and

---

* Bagdikian, *Columbia Journalism Review,* January–February, 1973.

those around him were beleaguered by hostiles in the press, in Congress, in the public at large. Deceit and secrecy, buttressed by propaganda, were the norm for Reagan. Even before the Iran-contra affair, his administration was regarded by many who pay attention to such matters as the most secretive in the nation's history.

During the Watergate scandal it took eleven months from the time of the original arrests before a special prosecutor, independent of the Justice Department, was appointed. By contrast, the decision to appoint a special prosecutor in the Iran-contra affair was made less than a month after the first word of the dealings with Iran.

That was only one example of riding on the grooves that were set in place by Watergate. Every step along the way in 1972, 1973, and 1974 there had been slow groping, by the White House itself, by the justice system, by the Congress, by the press. When Reagan's scandal occurred, the actors knew their various roles well. The script was more than a decade old, but it had been writ large.

Within a month of the November, 1986, revelations, committees in both the House and Senate were conducting hearings on the Iran-contra affair. Preliminary findings were rapidly released. A determination was made to establish special investigative committees, which were granted subpoena power, sufficient funding, and experienced staff members, some of whom had learned how to investigate the White House firsthand, during Watergate.

Again, the contrast with the earlier scandal was striking. Wright Patman had been unable to gain subpoena power in the summer of 1972; it was for that reason that his congressional investigation failed and there were no Senate hearings until the following year.

The press, too, knew what to do. It was common right off the bat in 1986 for individual news organizations to have twenty or more reporters working the story. Many, aside from the elite newspapers and magazines that worked hard on Watergate, contributed scoops this time. The television networks were no slouches, either. During Watergate, the excuse was made that investigative reporting was not visually effective. In 1987 no one made that argument. The networks jumped on the story.

Early, frequent soundings of public opinion lent encouragement to the investigators in Congress and the news media. The report of arms for the Ayatollah was not two weeks old when *ABC News* conducted what was, I believe, the first survey of opinion on the sale of weapons to Iran.

As noted, those poll inquiries were tough ones, eliciting widespread suspicions that Reagan had not been candid, and that despite his remarks, he was not interested in getting to the bottom of things. Other news organizations followed up with opinion polls of their own; so did Gallup and Louis Harris.

In 1972, no main news organization had a regular poll of its own. The chore of sampling public opinion was left mostly to Gallup and Harris, neither of whom could be considered aggressive in their questioning. Fifteen years later almost every elite media outlet had a poll of its own or was a partner in a poll. Thus, each week, and frequently more than once a week, new findings showing public concern and distrust of Reagan were aired.

In his remarks to *Time* magazine, Reagan warned that "the press has to take the responsibility for what they have done," implying that it was the news media's fault that Iran had not seen to it that the remaining American hostages were released. Such a comment was meant to have a chilling effect on coverage. But the existence of so many media polls showing that Reagan had lost credibility with the public created just the opposite of a chilling effect. They served as a prod to fuller media exploration of the scandal.

Every now and then Richard Wirthlin would say his surveys showed a rebound for the president. Sometimes the media polls showed one too, but they were so slight as to be negligible.

As the scandal moved along, the opinion polls remained an important factor in encouraging editors to continue vigorous pursuit of the story. In all probability, many editors did not realize the polls were having such an effect on them. Nevertheless, had the polls shown the public believing Reagan and resenting press coverage, the story would have gotten very different play, I am sure, from many news organizations.

REPUBLICAN GAINS AND SETBACKS

UNDER RONALD REAGAN, THE REPUBLICANS
moved toward becoming the majority party in the
United States. In 1985 and 1986 they reached virtual
parity with the Democrats, according to a number of
surveys. This political realignment was stunning because the
GOP had been so far behind for so long.

The Republican climb was rooted in a repudiation of the
Democrats as a party with few if any convictions and little
ability to govern, a belief that the Republicans, while not
likable, would certainly do better than their opponents at
managing the economy, and the strongly favorable personal

impression that Reagan made on a portion of the electorate. It had little if anything to do with political philosophy.

As of this writing, however, the Republicans have been set back, mostly by events of their own making. The deceit of the secret Reagan-administration dealings with the regime of the Ayatollah Khomeini and the reckless, prideful, unconstitutional administration intervention in Nicaragua appear to have made the Republicans damaged goods, as did the Watergate scandal in the seventies. The stock-market crash of October, 1987, compounded the problem, raising questions as to whether the Republicans could manage the economy after all.

Even before the Iran-contra revelations, the GOP bubble was bursting. Without any severe jolt, people's faith in the economy eroded rapidly in the spring and summer of 1986, signaling difficulty ahead for the party in power. In the U.S. Senate elections that fall, the Republicans were battered despite strenuous, highly focused campaigning for them by Reagan.

For the time being, therefore, as maneuvering for the 1988 presidential campaign got under way, majority status seemed beyond reach for the GOP. One item of significance, showing up in *Washington Post/ABC News* opinion polls, was that after leading the Democrats for several years as the party seen as better able to cope with the nation's main problems, the Republicans had fallen behind through most of 1987.

But in that measure and others, the GOP trailed by only small margins, despite the severity of the Iran-contra scandal. Electorally, a continued decline was no certain fate. In this age of distrust, voting for the many had often been a choice between the lesser of two evils. The Republicans' problem was that they had failed to attract people to GOP positions on issues, a weakness that was compounded by both the scandal and concerns over the economy. The Democrats, on the other hand, had suffered in recent years by giving the appearance of not standing for anything at all, and not being able to manage, either. Whether that would change in 1988 was unclear. Which was the lesser evil? Only time would tell.

Recent history is marked by elections in which for many people the choice is whom to vote against. A Baltimore columnist, Peter Jay, aptly described the dilemma as it applied to a Maryland governor's race in the 1970s. The candidates were Marvin Mandel, the Democratic incumbent, and Louise Gore, a Republican who was perhaps best known as the person who introduced Spiro T. Agnew to Richard Nixon. "Anybody but Marvin," Jay wrote, "except Louise."

Jay could have used the line in presidential contests, both before and afterward. Richard Nixon was elected in 1968 because of dissatisfaction with the Democrats, not because he was an appealing figure; Carter in 1976 because of abuses by Nixon and Ford; and Reagan in 1980 because of Carter's failed presidency.

In that last year, according to *New York Times/CBS News* Election Day voter polls, more than thirty-five percent of Reagan's support came from Democrats and independents who leaned Democratic. Many of these voters expressed serious doubts about Reagan but set them aside rather than go with Carter again.

From the start of his presidency, Reagan and Republican leaders tried to break the lesser-of-two-evils pattern and win support for themselves as well as rejection of the opposition. The method was Reagan oratory and constant propaganda— the assertion that things were going to go well, that the national spirit had been restored, that America was standing tall—and, frequently, a hard jab at the Democrats. The subsequent political realignment was proof that such an approach could work, within limits, especially when the opposition helped.

Along with Reagan, voters in 1980 also elected enough other Republicans to give the party a majority in the Senate for the first time in thirty years, helping smooth his path. Almost immediately, many Democrats in Washington tended to roll over and play dead—hardly challenging the president, supporting the virtual elimination of corporate taxation, slashes in taxes for the wealthy, cuts in programs for the poor and middle classes. If they quarreled some with Reagan's bellicose foreign-policy posture, they nevertheless supported his call for unprecedented military spending, which was to cost the country dearly for years to come.

Some Democrats did not go along. But, by and large, whether they did or not, few cried out. The lack of any strong Democratic opposition—the absence of a leadership debate, that is—weighed on public opinion, contributing heavily toward political realignment.

By the middle of 1981, Republican leaders were able to cite creeping progress in opinion polls and assert that they were on the road to parity. The claims seemed inflated, but there was no denying the trend.

In the period from 1972 through 1980, the Democrats had held an average twenty-five-point lead in party affiliation nationwide, according to most surveys. Over that time in the National Opinion Research Center's General Social Survey, for example, fifty-five percent of the people interviewed listed themselves as Democrats or leaning Democratic, thirteen percent as independents not leaning either way, and thirty percent as either Republican or leaning Republican. (The remaining two percent deemed themselves totally uninvolved.)

In ten polls done by the *Washington Post* and *ABC News* in 1981, however, that margin was cut in half, with fifty-two percent affiliating themselves with the Democrats, thirty-nine percent with the Republicans. Those findings were in line with those of other polls—Gallup, the *New York Times/ CBS News* poll, and others.

The recession of 1982 temporarily halted realignment. *Post/ABC News* polls that year showed Democrats picking up five points overall, and holding an average eighteen-point lead over the Republicans in party affiliation.

Subsequently, as impressions of an economic recovery took hold, the Republicans resumed their rise. Yearly averages in *Post/ABC News* surveys showed a sixteen-point Democratic advantage in 1983, a thirteen-point advantage in 1984. Then, with a burst in 1985, the margin was reduced to five points: forty-nine percent in our polls that year listed themselves as Democrats or independent-Democrats, forty-four percent as Republicans or independent-Republicans.

During the following year, the Republicans eked one or two points past the Democrats in two of six *Post/ABC News* polls taken through September. In the other four surveys, the Democrats never led by more than three points. The average for the period: Democrats forty-eight percent, Republicans forty-seven.

New York Times/CBS News polls had slightly different numbers that told the same story from 1981 to 1986: quick gains for the GOP in 1981, setbacks in 1982, recovery in 1984, and virtual parity in 1985 and 1986. On the average, those surveys showed the Democrats with leads of nine points in 1981, seventeen points in 1982 and 1983, eight in 1984, three in 1985, and four points in 1986.

Was 1986 a time for high hopes for the Republicans? Of course. But by the summer there were also strong signs that the party had progressed about as far as it could. As early as June I was able, looking at the data, to write in a column for the *Washington Post National Weekly* that the Republicans were so high that they "may have nowhere to go but down."

The main problem was that despite a general cheerfulness on the state of the economy at the time, and a high evaluation of Reagan's conduct of foreign affairs, the best that Republican candidates projected in upcoming elections was a standoff against the Democrats. Any jolt in either area had the potential to be extremely damaging for the GOP.

By the time of that writing, doubts about the economy were already in motion. In March, 1986, forty-two percent in the *Post/ABC News* poll thought the economy was getting better. Each of our polls after that showed a decline, sliding to forty percent, thirty-five percent, thirty-two percent, then, in September, thirty percent. In March, twenty-four percent felt the economy was getting worse; by September that figure had increased by ten points.

What those percentages meant in terms of the actual voting-age population was that between March and September the number of people who were optimistic about the economy dropped from about seventy-two million adult Americans to fifty-two million, changing places somewhere in between with the pessimists, whose numbers went up from some forty-one million to about fifty-eight million.

A trend like that had to put a knot in the stomach of any Republican analyst. The public mood, if not the economy itself, was nearing a recession level. A continuation was sure to bring a decline in Reagan's approval ratings and stop realignment in its tracks. Beyond these cold figures lay another problem for the Republicans. The switchers showed no interest in any GOP message, only in results—that is, in proof that the Republicans could manage the economy.

We seemed to be a nation fixed in Democratic New Deal beliefs but rejecting the Democrats as incapable of running the country, accepting the Republicans as caretaker managers. One poll I worked on, taken in January, 1985, shortly after Reagan's massive reelection victory, showed how strongly it was dissatisfaction with the Democrats, rather than any Republican appeal, that was accounting for realignment.

The president's approval rating at the time was at a peak, measuring sixty-eight percent, one of the top two or three scores we had ever found for him. But as was often the case, the approval rating was a superficial, misleading gauge of popularity.

In the survey we asked people to grade the Reagan administration A, B, C, D, or F on its handling of a wide variety of important issues. The results showed a belief that Reagan was doing decently but not superbly in dealing with the nation's main problem, the economy. The average citizen gave his administration a B for its overall handling of the economy, and a B for dealing with inflation. For its work in two other chief economic areas, unemployment and federal budget deficits, the administration got a low C.

On all other measures, the score was also a C: a C for reducing the chances of nuclear war, a C bordering on D for dealing with toxic wastes and other environmental problems, another low C for reducing poverty, and C for reducing crime, dealing with the Soviet Union, improving the quality of public-school education, and establishing a sound overall foreign policy.

I then matched the way people graded the administration with their vote in the Reagan-Mondale election the previous fall. Naturally enough, those who gave an overall score of A or B said overwhelmingly that they had voted for Reagan. But lo and behold, so did those who gave the administration the mediocre score of C. Among them, Reagan beat Mondale by a ratio of better than two to one. Only among people who gave Reagan Ds and Fs had the majority supported Mondale.

The message was not very complicated. When people judged Reagan according to what they wanted in a president, he got mediocre grades, even at a time when political leaders and most of the news media were lauding him as extremely popular. It was only when the public compared Reagan to his Democratic opposition that he did magnificently.

In dealing with findings like these, some commentators described Reagan's relationship with the American people as a political paradox, saying endlessly that he was a Teflon president whose unpopular policies did not rub off on him. We heard that for years; it became part of the Sunday political-talk-show litany.

It was an extremely misleading description, in my view. Certainly Reagan was personally more popular than his policies. People admired his courage, humor, and charm. But at the same time they saw him as a rich man's president, insensitive to the poor, to blacks, to working people generally, as caring more about industries that polluted than about cleaning up the pollution, as an ally of special interests throughout.

The Teflon theory was demeaning to the citizenry, making it appear that personality alone could induce them to give one of the most sweeping election victories in history, as they did Reagan in 1984, to someone whose policies they disliked. A more correct and less insulting interpretation would have been that while Reagan's policies were disliked, the Democrats were seen as being devoid of policies altogether. Why would an ordinary person vote for a rich man's president? What better reason than that, as undesirable as Marvin may be, he's still preferable to Louise?

The Teflon theory was based exclusively on what were regarded as extremely high approval ratings for Reagan. It should have been discarded by 1982, when those ratings sank to the low forties during the economic recession.

Frequently, the Gallup poll would note that Reagan's ratings were not especially high compared to most of his predecessors'. In early 1985, for example, Gallup reported that Reagan's scores during his first term were similar to those of Carter, Ford, Nixon, Johnson, and Truman during comparable periods, but substantially lower than those given to Kennedy and Eisenhower.

Such accounts were often duly reported in the news media, then ignored. Commentators raved about Reagan's ratings at times when they were no better than those of most of his predecessors. As for the paradox of his getting decent approval ratings while his policies were disliked, reviewers in the press often found it easier to make the public seem foolish, as though under some hypnotic spell, than to add another variable, such as general optimism about the economy, or repudiation of the Democrats, to the equation.

The Teflon theory was pretty much abandoned in 1987 when Reagan's ratings fell once again and stayed down, generally at or below fifty percent in most polls, because of the Iran-contra debacle.

In February, 1985, I undertook a fairly extensive examination of political realignment. In our *Washington Post/ABC News* poll that month, the people we interviewed divided up fifty percent Democrats or leaning Democratic, forty-four percent Republicans or leaning Republican, and six percent independents who did not lean in either direction.

We asked this cross-section of people to think back to 1980

and tell us what their political partisanship had been then. Fifty-seven percent said they had been Democrats or leaned Democratic, thirty-six percent said they had been Republicans or leaned Republican and seven percent said they had been nonleaning independents. While subject to the vagaries of memory, these proportions seemed quite close to the mark. Our sample was in line with other polls, both from 1985 and 1980.*

In all, about one of every five people in this survey—a figure equivalent to 35 million people of voting age—admitted to switching party affiliation in one direction or another since 1980.

Despite outward appearances, I found that part of that movement had been toward the Democrats. Among people who said they were Republicans five years earlier, nine percent thought of themselves as Democrats in 1985 and three percent as non-leaning independents.

That shift was dwarfed, however, by the move toward the GOP. Of those who said they were Democrats in 1980, eighteen percent listed themselves as Republicans in 1985 and three percent as pure independents. After cancelling out the effect of the movement toward the Democrats, the net result was a gain of about fourteen million people for the Republicans and a loss of about twelve million for the Democrats.

I then began to examine the switchers in some detail. What I found refuted some of the most widely heralded explanations of realignment, such as the perception that the Democratic party had become too liberal (a claim often asserted by Reagan and echoed by many in the Washington Democratic establishment), or that there had been a "reverse gender gap"—that is, an unbalanced, sharp movement by men toward the Republicans.

The main factor, once again, seemed to be that the Republicans in 1985 were regarded as better able than the Demo-

---

* Throughout in my discussions of party affiliation I am referring to how people identify themselves in public opinion polls, not to official voter registration figures.

crats to handle the nation's economy, as more efficient managers of government.

Hardly ever did distinctions between party policies or philosophy seem to account for an individual's move toward the Republicans. Many switchers did not seem aware of such distinctions; they did not follow public events that much. Among all people interviewed, only about one quarter knew that the Republicans had a majority in the Senate and the Democrats a majority in the House of Representatives. And the party switchers did even more poorly on this rudimentary test.

The survey showed quite conclusively, in my view, why it was wrong to think of ideology—either the Democrats being too liberal or the Republicans invitingly conservative—as a major factor in realignment. A minor explanation, possibly. But even that was unlikely.

One question we asked was this:

Overall, do you think the Democratic Party's stands on issues are more conservative than your own, more liberal than your own, or about the same as your own?

Among all people who said they were Democrats five years earlier, twenty-nine percent said the party's stands were more liberal than their own, and half as many, fourteen percent, said the party's positions were more conservative than theirs. Of that first group, four in ten (forty-one percent) had abandoned ship and moved toward the Republicans. That was a high proportion; there is no gainsaying it. But among those who thought the Democrats were more *conservative* than they themselves were, almost three in ten (twenty-eight percent) also switched. That, too, was a high proportion.

For this latter group, it seemed obvious that the switching was brought on by something other than political philosophy. Where they placed themselves and the two parties on a left-to-right scale was not what was pulling, or pushing, them to the Republicans.

If that was true for those who placed themselves as being

to the left of the Democratic party, logic suggested it could also have been true for those who placed themselves to its right. Perhaps many among that fairly large group switched for ideological reasons, but perhaps not. Luckily, the survey was rich enough to allow me to test the idea.

My examination showed that the main, almost all-encompassing reasons for realignment were a strong personal pull exerted by Reagan on some voters and a belief that under him, the GOP was better able than the Democrats to handle the economy. Yes, back once more to the dominance of the economy in people's political decisions.

Both groups of switchers were almost incredibly high on Reagan. He got a ninety-one percent approval rating from those who thought the Democrats more liberal than they themselves were, and a ninety-six percent rating from those who thought the Democrats more conservative. By comparison, he got a sixty-two percent rating among all people interviewed.

Both groups of switchers were far more enthusiastic about the direction of the national economy than the rest of the public. Among all people interviewed, those optimistic about the economy outnumbered pessimists by about five to three. But among the "Democrats are too liberal" group of switchers, the optimist-pessimist ratio was sixteen to one, and among the "Democrats are too conservative" group, seven to one.

On all other questions, the Democratic defectors invariably were more optimistic in their interpretation of current events than other Americans. Switching was most common in the younger, more impressionable age groups, suggesting that the extensive, uncontested administration propaganda had taken effect.

People who follow polls will realize that in concentrating on these switchers, I was dealing with a small number of people. There were ninety Democratic defectors who felt the party was more liberal than they were, and twenty-seven who felt it more conservative. Ordinarily, such numbers would not be large enough for important generalizations. But both these small groups held the same views, or nearly the same views, on almost every political question in the poll, views that often differed sharply from those of the rest of the population. On more than a dozen inquiries, these two small groups responded as though in lockstep.

Despite the small sample, therefore, the law of averages strongly suggests that the findings were almost certainly valid, that the motives of both sets of switchers were the same. When two coins turn up heads and tails in exactly the same pattern, and when the pattern for other coins is very different, it is most likely that something more than chance is at work.

Findings like these are not proof that ideology played only a small role in the political realignment during the Reagan years but they are about as close to proof as a public opinion poll can get. They are extremely important in the battle that is certain to occur among Democrats in 1988, as neoliberals and numerous consultants keep putting forth the message that Americans have moved to the right and that the only way a Democrat can win the presidency is to act like a Republican.

I have focused on those polls because they yielded rich detail to make the point that political realignment was *not* based on any attraction to the Republicans' political philosophy. It is never wise, however, to read too much into one or two opinion polls. In this instance, there is no need to do that. There is abundant supporting evidence.

On forty-six occasions from 1981 through May, 1987, the *New York Times/CBS News* poll asked people whether they regarded themselves as liberal, moderate, or conservative on most political matters. Across that period of time, there was some gradual movement, but in the wrong direction for those who maintain that the country has moved to the right.

In January, 1981, sixteen percent said they were liberal, forty percent moderate, and thirty-seven percent conservative, with seven percent failing to classify themselves. In

August, 1986—a moment that signified the height of political realignment in the *Times/CBS News* poll (as well as in the *Post/ABC News* poll)—nineteen percent said they were liberal and thirty-four percent conservative.

Thus, even when the Republicans were doing best, there was no apparent move to the right. And by May of 1987, with Republican partisanship declining, twenty-four percent in the *Times/CBS News* poll said they were liberal, thirty-two percent conservative.

Over a much longer period, the Gallup polls have made the same point. In 1985, Gallup reported that Americans were no more conservative politically than they had been ten years earlier.

The Gallup analysts drew their conclusions simply and directly. In asking their questions, interviewers offered a little introduction, saying that conservatives "are referred to as being right of center," liberals to the left. They then handed out cards in which people chose one of nine categories, ranging from far left of center to far right, to describe their own position.

Hardly any movement could be discerned over the decade; what little there was went against the conventional wisdom that there was a growing conservatism.

Percentage describing themselves as . . .

	. . . liberal	. . . moderate	. . . conservative	. . . not sure
in 1975	18%	42%	30%	10%
in 1985	20%	45%	28%	7%

Findings like these may be challenged on the grounds that the concept of political ideology is too lofty for many Americans, that people do not think about ideology, cannot define ideology, and, indeed, do not have any ideology, regardless of what they tell pollsters. Gallup had a response for that. Evidence that there was stability in people's ideological views came not only from assertions of it but from longstanding, consistent public positions, found in polls on such issues as school prayer, gun control, abortion, federal aid to parochial schools, and others. In other words, Americans were not only unchanging in their professed ideological positions from 1975 to 1985, but also in the measures that put their claims to the test.

During the Vietnam war, Richard Nixon tried to make it appear that people who opposed his government's actions were supporters of Hanoi. Of course, they weren't. In the 1980s, Reagan and his propagandists tried to make it seem that disaffected Democrats had become conservative Republicans. That wasn't true, either.

WHITHER THE DEMOCRATS?

Men in politics must never consider the present moment; they should always be looking toward the future. Yes, public opinion is quite movable! Yes, it undergoes abrupt and irresistible turns.

—Waldeck-Rousseau*

N 1985 THERE WAS A STARTLING STATEWIDE election in Virginia. At the height of the political realignment nationally and in a state where Republicans had been dominant since the sixties, the Democrats won the three top offices—governor, lieutenant governor, and attorney general. In two of those races, the candidates romped to victory.

The election exposed a latent Democratic strength and

---

* Pierre Marie René Waldeck-Rousseau, a French statesman of the nineteenth century.

GOP weakness that exist wherever Republicans have made sharp gains. In a nutshell, it demonstrated that for many party-switchers, the only real change was that they had become nominal Republicans instead of nominal Democrats. They were floaters whose vote could not be counted on by either party. Their calling themselves Republicans during the eighties made it appear that there had been enormous gains for the GOP; in actuality, those gains existed largely on paper.

What was most amazing was the composition of the Democratic team. The gubernatorial candidate, Gerald Baliles, was extremely bland. He had been serving quietly as attorney general, drawing little attention statewide. The candidate for lieutenant governor, L. Douglas Wilder, was a controversial black state senator who had threatened three years earlier to lead a rebellion if the Democrats failed to nominate a black for high office. And the candidate for attorney general was a woman, Mary Sue Terry, a state legislator who was virtually unknown.

In Virginia, voters select each statewide officer separately, not as a ticket. Baliles won by ten points, Wilder by four, and Terry by twenty-three.

Wilder was the first black elected to so prominent an office in the South since Reconstruction, Terry the first woman ever chosen to a statewide position in Virginia.

Researchers could find no successful team like this one—a white male, a black male, and a women—anywhere in the United States, ever. That it should happen in Virginia was stunning; that it should happen in 1985 at the peak of realignment more stunning, and that the candidates should win as easily as they did (while Wilder won narrowly, he was ahead all the way), even more stunning.

Furthermore, the Democrats won without any notable black voter turnout or disproportionate support from women. The black vote, in fact, appeared to have declined slightly from the election four years earlier, when there was no black candidate. In addition, preelection polls that I did for the *Washington Post* showed an almost insignificant gender gap in the governor's race in 1985, while in 1981 a skewed women's vote made all the difference for the Democrat.

It marked the second straight time that the Democrats took all three state offices, a surprise in itself. Before 1981, Republicans had held the governorship since the election of 1969; as of this writing, no candidate running as a Democrat has won a U.S. Senate seat in the Old Dominion since 1966. The GOP had made such steady gains since the days of the Harry Byrd Democratic machine that by 1981 Republicans had reached parity. A *Washington Post* poll that year found thirty percent listing themselves as Democrats, twenty-nine percent as Republicans, and the rest as independents. (Voters do not register by party in Virginia; what we know of partisanship comes mostly from election polls.)

Baliles, Wilder, and Terry benefited in part by facing three lackluster Republican opponents. The gubernatorial candidate was no more lively than Baliles and never got his campaign off the ground. The main attraction of the candidate for lieutenant governor seemed to be that he was not a black (indeed, his family roots were in the antebellum Virginia aristocracy). And the candidate for attorney general discredited himself early on, claiming in campaign literature to have once been a Washington Redskins football player when, apparently, his connection with the team had been nothing more than a tryout.

"White bread," these running mates were called, and their dullness allowed the Democrats to find the Achilles heel in the political realignment. The new Republicans, the switchers, were not very Republican at all. Used to crossing over to GOP candidates, they had no qualms about crossing over in the opposite direction.

In most of the country, GOP election victories traditionally have come in the face of strong odds. Commonly outnumbered by five to three or even greater proportions, Republicans could win only with the help of these crossover Democrats who, as the saying goes, "vote for the man, not the party."

Historically it has been a given that Republicans could count on extremely solid support from their own partisans, with defection on Election Day amounting to not more than ten or twelve percent of all Republican voters, often less. Reagan won about ninety-five percent of the GOP vote in 1984. At the same time, Democratic candidates knew they would lose a substantial share of their rank and file, frequently as much as twenty-five or thirty percent.

That pattern was wrecked in Virginia.

With my assistant, Kenneth John, I did one preelection poll for the *Washington Post* about five weeks before the Virginia election and then, in the final days, a "panel-back poll," reinterviewing as many of the same people as we could find. One advantage of the panel-back technique is that it tracks change in specific groups of voters, often finding a ferment bubbling under the surface that might otherwise go undetected. There was plenty of that, especially among Republicans.

Republicans were so shaky that a bare majority of them, fifty-three percent, were consistent enough to support the GOP gubernatorial candidate both times we talked to them. One of every three switched—either toward the Republican or away from him—in the few weeks between interviews, an expression of mass uncertainty and confusion.

Among Democrats, on the other hand, seventy-five percent supported Baliles in both interviews, and only twenty percent shifted preference from one survey to the next. That was not a bedrock firmness, but it was substantially more stable than the Republican vote.

What occurred in Virginia in 1985 was a precursor of the sweeping Democratic gains in the U.S. Senate elections a year later. In the South alone, four seats that had been held by Republicans—those in Florida, Alabama, North Carolina and Georgia—were taken by the Democrats despite sharp recent increases in the GOP ranks. There was, clearly, a certain hollowness in realignment.

▪ ▪ ▪

If a black and a woman could win high state offices running as Democrats in Virginia, then blacks and women can win anywhere in the United States. So can Jews, for that matter, who, without much notice, held eight seats in the U.S. Senate through much of the 1980s, including ones in states with hardly any Jewish voters.

The 1985 Virginia result and the success of black, female, and Jewish candidates elsewhere testify to a sharp decline in racial, sexist, and religious bias in the American electorate. Startling as it may sound, the presidency itself, and certainly the vice-presidency, seem within reach for blacks, women, or Jews, given appealing candidates.

Gallup polls from 1958 through 1987 track the trend:

Percentage saying they would vote for a qualified . . .

	. . . woman	. . . Jew	. . . black
in 1958	52%	62%	38%
in 1978	76%	82%	77%
in 1983	80%	88%	77%
in 1987	82%	89%	79%

This declining prejudice is one more piece of evidence working against the assertions by so many political leaders and commentators that there has been a move to the right on the part of the American voter.

If anything, what voters have demonstrated, in the midst of an alleged new conservatism, is a decidedly progressive and tolerant bent. In 1970, there were 10 blacks in the House of Representatives and 169 in state legislatures across the country. In 1987, there were 23 blacks in the House and 410 in the state legislatures. In all, there were more than 6,500 black elected officials in the United States in 1987, four times as many as there had been fifteen years earlier, according to a political-research organization, the Joint Center for Political Studies. In 1966, not a single large city had a black mayor;

by 1983, eighteen cities with populations of a hundred thousand or more had black mayors.

Similarly, in 1969 there were 10 women in the House, and 301 in state legislatures; in 1987 there were 23 in the House and 1,163 in the legislatures. Other democracies, such as Britain, Israel, and India, have chosen women for their highest elected office; it seems quaint to think that Americans would not do the same. Neither blacks nor women hold office in proportion to their numbers in the population. But that they have made substantial gains is indisputable. The doors of politics have opened wider in recent years.

The arithmetic in Virginia provided a model for the Democrats nationwide: keep rank-and-file defection of Democratic voters to a minimum, get a respectable chunk of the independent vote—a majority is not necessary—and attract the new, soft, crossover Republicans. Given the natural leaning of voters toward the Democratic party, that does not seem so hard to obtain.

Nevertheless, a Democrat has been chosen president of the United States only once in the five elections from 1968 through 1984, and only three times in the nine from 1952 through 1984. That kind of failure is colossal, tantamount to a heavyweight losing to a lightweight time after time.

After a while, it becomes reasonable to conjecture that the heavyweight may not be trying hard enough. Many Democrats themselves would offer that as an explanation for their dismal showing. On the left are a growing number who say the problem with the Democrats nationally is that party leaders have moved too far to the right, alienating and splintering the traditional Democratic constituency.

On the party's right are those who say the only opportunity for the Democrats is to present centrist candidates, meaning ones who look and talk a lot like Republicans, who are less interested than liberal Democrats of the past in programs aimed at bringing the disadvantaged into mainstream American life.

Election results do not solve this dilemma; the same evidence may be used to argue both sides. Did Hubert Humphrey lose because he was too liberal—or because he was loyal to Lyndon Johnson, refusing to separate himself from Johnson's handling of the Vietnam war? Did George McGovern lose four years later because of his ideology, or because he was seen as a feckless, irresponsible candidate who ran a poor campaign?

Similarly, was Walter Mondale trounced because he was perceived as a liberal—or because he failed to offer even a modest liberal agenda, running, in his own phrase, on a theme of a "new realism," code words meaning he had no new social programs in mind, no plan for relieving high unemployment?

Public opinion polls also fail to resolve the matter. They have constantly shown most voters stuck in a semi–New Deal mode, preferring the Democrats as the party that will protect Social Security, Medicare, the environment, the poor, the elderly. But the same polls show the Republicans seen as better able to keep spending and taxes down.

A Democrat who models his campaign on a literal reading of opinion polls is likely to find himself skeltering in all directions. Protect the environment, but don't raise taxes to do it. Help the poor, but don't raise taxes. Cut military spending, but only through elimination of waste, fraud, and abuse; don't weaken the national defense. Help the farmer, but not at the expense of the citydweller. Create a jobs program? Yes, as long as it entails no spending. The public wants a national health-care program, more emphasis on education, but where will the money be found? Better not to talk about it.

Public opinion, as expressed through polls, is a mean master for any Democratic candidate who thinks himself or herself as following in the steps of Roosevelt or Johnson or even Jimmy Carter. Small wonder that the party establishment has moved to the right; the reading of opinion polls and the advice of consultants has helped push them there.

In June, 1987, Arkansas governor William Clinton gave a pithy analysis of the key problem facing all Democrats who seek high office: "The great dilemma," he said, is "how to speak to the possessed and the dispossessed at the same time."

The polls impose few such constraints on Republicans. Never saddled with the goal of lifting the poor into the mainstream, it is easy for them to focus on fiscal soundness, low tax rates, and strong defense even at the expense of social programs, and to attack the Democrats as big spenders.

The piling up of massive budget and trade deficits under Reagan has made it even harder for Democrats to address the problems of the dispossessed. In 1981, the nation's total deficit went over a trillion dollars; by 1986 it had doubled. With sixteen cents of every tax dollar used to pay interest on the federal debt, and not a penny used to retire the debt, with another twenty-nine cents earmarked for military spending (and more of the tax dollar committed for that purpose in the years ahead), and with forty-six cents set for Social Security and other entitlement programs, there is little money for programs for the poor, for restoring the infrastructure, for protection of the environment. No money, that is, for a Democrat to talk like a Democrat.

This financial plight and the wary reading of public opinion polls take their toll on all Democratic candidates. As the 1988 presidential campaign got under way, even Jesse Jackson, the country's main spokesman for the underprivileged, could be seen drifting toward a more centrist position, saying the party needed both a left wing and a right wing to be able to fly, and recognizing that fiscal constraints made it impossible to do many of the things that needed to be done.

Faced with this quandary of "Where's the money?" the Democrats risk antagonizing large clusters of voters no matter which way they turn. Candidates who stand up for the poor, the elderly—for any socially desirable goals—leave themselves open to attack as big spenders who would force the middle class to pay for experiments aimed at elevating the poor. Those who don't, give the appearance of betraying the principles of their New Deal heritage.

▪ ▪ ▪

This hard choice made life difficult for Democrats in Congress during the Reagan years, with party leaders choosing to go in both directions. The argument may be made that the Democrats were somewhat successful in the practice of damage control from 1981 on. If social programs were curtailed, their diminution was substantially less than Reagan sought. The Democrats succeeded in stopping him from abolishing the Amtrak rail service and from drastically reducing mass transit aid, from selling off public lands, from gutting federal aid to education, from restructuring the budget into block-grant programs. On military matters, the Democrats, through negotiation, limited the number of MX missiles, and reined in Reagan's arms-sales proposals to Saudi Arabia, Jordan, and some other nations. It is entirely possible that some liberal Democrats are proud of their record under Reagan, feeling they have held off the worst that the Republicans could throw at them, and that it was time for a correction in course, anyway.

But in certain areas involving great outlays of money and important principles, the Democrats acceded beyond acceptable limits for a party committed to the greatest good for the greatest number. The tax breaks for large corporations and the wealthy could not have been enacted without approval in the House of Representatives, which was overwhelmingly Democratic. If Democrats improved on compensation for the unemployed, they defaulted when it came to reducing joblessness. On low-income housing, federal spending for programs administered by the Department of Housing and Urban Development was slashed from $26 billion in the 1981 fiscal year to less than $11 billion in 1987. According to the *New York Times,* new units of federally subsidized low-income housing decreased from more than 300,000 in 1979 to 87,000 in 1987. Yet in a series of votes during that period, Democrats approved unprecedented military spending.

Politically, the Democrats' record was even worse, making no sense to voters. Warned by the polls and the consultants that public opinion is treacherous, that the label "liberal" is a stigma, they have done little to advertise their occasional attempts to rein in Reagan. On the matter of how to position themselves in seeking public office—as liberals, as near-Republicans, or as something in between—the Democratic right was the voice most heard. Failure to trust the people led liberal Democrats to silence, inducing them to avoid discussion of socially desirable democratic goals, making them appear feckless. They gave away the high ground.

Housing for the poor, jobs programs, protection of the environment receded as national goals, seldom the subjects of spirited leadership discussion. Once elected, many Democrats in Washington may have worked seriously on such issues. But they generally avoided talking about or running on them, afraid to be tarred as big spenders, agents of "special interests."

As time passed, this Democratic party plight worsened. Gradually, the nature of issues brought to the public for debate shifted. "The Great Society is dead," proclaimed the *Wall Street Journal* in an editorial in 1986. For all that the Democrats in Washington spoke about it, it certainly was. Democrats who believed that social-welfare programs had been worthwhile, if not a total success, failed to defend them on their merits and talked instead about "workfare."

One of the most baffling developments in recent years was the silence of many Democrats in the face of charges that they sided with special interests, and the glee of other Democrats in making such accusations. By any traditional definition, and certainly that of ordinary citizens, special interests are the nations' powerful, moneyed interests—big business, oil, the top *Fortune* companies. In recent years, however, the term has been used to describe assorted Democratic constituencies: blacks, the poor in general, environmentalists, the women's movement, homosexual-rights groups, labor—elements that are either downtrodden and lacking in power and money, or so large that help for them can only be in the national interest.

To call these groups special interests is a perversion of the term as it is understood by most Americans. In polls during the 1984 presidential campaign it was Reagan, not Mondale, who was seen by the majority as the candidate of special interests. Asked by *Post/ABC News* interviewers in two separate surveys which one, Reagan or Mondale, would do a better job of insuring that "government programs and policies are fair to all people," more than half chose Mondale both times, while only four in ten chose Reagan.

More directly, Reagan was seen by about two to one in these surveys as siding with special interests, while a majority, on the other hand, saw Mondale as siding with the average citizen *against* special interests. Americans voiced such feelings despite the fact that it was Mondale who had been labeled the special-interest candidate—a charge initially lodged by a fellow Democrat, Gary Hart, during the presidential primaries, and one that Mondale never effectively refuted.

For 1988, Democrats were being cautioned about the special-interest problem again, with the warning coming from Democrats themselves as much as from Republicans. Strikingly, the advice was not that candidates should respond to the charges, but rather that they should make it clear that they were *not* catering to the working man or woman, or to the poor, or to blacks.

A group that seemed formed especially to move the Democrats toward the right, the Democratic Leadership Committee, was organized in 1985. At a meeting in Atlanta in June, 1987, its president, Charles Robb, the former governor of Virginia, sounded the cry:

> If the nominating race degenerates into an unprincipled bidding war for the support of activists and pressure groups . . . if their narrow demands, however worthy, divert our candidates from the issues of concern to the American people . . . if our party's platform becomes a hodgepodge of special pleading . . . then we will almost certainly be disappointed next November 9.

Through some peculiar reasoning, Robb and many establishment Democrats were arguing that only by rejecting *worthy* demands of their own constituencies could the Democrats capture the presidency.

For public consumption in most of the 1980s, many Democrats concentrated on making themselves appear fiscally responsible, and on criticizing Republicans. They neither promoted nor rejected the principles that in the past had drawn voters to the Democrats.

For years in our *Washington Post/ABC News* polls we had been asking people which was a greater danger: excessive spending on social programs by the Democrats, or excessive cuts by the Republicans. Other pollsters, including ones commissioned by the Democratic party, had been making the same inquiry. Invariably, the greater danger was seen as Republican cuts.

Leading Democrats had to know of such findings. Nevertheless, as the opposition party, their theme in Washington was silence, their hope was that they themselves would slide by to live another day, and, possibly, that the Republicans might self-destruct.

In midcourse during the Reagan years, shortly after the trouncing of Mondale, the Democrats appeared to have destroyed themselves instead. A February, 1985, *Washington Post/ABC News* poll asked people which party could better provide leadership for the nation; in response fifty-four percent chose the Republicans, only thirty-three percent the Democrats.

That survey also showed the Republicans seen as far better able to reduce the federal budget deficit despite the fact that it had by then doubled under a Republican administration. Republicans under Reagan were believed better able to control government spending, better able to hold down taxes.

Almost amazingly, considering the Reagan record, Republicans were judged as able as the Democrats to cope with unemployment. Perhaps no individual poll finding showed how far the Democrats had fallen as that one. In a 1981 *Post/ABC News* survey, the Democrats were seen by a five-to-three ratio as better able to reduce unemployment; in one of our 1982 surveys they led by more than two to one. But in February, 1985, the Democrats were chosen by forty-five percent and the Republicans by forty-five percent. Gallup polls showed the same deterioration

Later on, in February, 1987, the *New Yorker* magazine referred in its "Talk of the Town" column to the Democrats as "having with a few exceptions been almost in political hiding for the last six years" and hoping at the last "that the public will return to them almost by default."

That same month, in a meeting of Democratic state chairmen and the national party's executive committee, a Texas populist, Jim Hightower, ridiculed the years of drift. "They say we've got to get moderate, nominate someone who doesn't say much, who says it with a slightly southern accent, who espouses strong conservatism with just a little dash of compassion thrown in," Hightower said, according to a *New York Times* account. "They've described a liberal Republican basically, sort of a George Bush with chest hair."

The situation then was not as bad as it had been earlier. Some Democrats in Washington were emerging from hiding. A new Speaker of the House, James Wright of Texas, was personally drawing attention to the plight of the homeless; he was also hinting at a move to keep the highest-income Americans from getting the full benefits of the previous year's tax reform. An expensive measure to restore sanitation to the nation's water was enacted over a presidential veto. A catastrophic-illness health plan, a major expansion of Medicare, also drew strong Democratic support.

Finally, in 1987, through such actions and other appeals to the public, there were signs that a few Democrats were beginning to speak out on behalf of traditional party principles. Whether they would prevail was unclear, but at least a national debate seemed in the offing.

Some Republicans, also with opinion polls at their disposal, were moving in the same direction—or at least wanted to give that appearance. Early in 1987, Senate Minority Leader Robert Dole, a presidential candidate, said in an address to the Republican National Committee, "We are a sensitive, compassionate party . . . just as concerned with health care as the Democrats. . . . Let no one say this party is going to turn its back on the elderly."

The polls, it seemed clear, were pulling both parties toward a pre-Reagan stage, at least in the early campaigning for 1988. And when the polls weren't pulling, they were pushing. Almost all the candidates seemed poll-driven. That was especially true among the field of Democrats.

On the evening of July 1, 1987, the Democratic candidates gathered for their first joint debate of the campaign, in Houston. There were seven of them, including Joseph Biden, the Delaware senator who dropped out less than two months later. (Not present, of course, was Gary Hart, who had dropped out earlier, only to reannounce his candidacy at the close of the year.) The Iran-contra hearings were in full steam at the time, and Reagan had been taking a beating in the opinion polls. Earlier that day he had nominated a controversial appeals-court judge, Robert Bork, to fill a vacancy on the Supreme Court.

The candidates quickly launched into criticism of Reagan, and several were particularly strong in their attacks on his Strategic Defense Initiative. The sweeping tax reform of the previous year, which had been so lauded by leaders of both parties at its passage, drew rebukes as well, and the best that was said of it, by one of its original proponents, was that it was at least an improvement on the previous tax code.

For people who had been following national politics, the singling out of the space shield as an item for strong criticism was perhaps a little surprising. Many scientists were in strong opposition to it, but the political debate until then had been a quiet one, fought mostly in Capitol corridors. Even more astounding was the attack on tax reform, which had been so widely celebrated.

But for those who followed the opinion polls, the attacks were easily understandable. Most people in surveys had expressed approval of the space shield in theory, but were more interested in reduction of nuclear weapons than in the development of the costliest and one of the most dubious weapons systems ever conceived. On taxes, the polls had shown the 1986 reforms to be one big question mark in the public mind, their effect not yet clear to the individual citizens.

In other words, both subjects were ripe for debate, and the candidates seized on them. To the surprise of some commentators, for every statement in the debate that came out as sounding liberal, the candidates drew loud applause. One newspaper columnist* wrote, "Perhaps the most interesting thing about this encounter was the audience. It was amazingly responsive and liberal. The most unscrupulous and resourceful candidate-promoters could hardly have flown or bused in that many enthusiasts from Massachusetts or other centers of dangerous secular humanism. . . . If Houston is any measure, the Democratic party is not a party that is searching for a centrist or a pseudo-Republican. They sounded like people who know exactly what they want."

As for the Bork nomination, which had been expected for several weeks, and which was bitterly opposed by civil-rights groups and everyone else on the liberal side of the spectrum, not a word was said by any candidate in the debate. The Democrats in the Senate, with help from some Republicans, eventually got to Bork, overwhelmingly rejecting his nomination in October. But on this night, not one of the seven men seeking to lead the nation so much as mentioned his name. Perhaps it was just too soon, and no polls on him were in hand.

---

* Mary McGrory, of the *Washington Post.*

EPILOGUE

I WOULD LIKE TO GO BACK TO THE WORDS OF Thomas Jefferson cited at the beginning of this book, on the tension between government and public opinion in a democracy. On the one hand, as Jefferson put it, government degenerates when trusted to the rulers of the people alone. That maxim is terribly relevant today. As a nation, we may not be leaving our affairs totally to "the rulers," but we have gone a long way toward it. The result, more often than we would like, is a leadership whose goals are not those of the people, and whose methods—the only ones that could allow them to succeed—frequently include secrecy, demagoguery, and manipulation.

On the other hand, public opinion is most certainly as powerful now as it was when Jefferson called it an agitating force that "cannot be resisted," which is needed "to keep the waters pure." Public opinion almost invariably does have its way—once the people become aroused. Such was the lesson in the U.S. withdrawal from Vietnam, the resignation of Richard Nixon, the election defeat of Gerald Ford, and in the numerous, often dramatic, reversals of policy that Ronald Reagan was forced to make as president. But seldom does the public get aroused, or stay that way for long.

In one sense, the thoughts of Jefferson are somewhat comforting. Governments have always tried to keep the people uninvolved and lethargic, and they always will; the present leaders' efforts are not a sign of some recent American collapse or decadence. "The natural progress of things," Jefferson wrote, "is for liberty to yield and government to gain ground." If he is right about that, today's relationship between government and the citizenry becomes more intelligible, part of the weave of history. If current leaders try to enact their own agenda rather than the public's—well, what else is new?

But to say a problem has always existed does not make it less real. When leaders substitute public relations for public debate, when officeholders, candidates, and political parties encourage stupor, and when, as a result, the public is ill-informed and distrustful, with almost half failing to vote— then, when all is said and done, it is just not satisfactory to accept that things have always been that way.

Under such circumstances it makes little sense to encourage wider public participation in public affairs; the "get-out-and-vote" cry every four years is misfounded. When people are unprepared to exercise sound judgment, they are easier to manipulate. Shrewd politicians may well create a democratic tyranny of the majority.

Jefferson's solution—to create an informed citizenry that can exert "control with a wholesome discretion"—is the correct one. But it is a goal that remains as distant today as it must have appeared then. And it will stay out of reach as long as leaders remain afraid of the people.

▪ ▪ ▪

After abandoning his race for the Democratic presidential nomination in February, 1988, Bruce Babbitt, the former governor of Arizona, laid out the problem in an article in the *Washington Post*. The candidates were all vague and "consensus-oriented," Babbitt wrote. As evidence, he cited their nonreaction to the continuing demonstrations by Palestinians in Israel—a matter of great urgency that American leaders, one would think, were obligated to address. "The Democrats had nothing to say about it," he wrote. (Neither, it may be added, did the Republicans at the time.) "Our process inhibits risk-taking," Babbitt said. "Part of it is the desire for a winner among our constituency groups. . . . They don't want us to emphasize any differences, stir any debate."

The public is not likely to develop a "wholesome discretion" unless the people at the top do stir up debate, and keep it stirred. There is no scarcity of good men and women among our national leaders, regardless of how things sometimes appear. Many of them frequently demonstrate personal and political courage, and act out of principle, not expediency. But almost all of them are terrified of public opinion.

Some intelligent leaders have always known that they are served best by openness, candor, and vigorous debate, not simply by creating an impression of openness and candor through platitudes and thirty-second advertisements. Candidates and those in power should get the message that real debate holds political rewards. Should that occur, there will be a lot of stirring and a more informed, participating citizenry. Progress may be slow, and clashes frequent. National problems will not disappear or be easily resolved. But a genuine respect for government would emerge, and we could say, legitimately, that it is morning in America.

INDEX

italicized page numbers refer to charts